Executive's Guide to Government

How Washington Works

A. Lee Fritschler
Chairman, U.S. Postal Rate Commission

Bernard H. Ross
The American University

Winthrop Publishers, Inc.
Cambridge, Massachusetts

Library of Congress Cataloging in Publication Data

Fritschler, A Lee
Executive's guide to government.

Includes index.
1. Business and politics — United States. 2. United States — Politics and government. I. Ross, Bernard H., joint author. II. Title.
JK467.F74 353'.0002'4658 79-25753
ISBN 0-87626-251-5

cartoon credits

p. 7: © 1979 Mobil Corporation. Reprinted by permission.

p. 23: © 1975 THE NEW YORKER MAGAZINE, INC. Reprinted by permission.

p. 43: © 1976 Mobil Corporation. Reprinted by permission.

p. 47: Reprinted by permission of Scripps-Howard Newspapers.

p. 62: Reprinted by permission of *Update,* the Westchester County government employee newsletter.

p. 79: © 1966 THE NEW YORKER MAGAZINE, INC. Reprinted by permission.

p. 86: © 1966 HERBLOCK. *The Washington Post.* Reprinted by permission.

p. 118: Reprinted by permission of *The Los Angeles Times* Syndicate.

p. 152: Reprinted by permission of THE CHICAGO TRIBUNE-NEW YORK NEWS SYNDICATE, INC.

p. 163: Reprinted by permission of Cartoon Features Syndicate.

p. 192: Reprinted by permission of United Features Syndicate.

17 Dunster Street, Cambridge, Massachusetts 02138

10 9 8 7 6 5 4 3 2 1

For

Susan

Craig, Katherine, and Eric

and

Marlene

Jeffrey, Joanne, and Carolyn

contents

preface

The relationship between government and business is often confusing and antagonistic. This book demystifies the complex processes of government decision-making and regulation. It shows interested individuals how to be effective in dealing with government.

The book assists executives knowledgeable about management of their own corporations but who need to know how their corporations affect and are affected by government. It is a book for present and future corporate leaders—individuals who know that corporate success depends on having the management skills necessary to deal with major forces in the corporate environment. In contemporary government and business relations these facts emerge:

1. Government decisions impact nearly every management decision made by corporate executives;
2. business executives spend more time on government matters each year;
3. successful business executives need to know as much about how government operates as they know about their own corporations; and most importantly,
4. government not only regulates and investigates business but supports it and has become its single biggest customer.

Business executives have good reason to want to know more about government and how it functions. Governments have become central to the environment in which executives operate. Government spending decisions and regulations shape and even change executive decisions on what is produced, how it is produced and distributed, and who is involved in production processes. There is much to be gained in learning how government makes decisions on spending—increases and cutbacks—and how it decides which areas of public policy are to be emphasized and which are not.

This book takes the mystery out of government for business executives and students of business, and describes in detail:

How government decisions are made.
How you as a business executive can navigate the system.
What the major similarities and differences between public and private sector management are.
How government regulations are developed and who develops them.
How national government policies filter through to state and local governments.
Who the most powerful government actors are and how they affect decisions.
What the prospects are for reforming government decision-making.

In a systematic way, this book shows how policy is made by governments at all levels, with the emphasis on the decision-making systems of Washington. We recognize that government is now a major force in the affairs of business and, by manipulating numerous rewards and penalties, has the capacity to affect materially the environment in which business operates. Government spending for research, development, and contracting runs into tens of billions of dollars a year. Most major industries operating today were started as a result of some important government decisions. Aircraft manufacturing, airlines, computers, road and rail transportation, and a wide variety of space-age industries were launched directly, or at least stimulated by, the actions of governments.

Business executives, whether or not they like government, must learn to live and cope with it if they want to succeed and prosper. This book provides business executives and students of business with the knowledge and understanding to operate in the complex and changing government environment. Business executives will be able to identify those decision-making systems which affect their corporate or industry interests. Using this information they can make sound judgments and take the necessary steps to insure that their corporation's interests are fully and fairly represented in the decision-making process.

The book contains an abundance of useful information for executives on the size and structure of the public service, the types of people who work for government, an analysis of what motivates them, and a detailed examination of various reform proposals recently implemented or under discussion. A major section is devoted to the differences between management in government and management in business. Business-government relations in the United States have traditionally been characterized by a debate between business and government executives over what business management techniques should be transferred into government operations. We evaluate the prospects for implementing more business techniques in government and analyze those techniques already in use.

In a series of valuable appendices the authors provide practical and detailed information on:

- How to register as a lobbyist.
- Who should register as a lobbyist.
- How to form a Political Action Committee.
- How to use the *Federal Register* and the *Code of Federal Regulations.*
- How a bill becomes a law.
- Washington-based organizations of importance to business executives.

Our goal has been to make this book useful to a wide variety of individuals in business and to those preparing themselves for business careers. It is a book for top-level and middle-level executives and for students of business-government relations, whether in schools of business management or schools of public management.

The first two chapters, "Business and Government: Some Fundamentals in the Relationship," and "The Personnel of Public Management," are of vital importance to the business community. They serve as an introduction to the complexities of public management and to the challenges of decision-making in government. Chapters three and four, "Government Rules and Regulations: What, Why, and From Where," and "The Management of Government Regulations," provide a clear historical perspective on government regulation of business. They show how business has worked with government in developing the regulatory process. In addition, these chapters supply much needed information on the prospects of regulatory reform and the politics inherent in the process.

The chapters that follow carefully pinpoint who is involved in government decision-making, what institutions they represent, and how the system looks from the perspective of an outsider eager to make an impact on these systems. "The Decision-Making System in Operation" gives a step-by-step description of how decisions are made and presents effective strategies for influencing them. Covered are such issues as how these systems compete for a share of the budget and for control of programs. The processes used to change these systems and government policies associated with them are also discussed. "Business Executives and the Intergovernmental System" explains how the U.S. governmental system fits together and shows how federal policy is closely integrated with state and local policy. Business executives should understand the relationships between national, state, and local governments in domestic policy-making. Close to 90 billion a year in federal money is spent on domestic aid programs to state and local governments, and most of this money finds its way into the private economy. Private sector executives need to understand better the processes governing these important decisions.

Over the past several years, various reforms have been discussed and instituted. Advocates claim that these measures will help to improve both the external and internal operations of government. Chapter nine, "Strengths and Weaknesses," and chapter ten, "Two Approaches to Reform," look at these reform proposals and examine the likelihood of their success and failure. If the government fails to respond to the most critical problems of our times, the fundamental premises and processes on which government decisions have been built might change dramatically. "Reforms in the Intergovernmental System" offers informed analyses of what to expect should important issues such as energy availability, rising inflation, and municipal financial viability fail to be resolved by the decision-making systems as they currently function. The final chapter of the book, "Business and Government in the Future," takes a hard look at decision-making processes as they may affect business-government relations in the future.

This book is an outgrowth of some ideas the authors developed while working in executive development programs for major U.S. corporations. The College of Public and International Affairs at The American University has been offering government decision-making programs for business executives for many years. The authors have been active in those programs, and many of the ideas in this book come from discussions with business executives who have participated in these programs. Several of our colleagues at American, at other universities, and in corporations read drafts of this manuscript.

Stanley L. Kroder and Frank C. Parson of IBM, Kenneth O. Michel of General Electric, Peter Malof of the Brookings Institution, George C. Lodge and J. Ronald Fox of the Harvard Business School, Andrew W. Boesel of the U.S. Office of Personnel Management, Susan J. Tolchin of George Washington University, Charles H. Levine of the University of Maryland, Edwin M. Epstein of the School of Business Administration, University of California, Berkeley, and our colleagues at The American University, Murray Comarow, Cornelius M. Kerwin, Bernard Rosen, and James A. Thurber, read all or parts of the manuscript. Their comments were pointed and thoughtful; most of them have been incorporated in the text.

Professor Marshall E. Dimock read the manuscript with great care and made several suggestions for improving both its content and organization. We are grateful to him for his willingness to give us the benefit of years of teaching and writing experience, especially in the fields of public management and business-government relations. John D. Young, a colleague at American and a person with years of top management experience in both government and business, contributed much to this book. The authors spent many hours discussing the intricacies of government decision-making with Dr. Young and have also attended a number of seminars he has conducted for both public and private executives. His insights into the complexities of public management and some of the differences between public and private management are evident throughout the book.

Charles E. McKittrick, Jr., Vice President for Governmental Programs of the IBM Corporation, was instrumental in the creation of the executive development program for business executives at American University. His commitment to executive development and his professional and intellectual interest in the processes of government decision-making were important to us as we wrote this book.

Our thanks go to several people at Winthrop Publishers: Alex Greene, Business Editor; Herbert Nolan and Lori Lienhard, Production Editors; Roger Ratliff, Marketing Director; and certainly to James J. Murray, III, President, who prodded and encouraged us in Phoenix, Cambridge, and Washington, DC.

Our wives, Susan Torrence Fritschler and Marlene Ross, read the manuscript and improved it in numerous ways. Carol N. Singer, Alicia Sheridan, and Michael C. Wilson contributed to the book as research assistants. And a group of talented, patient people typed more drafts of this manuscript than even the authors care to remember. Our thanks for these efforts go to Carol Frisbie, James Oppenheim, Stephanie Papadopoulos, Codelle Rosenberg, Martha E. Rothenberg, and Madoline Stack. Although the book contains the thoughts and labor of these individuals, only the authors are responsible for the outcome.

Washington, D.C.

A.L.F.
B.H.R.

Executive's Guide to Government

one

Business and Government

Some Fundamentals in the Relationship

Government agencies don't understand business.

My industry is regulated up to its neck. You are regulated up to your knees. And the tide is coming in.

Chief executive officers must talk directly to government officials.

We keep getting involved in policy areas after it is too late.

We should cease to be patsies and raise hell.

These comments by the chief executive officers of some major corporations indicate the suspicion and resentment that characterize business-government relations today.[1] Corporate executives have good reasons for their concern with government and their organizations' relationship with it. Government has become a significant force in the business environment. Its regulations shape and even alter executive decisions on what is produced, how and where production occurs, who is hired or fired from production processes, and how the output of production is distributed. Not surprisingly, as government has become more involved in the vital processes of private-sector management, distrust and antagonism toward government has grown.

Business executives are uncomfortable with government. It not only regulates them, but it does so in baffling and frustrating ways through a profusion of agencies. The differences in the goals, purposes, and management processes of government and business help to feed this climate of confusion and mistrust. Governments are staffed differently; government employees are motivated differently. Managing to achieve social goals instead of production and profit-inducing goals seems ambiguous and even aimless to business executives. These are only a few of the barriers the two communities must overcome before they can begin to understand each other.

There is a curious paradox in business-government relations today. Government regulates business, yet for over two hundred years government also has subsidized and protected business in crucial ways. Regulations have fostered the environment in which business operates. Without the protection of property, patents, and contracts, and without banking and currency regulations, the business system would collapse. The government also has provided technical assistance, funds, and contracts to start some industries, to protect others, and to bail out some that were close to bankruptcy. This positive government activity on behalf of business has led some observers to conclude that we have moved from a relatively free, competitive enterprise structure to a structure of "corporate socialism," a system of government support for industry instead of the standard socialist approach of government ownership of the means of production.[2]

Although it has grown in intensity in recent years, business executives' antagonism toward government is not new. One professor of business administration recently wrote, "The most characteristic, distinctive and persistent belief of American corporate executives is an underlying suspicion and mistrust of government."[3]

Why has this antagonism developed? Why should a group that has benefited from government policies be in the forefront of antigovernment criticism? Why should a group that has enjoyed such a privileged position in society feel this way today? Answers can be found in the changes in the relationships between government and business in recent years and the ways in which these changes are perceived by both business and government executives.[4]

Unfortunately, the debate between these two groups today is longer on rhetoric than reality. Business executives know little about the problems of government management, and government often displays little understanding of the problems of business management and economic development. Successful management of both government and industry and of the processes that bring them together are important to economic growth and national development. There is a good deal riding on improving the operations of government. There is even more riding on the ability of these two social giants to work out viable, productive relationships suitable to the times.

Business executives are not the only outspoken critics of government. Presidential candidates are often more critical of the federal bureaucracy than the most vitriolic captains of industry. Campaign rhetoric repeatedly accuses bureaucrats of being slow, inept and wrong, while successful policy implementation is usually attributed to the wisdom and skills of elected political leadership. Proposition 13 and the tax-cutting and tax-limiting movements show the impact of this rhetoric on the public. In a recent newspaper poll, 80 percent of those responding said that the federal government employs too many people, and 63 percent of those said "far too many." That same survey asked how the public would cut local services to allow tax reduction; 24 percent said they would like to see government pay, pensions, waste, and the number of government workers cut before anything else.[5] Government programs and employees are under attack; business executives are not alone in their dissatisfaction with government.

Love and Hate: Business-Government Relations Over Time

Certainly, large, new regulating programs inefficiently managed are upsetting, troublesome, costly, and open to criticism. Business executives, however, have reasons to want to be close to, and supportive of, government. It is tough to be critical and supportive at the same time. The nature and the shape of government regulations can dramatically affect the success of business operations. Almost all business depend on some government regulations for their success—some regulations hurt, but the bulk of them help. Aid and support of business by government through regulation has been an important part of our system from colonial times. The earliest businessmen on this continent, were pragmatic:

> To these men, the new phrase "laissez-faire" probably represented a meaningless doctrine. Rather, they stood for dispersed private activity when the capital required was within the grasp of the individual, state initiative when the capital required was too great for a small group of individuals, and at all times, public policy favorable to maximum exploitation of economic opportunities with minimum capital expenditure.[6]

These early capitalists set a pattern that has persisted for two hundred years. What has changed in the last two decades is the intensity of government involvement in the economy and the inclusion of broad social goals in the regulatory process.

An important consideration for businessmen today is that governments—national, state, and local—now spend over a third of the gross national product each year. The federal government alone spends well over $100 billion annually in contracts with industry. The inclusion of state and local government expenditures would almost double that figure.[7] Most major U.S. corporations estimate that about 20 percent of their gross domestic sales are to governments, either directly or indirectly. For many corporations, government has become the prime customer. This high level of expenditure heightens the love-hate relationship between business and government.

The twin horns of government—regulation and support—make it imperative that business executives learn more about government and how it operates. Knowing how the government identifies problems and needs, how it legislates responses to these needs and problems, and how it initiates, passes, and implements legislation is essential for effective corporate management.

The increased role of government in corporate life in the last fifteen years has caused corporations to add new functions to executive management and, in some cases, to reorganize management structures altogether. Many corporations are now moving to make the government relations aspect of corporate affairs more systematic, more prominent, and more productive. In the past, government relations were often chaotic and unplanned, handled in ways not characteristic of good, systematic corporate management. For several years now, highly trained corporate executives have moved deliberately to analyze and improve marketing, personnel relations, production, and other standard segments of corporate activity.

The Atlantic Richfield Company, for example, has organized itself to deal with state, local, and national governments. A computer-assisted information system analyzes pending government actions and communicates them quickly to people throughout the organization.[8] This innovative approach is described in a report by the Conference Board, a business-supported research organization. The report also contains suggestions on how other companies might replicate the Atlantic Richfield program.

Other corporations have also created units to deal with government impacts on corporate activities. Recently, the Mobil Oil Company opened a top-level department to focus on government regulations. Moreover, many corporations are opening their own Washington offices or joining the growing number of trade associations that are moving their headquarters to Washington. The Washington office of the Ford Motor Company had four employees in the mid-sixties; it now has a staff of over forty. It has been estimated that 1,800 trade associations are now in Washington, and over fifty per year are moving to the Capital. By the year 2000, Washington could be the financial center of the nation.[9]

The social and ideological underpinnings of the corporation have changed dramatically in the last several years. George C. Lodge of the Harvard Business School argues that the traditional ideology of the United States, characterized by the natural laws formulated by John Locke in the seventeenth century, has begun to give way. Lodge sees us moving from an ideology based on individualism and property rights, a market driven by competition and consumer desires, a limited state, and scientific specialization and fragmentation to a new ideology based on communitarianism, a system where political and social issues often supersede property rights, where community needs are more important than individual or consumer desires, where there is active intervention by the state, and where interdependence assumes more importance than independence.[10]

These shifts provide the ideological basis for government regulatory action in areas where there has been little or none in the past. Professor Lodge's comments suggest that we are now entering a new and different era where the corporate environment will be much more complex, controversial, and demanding. How well corporate executives cope with their government-active environment will provide a new measure of their corporate and professional success.

Government and Corporate Management: The Underlying Differences

To improve corporate management of government relations, executives first need to grasp the differences between public and private management. Some businessmen or business school deans, however, question whether management in the public and private sectors *is* substantially different. Arjay Miller, former Ford Motor Company executive and Dean of the Stanford Graduate School of Business, has argued that government is becoming more like business. Governments "have to deal with scarce resources in the public sector—money, land, air, water" and that is what private business has been doing all along.[11] The opposing point of view was summarized many years ago by the late Wallace Sayre of Columbia University, who said that business and public management are alike in every unimportant respect. Both views are partially correct. Business management techniques are increasingly important to government, but there are substantial differences in the environments in which private and public managers work. These differences dictate important differences in the application of techniques.

The chief personnel officer of the federal government described the differences between public and private management:

> While there are many similarities between public and business management, there are also a number of critical differences. For example, the private manager's major concern is profitability, while in the public sector managers must contend to a greater extent with more ambiguous measures of impact such as social values, the general public interest, accountability to both the law and elected and appointed officials, and the needs of specially targeted groups or individuals. The decisionmaking process in the public sector, given the demand for openness and the ability of competing groups or individuals to have access to the process, is at least different in degree from what exists in the private sector.[12]

There is a place for business management techniques in government, and there is a need for business executives to work in government from time to time, as many do. The differences in the two environments, however, often produce frustration and even despair. Professor George A. Steiner has noted these feelings about government by some businessmen:

> I have seen businessmen come to high executive positions in Washington with unsullied reputations for superior managerial efficiency and, after a short time, leave in frustration because the governmental managerial task baffled them. Managing in government is far different from managing in business, aside from the difference in rationality and efficiency. The entire milieu is different. Requirements for managerial success are different. The rules of the game are different.[13]

Steiner points out that this does not mean that sound business practices cannot be applied in government, but these practices must be applied in quite different ways and the result is likely to be quite unexpected.

Perhaps the most fundamental difference between government and private bureaucracies is their contrasting functions. Private bureaucracies are created for a specific, carefully defined purpose: to produce a product or deliver a service and to do so at a profit. Public bureaucracies, on the other hand, are created to represent and serve powerful constituencies in American life. They participate in government decision-making on behalf of various groups in society.

Public agencies are constantly under pressure to provide a satisfactory level of services to their client groups. In any large government today, there are departments and bureaus representing most major interests in society. There is also diversity within the large departments. The Department of Commerce, for example, contains the National Oceanic and Atmospheric Administration (part of which was formerly the Weather Bureau), the Maritime Administration (with jurisdiction over the Merchant Marine), the National Bureau of Standards, the National Fire Prevention and Control Administration, the Patent and Trademark Offices, the Economic Development Administration, as well as the functions one normally associates with the word *commerce.* The secretary of commerce spends much time responding to the diverse client groups that have interests in the diverse agencies under her supervision. The cabinet secretary responsible for the efficient functioning of a department does not expect the various interests represented in the department always to operate in harmony, any more than one would expect these interests to work harmoniously in society at large.

"I've learned a great deal in my 35 years with the company. Unfortunately, most of it is about government regulations."

A public bureaucracy is the image of the society that created it. Although cabinet secretaries work for and are appointed by the same president, there is no reason to expect them to agree on most issues. To be successful, the secretaries of labor and commerce must share and represent the views of their constituents. They are likely to agree no more and no less than their respective clients—labor and business—agree in the world outside of government.

These fundamental conflicts in interests and goals within departments are likely to be difficult and perplexing for executives accustomed to private-sector organizations. Internal conflicts there are far from uncommon, but in the private sector authority for internal conflict resolution is more clearly defined and centralized. It is easier to resolve internal disagreements.

There is no central core of authority in public bureaucracies. In government, even the fundamental goals and purposes of a department are likely to be at odds with one another. The solving of conflict by temporary solutions and fragile alliances is more common in government management than in corporate management.

Take the U.S. Department of Agriculture as an example. The secretary of agriculture and his staff sit atop a bureaucracy that represents many conflicting interests. It is a department for all farmers, with the mission to improve agricultural production and the state of American agriculture. The techniques for achieving this are often hotly debated between large corporate farms and smaller family-run farms. Furthermore, the department is also charged with regulating farm production and output through its responsibility for meat and food inspection. It runs large school lunch and nutritional programs, as well as a major welfare program, food stamps. The Farmers Home Administration, another division of the department, is one of the ten largest banking institutions in the United States. Yet nearly one-half of all the employees of the Department of Agriculture work for the U.S. Forest Service. Often the interests of the farmer and those of welfare, consumer, and conservation groups collide. Being secretary of agriculture can be a frustrating task. Most of the major issues of food production, regulation, food consumption, and conservation fought in society's political arena are debated forcefully within the department.

To some extent, the intense frustration of government executives is a new phenomenon. In the 1950s and 1960s, the Department of Agriculture had only a few client groups representing the diverse interests of the American farmer. While that community often lacked unanimity, the levels of disagreement within the department were nothing like they are today, when the department serves a vast, multifaceted clientele. A reporter recently wrote that the Department of Agriculture's "clients include food stamp recipients, school children, timber companies, food processing corporations and consumers. Minor decisions at Agriculture can send billion dollar shock waves through the U.S. economy."[14] This is a substantial change from the halcyon days when agriculture production and support for the farm community was the dominant departmental activity.

Operational Differences in Private and Public Management

Beyond the fundamental differences in the purposes of public and private bureaucracies, there are major differences in the ways the two function.

One often hears the criticism that public programs and governmental agencies do not have clearly stated goals and objectives. In fact, this is often true when compared to private organizations. Public agencies usually have their goals and objectives set for them by legislative bodies that create and fund the agencies. A legislative body also passes further legislation that the agency is responsible for implementing. The legislation has stated goals and objectives, but these are often vague and ambiguous. Legislative terms like "*quality* education," "*adequate* transportation," "*decent* housing," and "*safe* streets" are difficult to translate into meaningful operational objectives. In fact, these terms are often used only to insure passage of the legislation. Conflicting groups in the legislative process cannot agree on specifics, so it is often necessary to avoid specifics, pass the legislation, and leave operational matters till later. Agency executives have to sort out real objectives from rhetorical ones. Out of the vague and often conflicting statements in the law and in the legislative debate must come goals that can be used to define efficient operations. Usually this is impossible.

The U.S. Postal Service is a striking example of the contrasts between business and government management problems. In many ways, the Postal Service is like a typical business organization. Specific, operational goals can be set, and the efficiency of the system in attaining those goals can be assessed by standard, statistically based measurement techniques. One can, for example, determine time and costs of moving a letter or a package from address A to address B. With that information, it becomes feasible to measure efficiency and, over time, management improvement or degeneration.

The Postal Service becomes much less like a business organization and more like a government organization when one examines the social policy it is required to implement. One aspect of that policy is the proposition that all United States citizens should receive the same level and quality of government services no matter where they live. This has been interpreted to mean that everyone should have the same access to a post office—as well as to other government services—whether one lives in rural Winterset, Iowa or in suburban Chevy Chase, Maryland. To breathe life into that policy, the Postal Service has to maintain service in areas where it is not profitable, and some argue that they must continue to operate post offices in virtually every crossroads in America.

The postmaster general has a list of a few thousand post offices that do not pay their own way and are not essential to the efficient maintenance of the total system. Using business management techniques, the postmaster general can determine that a facility in Crossroads America moves fewer packages and letters and sells fewer dollars worth of stamps than it costs to heat, light, and staff the building. Yet a business-like decision to close the facility cannot be made, and these offices are often kept open to fulfill the policy of equal service for all—rural, suburban, or central city residents. Decisions by the postmaster general to close postal facilities can be appealed to an independent regulatory commission, the Postal Rate Commission (PRC).

The Postal Rate Commission has ruled that the Postal Service may not close nine rural post offices simply for economic reasons. Pointing to the congressional mandate that other factors be taken into consideration, the PRC ruled that the effect on the community of closing these post offices has to be a part of the decision. These facilities provide important community-supported communication functions beyond the delivery of mail, according to the Commission.[15]

The Postal Service is additionally challenged by the tradition that it support or subsidize certain types of mailings by carrying them at low rates. No amount of sound business management analysis will correct this situation. These are matters of social policy, not management. Over the years, the government has decided that it should take a role in encouraging business, non-profit organizations, charities, and educational insitutions through the subsidization of a distribution system for their advertising and publications. The business community, especially advertising agencies and publishers, strongly concur in this judgment.

Financial losses incurred by the Postal Service are made up by Congress. Putting the Postal Service on sound business management techniques would be relatively easy in management terms. However, as in most government programs, good management considerations in the Postal Service often must give way to the nettlesome and complicated issues of social policy and political feasibility.

The business executive coming into government soon recognizes that there is a point where business management techniques become ineffective and social policy considerations or politics take over. It is as if there is a continuum, with business management techniques on the one end and politics on the other, and at some point along that line, management techniques are overshadowed by the need to respond to social considerations. Agencies fall at different points along that line, and that point can shift at different times. A good example of a government program or agency run very much like a business organization at one time was the National Aeronautics and Space Administration (NASA) during the manned-flight space program days. In those days, the environment in which NASA operated was not at all characteristic of the environment in which most government agencies function or, in fact, of the environment in which NASA operates today. In the early 1960s, the president of the United States gave NASA a clear, one-sentence mission: Put a man on the moon by the end of the decade. There is virtually no way to misinterpret that. Furthermore, this presidential quest became a national quest; few people in the American public disagreed with the goal. With that kind of national consensus, the funds to achieve success came relatively easily. NASA achieved its goal. In terms of management objectives, NASA had an easy task. Complex management systems and engineering techniques were deployed as they are by a large, well-run corporation. And NASA's mission was successfully accomplished on time.

Things have changed for NASA. Today it is very much like other government programs. Its mission is unclear. There is major debate and conflict over what its goals and timetable should be. And it has to compete forcefully with other government programs for its share of the national budget.

A large part of all governmental budgets today is devoted to human-services programs, which seek to combat some of the nation's major social problems. Different people from different groups in different regions of the country view these problems in varying ways. This means that only the most general statements of program goals will satisfy a large enough number of people to insure program passage and funding. In summary, government management problems are complicated by generalized, difficult-to-measure mandates. In the 1940s, for example, Congress mandated "adequate housing" for all Americans. Two obvious questions government managers had to answer in the early stages of implementation were: "What is *adequate?*" and "By when?" A further complexity arises in the implementation stages because several agencies of the federal government become involved, and in most U.S. domestic programs, state and local governments become active participants.

Business corporations have an easier time establishing goals and objectives. Fewer social issues are involved in corporate product lines. Besides, if a corporation wishes to state its objectives in very precise terms, it has universally agreed upon language to use. Whether stated in terms of net profits, gross sales, new branch offices, stock prices, or mergers and acquisitions, there is a common understanding by those concerned of what is to be achieved. In contrast, social programs, with their vague or ambiguous objectives, are difficult to evaluate because there are no common standards of measurement. Successful program achievement to one observer is merely a satisfactory performance to another.

Business corporations use much more quantifiable objectives than "adequate health care" to measure their success. Sales, profits, and production are measurable indicators of goal attainment. Efficiency in operations is easier to attain, for promotions, bonuses, and raises can be made dependent upon these quantifiable measures of productivity.

Rewards for public-sector personnel are based on achievements other than sales or profits. Consequently, few quantifiable incentives or objectives are involved in salary determinations.

The federal government does have a productivity measurement system, however. Since 1970, twenty-eight government functions are measured each year. Analysis of these functions shows a 1.2 percent a year increase in government productivity, compared to a 1.3 percent a year increase in the nonfarm private sector. The problem with the comparison is that the functions measured in the government index are the type of functions most easily measurable and probably least significant in terms of total government output. For example, printing and duplication costs are part of the index. The number of claims processed by the Social Security Administration (SSA) in a given period of time is another part of the measurement. Incidentally, SSA's productivity increased over 30 percent in the eight years between 1968 and 1976. Government compares favorably with the private sector in the areas that can be quantified in this way, but the measurements do not go very far in addressing the question of effectiveness of government.[16]

Business Executives' View of Government Management

Several differences between public and private management are especially apparent to those who have worked in both. One is the difference between a system driven by profit motives and one based on reciprocity. In the private sector, business executives are usually motivated and guided by the desire to earn a profit for the company. Their decisions can be based upon the objective, and others can be persuaded to a similar point of view if the profit motive is fairly well articulated. In the public sector, without a profit motive, other inducements must be found. Often these are nothing more than the principle of reciprocity. If one administrator, staff member, or lobbyist can do something for another participant in the decision-making process then there is an implied agreement that at some future, undeclared date the favor will be reciprocated.

W. Michael Blumenthal, secretary of the treasury under President Carter and former chief executive officer of Bendix Corporation, discussed some of the challenges a business executive faces coming into government.[17] The difference between appearance and reality is much greater in the public sector. As there is a bottom line in business, the reality of what you do takes precedence over the way you do it. In government the opposite is often true. How you do something may create an image of power more potent than what you have actually done. The perception others have of what you do enhances your bargaining position and consequently your ability to achieve your agency's or your personal goals.

Another difference cited by Blumenthal was the inability of government managers freely to change their minds. Business executives armed with new facts, better advice, or revised forecasts often alter their decisions and steer businesses or product lines in a new direction. However, when public-sector executives change their minds, often because of new or more recent data, they are accused of being weak, indecisive, and inconsistent.

In the private sector, managers can hire people because they are good administrators. They can also close plants, reassign personnel, and terminate programs. Blumenthal found a very different situation in the Treasury Department. Many of the managers working for him were covered by the Civil Service. They were not necessarily chosen because they possessed any managerial skills; rather, most of them were employed because they had specific knowledge in a function or a program area. Moreover, Blumenthal found how difficult it was to hire, fire, reward, and transfer any of his middle-management staff. To drastically change or terminate a program, he would first have to navigate a maze of interest groups, client groups, congressional committees, and in many instances his own employees, all of whom had some personal reasons for perpetuating the targeted program.

The motivation of employees was a major difference detected by the secretary:

> That then leads you to the old question of motivation. In private industry you have many ways of motivating people. I can say to a young person coming up the ladder, as I did, you're doing a hell of a job, and though you're only twenty-seven years old, you've demonstrated that you have the maturity and the ability of a thirty-five-year-old, you have the wisdom of a forty-year-old, and I see in you the potential to be the chairman of this company some time, even though you're only twenty-seven, so I'm going to move you around very quickly. I'm going to raise your pay to keep you in the company. I'm going to reward you at the end of the year with a bonus if you do a certain job. You could earn a big bonus. And I can set up a system in the company to pick out the bright young people to do that with, and really develop quality in the company.
>
> That's impossible in the government. If I do it with one, all the other twenty-seven-year-olds say, what about me? If you say well, you're not as good, you may quite possibly be sued. So it just cannot be done. You have almost no control over selection. Hiring goes off a list. And to go outside that system involves more bureaucratic footwork than it is worth.[18]

Finally, there is the problem of what Blumenthal called "the inverted pyramid." In the private sector, the work load resembles a pyramid, with top executives working hard and delegating tasks downward to their hand-picked departmental staffs. In the public sector, Blumenthal suggests, the pyramid has become inverted. "Government bureaucracy, in terms of work load, is an inverted pyramid. The amount of work varies with how far up you are—the people at the top do most of the work and have most of the pressure and cannot delegate."[19]

Blumenthal sees the top managers in government as hard-working, competent executives who are overloaded, underpaid, and trapped by being unable to right the pyramid so that they can get the type of management help they need to begin redistributing the work load.

Roy Ash, who headed the Office of Management and Budget after having been the chief executive officer of Litton Industries, went to the heart of the problem: "Just imagine yourself as chief executive officer where your board is made up of your employees, customers, suppliers and competitors. How would you like to run that business and try to be effective?"[20]

Constitutional Limitations on Government Management

In government, modern managers and the techniques they use must be tested against the fundamental goals of the U.S. Constitution. That document, written nearly two hundred years ago, sought to achieve a representative system of government that would operate openly and fairly. The major goal of the framers of the Constitution was to divide power, yet avoid what they regarded as the potential dangers of democratic government: mob rule and excessive influence of factions. The mood of the day and the motivation of the drafters was to divide and limit power, to make it difficult to generate executive management strength.*

The experience under the English kings had taught the founding fathers a lesson in power politics. The U.S. Constitution was their response. It was carefully drafted to insure that government would be composed of many different competitive centers of power, thereby eliminating the danger of control by a few.

Power in the Constitution is divided in several ways, between national government and states, between two houses of the legisla-

* The concern of the drafters and signers of the U.S. Constitution for devising a system in which power centers would be controlled—allowed to exist and compete but not exert excessive authority—is seen clearly in one of James Madison's contributions to the national debate on the adoption of the Constitution, *Federalist 10.*

ture, between the legislature and the president, and between all of them and the courts. Creating a modern executive management system against this constitutional backdrop is not easy. Nearly all the demands of modern management call for strengthening the decision-making authority of chief executives, and this runs counter to the philosophy of the Constitution.

Public and private organizations have very different requirements when it comes to what the public is entitled to know about their method of operations. Public organizations provide a public record of almost all of their activities for everyone to see. Legislation is, of necessity, proposed and adopted after open hearings are held. Proponents and opponents are allowed to testify. The transcripts of these hearings are published, as are the voting records of the legislators. Agencies hold open hearings whenever a rule is written affecting the implementation of a program. Judicial review is always a real possibility should agencies violate established procedures.

The openness of public agency decision processes is often criticized for not being open enough or for being open only to the "wrong" people. Common Cause recently named seven of the forty-seven federal agencies covered by the Sunshine Act of 1977 as the "Secret Seven." In a study of all those agencies, Common Cause reported that in one year, March 1977 to March 1978, 36 percent (813) of the 2,232 meetings held were closed to the public; 26 percent (583) of the meetings were partially closed to the public; and 38 percent (846) of the meetings were open to the public.[21] But even the "worst" government agencies are more open than most business corporations. Corporate deliberations for the most part are conducted in closed meetings with few if any public or consumer representatives present. The minutes, discussions, and results may be circulated to a select group of decision-makers within the corporation, but not to the public at large. In fact, should the results of some of these meetings become public, charges of industrial or corporate espionage would follow.

Public organizations not only conduct most of their business in public, but all their documents are open to scrutiny. Budgets, job descriptions, salaries, records of revenues and expenditures, and lists of grants and contracts awarded are considered public information.

The media devotes much of its attention to government activity. As most of the government's business is conducted in a highly visible environment, hearings, legislation, regulation, budgets, and expenditures are common subjects reported by journalists and television newscasters. The glare of publicity is often difficult for the government executive to take, although most view it as a healthy imperative of democratic government. The following humorous path of a government directive from the executive staff meeting to the press is the result of one wit's frustration with the press. Surprisingly, it comes from the government's most secretive agency, the CIA:

> DIRECTOR'S STAFF MEETING: "Tomorrow afternoon at about 1500 hours, Halley's Comet will be visible in the area, an event which occurs once every seventy-five years. Employees who wish to witness this phenomenon should assemble on the quadrangle in front of Headquarters and a representative of DDS&T will explain it to them. In case of rain, we will not be able to see anything, of course. In that instance, interested personnel may see films of it in the auditorium."
>
> DIRECTORATE STAFF MEETING: "By order of the Director, tomorrow at 1500 hours, Halley's Comet will appear above the quadrangle in front of Headquarters. If it rains, employees should assemble in the auditorium where the rare phenomenon will take place, something which occurs only once in 75 years. DDS&T will film it."
>
> OFFICE STAFF MEETING: "DDS&T has arranged for the phenomenal Halley's Comet to appear in the auditorium at 1500 hours tomorrow. In case of rain on the quadrangle, the Director will speak to all employees, something which occurs once every 75 years."
>
> DIVISION STAFF MEETING: "Tomorrow at 1500 the Director will appear in the auditorium with Halley's Comet, something which happens once every 75 years. It it rains, the DCI will order the comet onto the quadrangle in front of Headquarters."
>
> BRANCH MEETING: "When it rains tomorrow at 1500 hours, the phenomenal 75-year-old Dr. Halley, accompanied by the DCI, will drive his comet around the quadrangle in front of the auditorium."
>
> RUMOR MILL: "Some guy named Halley, who parks his old comet in front of Headquarters, is going to be named the new Director tomorrow at a 3 o'clock meeting in the auditorium. I think he's got some connection with DDS&T."
>
> WASHINGTON (AP): INFORMED SOURCES IN THE INTELLIGENCE COMMUNITY REPORTED TODAY THAT A SHAKE-UP OF TOP CIA LEADERSHIP IS PLANNED BY THE WHITE HOUSE. A LEADING SCIENTIST IS EXPECTED TO BE NAMED.

Continuity of Government Managers

Democratic government requires periodic elections of top officials. Those successful at the polls are encouraged by the electorate to restructure and staff their jurisdictions in a manner consistent with their policy goals and working style. Although it is difficult to change the structure of government, it is easy to change the top personnel. Over 1,000 top-level management appointments are made by a new president, about one-half of which require U.S. Senate confirmation. These changes often place public organizations at a great disadvantage when compared to private organizations. New executives, many of whom have not worked in government before, have to learn the rules and regulations of their new organizations. This takes time. Middle-management executives and clients of these agencies find a lack of continuity in agency policies and procedures which causes delay and confusion. Two to three years is the average length of service for these new officials. Such instability and inexperience in the top echelons creates major impediments to good management.

Business corporations are generally more orderly when they replace top executives. Rarely do they remove the top echelon all at once, down to and including the managers of the major operating departments. Even in cases of wholesale changes, the new top executives often come from within the organization. This tends to reduce the shock waves and insure continuity and corporate stability in the eyes of the employees, stockholders, and customers.

Notes

1. The quotations are from a series of conferences held between 1973 and 1975 by the Conference Board, a prominent business-supported research organization. These quotations and an analysis of the proceedings can be found in Leonard Silk and David Vogel, *Ethics and Profits: The Crisis of Confidence in American Business* (New York: Simon & Schuster, 1976).

2. See John Kenneth Galbraith, *The New Industrial State* (Boston: Houghton Mifflin Co., 1967) for a clear statement of this position.

3. David Vogel, "Why Businessmen Distrust Their State: The Political Consciousness of American Corporate Executives," *British Journal of Political Science 8* (August 1978): 45.

4. See Charles E. Lindblom, *Politics and Markets: The World's Political-Economic Systems* (New York: Basic Books, Inc., 1977), especially Chapter 13, "The Privileged Position of Business."

5. Barry Sussman, " 'Tax Revolt' Targeted at Poor Service," *Washington Post,* 1 October 1978.

6. Thomas C. Cochran, *Business In American Life: A History* (New York: McGraw-Hill, Co., 1972), p. 116.

7. See Michael Bell and L. Richard Gabler, "Government Growth: and Intergovernmental Concern," *Intergovernmental Perspective,* 2, no. 4 (Fall 1976): 8. It is not unreasonable to estimate that many major corporations earn 10 to 25 percent of their gross revenues from direct and indirect sales to public institutions.

8. Phyllis S. McGrath, *Action Plans for Public Affairs* (The Conference Board, Inc., 845 Third Ave., New York City, 10022, 1977).

9. Steven V. Roberts, "Trade Associations are Flocking to Capital as U.S. Widens Its Role," *New York Times,* 4 March 1978.

10. See George C. Lodge, *The New American Ideology* (New York: Alfred A. Knopf, 1975.)

11. "Big Picture is Not Just the Profit," *Washington Star,* 17 July 1978.

12. Letter to John S. Day, president of the American Assembly of Collegiate Schools of Business, from Alan K. Campbell, chairman, U.S. Civil Service Commission, 28 September 1977. Campbell became director of the Office of Personnel Management when the Civil Service Commission was abolished in January 1979.

13. George A. Steiner, *Business and Society,* 2nd ed. (New York: Random House, 1975), p. 384.

14. Dan Morgan, " 'Plain, Poor Sister' is Newly Alluring," *Washington Post,* 4 July 1978.

15. U.S. Postal Rate Commission, in the matters of Lone Grove, Texas, et al., 7 May 1979.

16. The figures cited are from Alan K. Campbell, chairman, U.S. Civil Service Commission, "What's Right with Federal Employees," *Civil Service Journal,* 18, no. 4 (June 1978): 6–12. Additional data and analysis are available from the Federal Productivity Commission, Washington, D.C. For an analysis of productivity measurements in state and local government, see Harry P. Hatry, "The Status of Productivity Measurement in the Public Sector," *Public Administration Review* 38 (January–February 1978): 28–33.

17. "Candid Reflections of a Businessman in Washington," *Fortune,* 29 January 1979, pp. 36–49.

18. Ibid., p. 40.

19. Ibid.

20. Gordon Chase, "Managing Compared," *New York Times,* 14 March 1978.

21. Larry Kramer, "Common Cause Grades 'The Secret Seven,' " *Washington Post,* 31 August 1978.

two

The Personnel of Public Management

Stability in government management programs is the responsibility of the bureaucracy, especially the career public servants. For business executives and others who deal with government, these are the key people. Often criticized—sometimes rightly—civil servants as a group, their environment and working habits, are not well known to the public. Too often, they are inaccurately regarded as one large group with common characteristics. Actually, these bureaucrats are a large and diverse group. Who they are, where they work, how they operate, what their pay and incentive systems are, and what type of training they receive are essential pieces of information for business executives.

The size of the federal bureaucracy is a good place to start. The number of federal employees has, over the past twenty years, been an important political issue. Most presidential candidates campaign against the size of the federal bureaucracy, claiming it is too large, too bloated, and too inefficient. To come to grips with the federal government, one must first examine some numbers.

At present, 2.8 million civilians work for the federal government. This figure has not changed significantly since 1967. The mix of agencies for whom these people work and their distribution across the agencies is often a surprise to people who have not looked at the data before. The three largest agencies in terms of civilian employees—the Department of Defense, the Postal Service, and the Veterans Administration—employ close to 2 million of the 2.8 million employees of the federal government, or about 70 percent of the civilian work force. To make a significant reduction in the size of the federal bureaucracy, the president must concentrate on these three agencies.

Table 2.1

Civilian employment of the federal government, executive agencies (April 1978)	
Total, all agencies	2,815,127
Executive departments and independent agencies:	
Department of Defense	982,093
U.S. Postal Service	650,648
Veterans Administration	231,110
Health, Education and Welfare	159,114
Treasury	138,126
Agriculture	120,227
Interior	75,809
Transportation	74,505
Justice	53,723
Tennessee Valley Authority	43,420
Commerce	40,140
General Services Administration	37,749
State	30,052
National Aeronautics and Space Administration	23,965
Labor	20,998
Energy	19,704
Housing and Urban Development	17,877
Environmental Protection Agency	12,587
Civil Service Commission	8,897
Small Business Administration	6,029
Smithsonian Institution	4,251
National Labor Relations Board	2,919
Nuclear Regulatory Commission	2,908
Equal Employment Opportunity Commission	2,349
Federal Communications Commission	2,134
Securities and Exchange Commission	1,984
Federal Trade Commission	1,778
Executive Office of the President	1,618
Board of Governors, Federal Reserve System	1,478
National Science Foundation	1,351
Consumer Product Safety Commission	978
Civil Aeronautics Board	819
Federal Maritime Commission	312
(Total)	2,771,692
Number with other agencies, boards, and commissions: 43,435	

Source: U.S. Office of Management and Budget

Only about 330,000, or under 12 percent of the total civilian work force, is employed in the Washington metropolitan area. The federal government is a broadly decentralized bureaucracy with most of its employees working in the ten regional centers, in other cities in the U.S., and around the world. The Washington, D.C. metropolitan area is only the very tip of the employment iceberg.

The concern that businessmen often voice about a huge, centralized, and growing federal bureaucracy is at least partially unwarranted. With almost 70 percent of the federal work force employed by three departments and with almost 90 percent of the employees working outside the Washington area, it is difficult to substantiate claims that the federal system is overcentralized. And measured against GNP or population growth, the federal bureaucracy has been declining over the past several years. In 1952, there were 16.3 federal employees for every 1,000 people in the United States, and today there are about 13 federal employees (table 2.2). Even the real figures show no significant change in well over a decade.

It can be argued that figures of federal employment do not accurately reflect the size of the federal government, for these numbers do not show the vast army of people dependent upon the federal government for a job. It has been estimated that between 3 and 4 million people are not on the federal payroll, but derive their salaries from government grants and contracts. This estimate includes those employed by state and local governments as a result of federal programs; it also includes university faculty on government research projects and employees in the private sector working as a result of a government contract with industry. The Defense Department, which keeps the best figures on these matters, estimates that over 2 million people "receive salaries funded by DOD through research and service contracts and DOD procurement and construction activities."[1]

The big growth area in public employment is in state, county, and local governments. In 1976, the total was about 12.2 million. Over 3 million people work for the fifty state governments, which is more than all civilians in federal employment. And about 9 million people work for cities, counties, towns, and villages across the country. The number of state and local employees is growing very fast. Whereas the number of federal employees per 1,000 population has decreased since the early 1950s, the number of state and local employees per 1,000 population has increased in that period by over 117 percent (table 2). A total of 15 million people work in the public sector today. That is about one out of every six nonfarm jobs in the United States.

Government personnel perform a wide variety of functions. The federal government alone employs almost every known professional, skilled, and unskilled type of employee. Of the total of 15 million public employees in this country, however, over 40 percent are working in public school systems. Public education is the major function of government in the United States in terms of the number of personnel employed (figure 2.1)

Table 2.2

Government Employment and Population, 1948–1978

Fiscal year	Government employment				Population	
	Federal executive branch [1] (thousands)	State and local governments (thousands)	All governmental units (thousands)	Federal as percent of all governmental units	Total United States (thousands)	Federal employment per 1,000 population
1949	2,075	3,906	5,981	34.7	149,767	13.9
1950 [2]	1,934	4,078	6,012	32.2	152,271	12.7
1951 [2]	2,456	4,031	6,487	37.9	154,878	15.9
1952	2,574	4,134	6,708	38.4	157,553	16.3
1953	2,532	4,282	6,814	37.2	160,184	15.8
1954	2,382	4,552	6,934	34.4	163,026	14.6
1955	2,371	4,728	7,099	33.4	165,931	14.3
1956	2,372	5,064	7,436	31.9	168,903	14.0
1957	2,391	5,380	7,771	30.8	171,984	13.9
1958	2,355	5,630	7,985	29.5	174,882	13.5
1959	2,355	5,806	8,161	28.8	177,830	13.2
1960 [2]	2,371	6,073	8,444	28.1	180,671	13.1
1961 [2]	2,407	6,295	8,702	27.7	183,691	13.1
1962	2,485	6,533	9,018	27.6	186,538	13.3
1963 [3]	2,490	6,834	9,324	26.7	189,242	13.2
1964 [3]	2,469	7,236	9,705	25.4	191,889	12.9
1965	2,496	7,683	10,179	24.5	194,303	12.8
1966	2,664	8,259	10,923	24.4	196,560	13.6
1967	2,877	8,730	11,607	24.8	198,712	14.5
1968	2,951	9,141	12,092	24.4	200,706	14.7
1969 [4]	2,980	9,496	12,476	23.9	202,677	14.7
1970 [2]	2,944	9,869	12,813	23.0	204,878	14.4
1971 [2]	2,883	10,257	13,140	21.9	207,053	13.9
1972	2,823	10,640	13,463	21.0	208,846	13.5
1973	2,775	11,065	13,840	20.0	210,410	13.2
1974	2,847	11,463	14,310	19.9	211,901	13.4
1975	2,848	12,025	14,873	19.1	213,540	13.3
1976	2,832	12,410	15,242	18.6	215,078	13.2
1977 (act.) [5]	2,789	12,286	15,075	18.5	217,329	12.8
1978 (est.)	2,805	([6])	-----------	17.8	219,068	12.8
1979 (est.)	2,803	([6])	-----------	17.3	220,821	12.7

[1] Covers total end-of-year employment in full-time permanent, temporary, part-time, and intermittent employees in the executive branch, including the Postal Service, and, beginning in 1970, includes various disadvantaged youth and worker-trainee programs.

[2] Includes temporary employees for the decennial census.

[3] Excludes 7,411 project employees in 1963 and 406 project employees in 1964 for the public works acceleration program.

[4] On Jan. 1, 1969, 42,000 civilian technicians of the Army and Air Force National Guard converted by law from State to Federal employment status. They are included in the Federal employment figures in this table starting with 1969.

[5] Data for 1949 through 1976 are as of June 30; for 1977 through 1979, as of Sept. 30.

[6] The percentages shown for these years are consistent with reasonable estimates based on recent trends in State and local government.

Source: U.S. Office of Management and Budget

Figure 2.1.

Functional distribution of governmental employment, October 1976

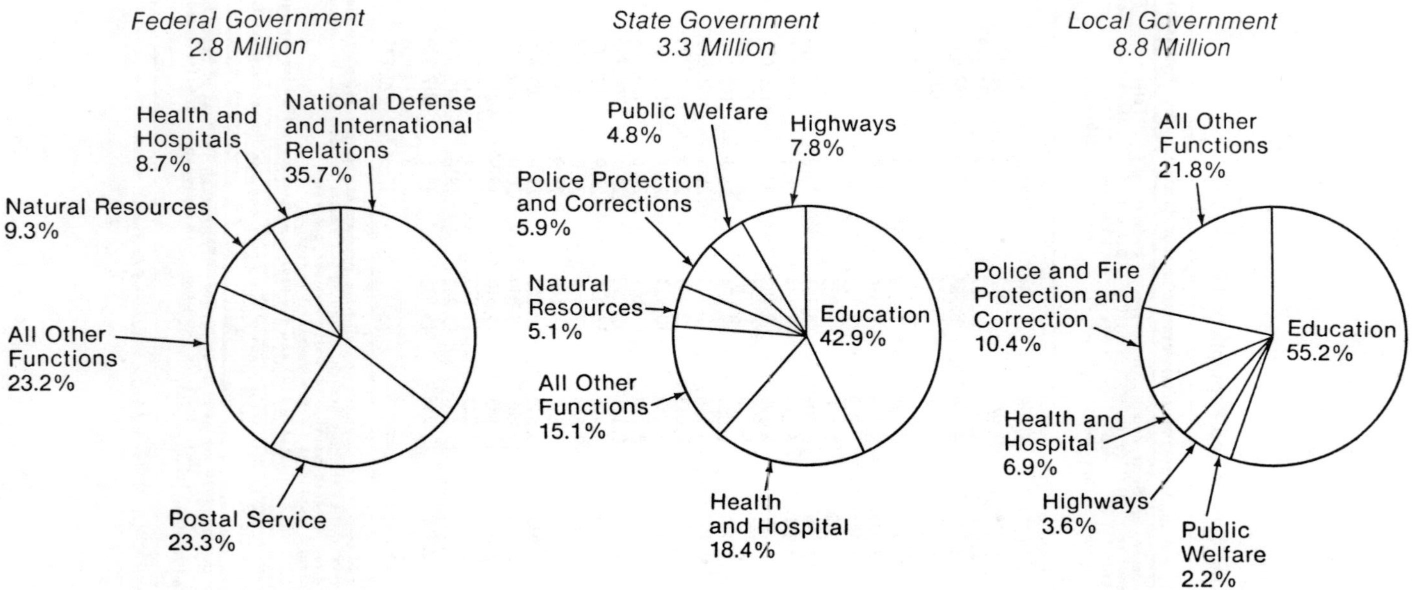

Source: U.S. Bureau of the Census

The regulatory bodies that oversee business practices in a variety of fields have far fewer employees than is generally believed. Table 2.3 gives the number of all employees, professional and nonprofessional, of five long-established regulatory commissions over a period of eighteen years.

Table 2.3

Paid civilian employment in the federal government by agency, 1960

Agency	*1960*	*1970*	*1973*	*1978*
Civil Aeronautics Board	755	682	661	834
Federal Communications Commission	1,403	1,537	1,703	2,083
Federal Trade Commission	782	1,330	1,410	1,626
Interstate Commerce Commission	2,381	1,755	1,765	2,037
Securities and Exchange Commission	–	1,657	1,971	2,082

Source: U.S. Government Documents

Two relatively new regulatory agencies that have major impact on the business community are the Environmental Protection Agency (EPA) and the Occupational Safety and Health Administration (OSHA). OSHA employs 2,817 people, and the EPA employs 9,600 people. OSHA recently reported a large and growing backlog of complaints. It has a waiting list of 5,000 complaints from workers and other government agencies. The agency employs 1,500 compliance officers currently, but would require over three times that many just to investigate the complaints now coming in.[2]

The percentage of GNP expended by government is perhaps a better indicator of government size than is the number of government employees. In 1949, federal expenditures were 16 percent of GNP, and in 1976 they were 23.2 percent. This increase of 45 percent was exceeded by the increased portion of GNP spent by state and local governments (table 2.4). Although this is substantial growth, it is not nearly as high a percentage of GNP as government expenditures in other developed nations. The United States ranked fifteenth out of twenty-three countries. The study in which these figures were compiled and analyzed concluded, "It does appear that the international trend is toward increased governmental responsibility and that the United States is far from the vanguard of the movement in terms of size and growth."[3]

Table 2.5 shows federal expenditures as a percentage of GNP. It also indicates how the mix of expenditures has changed, especially in

Table 2.4

An elastic yardstick for measuring the growth of government 1949–76

	1949	1976	Percent change from 1949 to 1976
Dollar expenditures (in billions)			
Federal	41.3	390.6	845.7
State–Local	18.0	185.0	927.3
Total	59.3	575.6	870.7
Public expenditures as a percent of GNP			
Federal	16.0	23.2	45
State–Local	7.0	11.0	57.1
Total	23.0	34.2	48.7
Public expenditures as a percent of GNP adjusted for price changes			
Federal	17.6	22.8	29.5
State–Local	9.3	10.9	17.2
Total	26.9	33.7	25.3

Expressed in 1972 dollars.

Source: U.S. Advisory Commission on Intergovernmental Relations, Washington, D.C., Intergovernmental Perspective 2, no. 4, (Fall 1976): 9.

Table 2.5.

Federal sector expenditures as a percent of GNP

Description	*1947–49 average actual*	*1957–59 average actual*	*1967–69 average actual*	*1977–79 average estimate*
Defense purchases	4.3	9.9	8.7	4.9
Nondefense purchases	2.0	1.6	2.4	2.8
Domestic transfer payments	3.4	3.9	5.1	8.9
Foreign transfer payments	1.3	.4	.3	.2
Grants-in-aid to state and local governments	.7	1.1	2.0	3.6
Net interest paid	1.7	1.2	1.3	1.7
Subsidies less current surplus of government enterprises	.2	.6	.6	.4
Total expenditures	13.8	18.6	20.4	22.4

Source: U.S. Budget for Fiscal Year 1979 (Washington, D.C.: U.S. Government Printing Office, 1979).

the defense and domestic transfers categories. The latter has gone up dramatically, largely because of increases in Social Security and Medicare obligations, while defense expenditures declined as U.S. activity in Vietnam subsided.

Bureaucrats at the Top

The number and characteristics of top-level executives in the federal civil service is a complicated picture. There are approximately 8,400 senior-level managers or executives in the service who are responsible for the management of over 2 million civilian personnel (table 2.6). (The Postal Service is not included in these figures). They are also responsible for the administration of a budget in excess of $500 billion per year. In addition to the 8,400 managers, there are around 400 cabinet secretaries, assistant secretaries, and similar high-level appointees, who require confirmation by the U.S. Senate.

Table 2.6

Senior-level managers in the U.S. civil service

Executives	*Career*	*Noncareer and presidential appointments*	*Others excepted*[a]	*total*
GS–15 properly classifiable at supergrade	400	20	0	420
Supergrade and equivalent	3,750	400	3,700	7,850
Executive level V	25	72	13	110
Executive level IV	2	25	11	38
Total	4,177	517	3,724	8,418

[a] Positions excepted from competitive selection because they are scientists, engineers, and other highly technical specialists.

Source: U.S. Civil Service Commission, September 1978

The 8,400 senior personnel are divided into three groups. The largest, over 4,100, are the career civil servants, who are appointed on the basis of open competition without presidential participation. This corps of career managers, with many years of experience in government, is the main, continuing support system for federal management. They are paid according to the General Service Schedule (table 2.7) at the levels GS 15–18. Fewer than thirty are on the Executive Service Schedule, the salary system used for cabinet-level appointments.

Table 2.7

Salaries of U.S. civil servants

General Schedule (GS)
per annum rates and initial and top steps

	Step 1	*Step 10*
GS–1	$ 6,561	$ 8,532
2	7,422	9,645
3	8,366	10,877
4	9,391	12,208
5	10,507	13,657
6	11,712	15,222
7	13,014	16,920
8	14,414	18,734
9	15,920	20,699
10	17,532	22,788
11	19,263	25,041
12	23,087	30,017
13	27,453	35,688
14	32,442	42,171
15	38,160	49,608[a]
16	44,756	
17	52,429[a]	
18	61,449[a]	

Executive Level Schedule (ES)

I.	$66,000
II.	57,500
III.	52,500
IV.	50,000
V.	47,500

[a]The rate of basic pay payable to employees at these rates is limited to the rate payable for level V of the Executive Schedule, which is to remain at $47,500.

Source: U.S. Office of Personnel Management, Washington, D.C., 1979

The second largest group of executives (3,724) are differentiated from the first group mainly in the manner of selection. They are specialists, often scientists or engineers, needed for top-level jobs in agencies like the Tennessee Valley Authority and the National Bureau of Standards. This selection process is also outside the sphere of presidential influence, but it is not openly competitive. All but twenty-five are paid at the supergrade, GS 16–18 level.

In the third and smallest category are about 500 executives. These are the managers, some of whom are appointed by the president, the remainder by cabinet officials. This small group of managers does not hold cabinet rank, and their appointments do not require Senate confirmation. They serve at the pleasure of the president or the cabinet official and are usually replaced after a change in administration.

A major problem in government management is the relationship between the career and noncareer executives.[4] Not only is the rate of turnover troublesome, but equally difficult is the interest of the high-level appointees in making their mark on public policy in the short time period they serve. The result is that few devote much attention to management problems, where the rewards are meager and usually unnoticed by the public. Instead, they concentrate on the more grandiose, more attractive problems of policy design, which attract more public attention.

Presidents are not exceptions to the rule; they generally avoid the tough managerial questions, for they lack glamour and public interest. Recent presidents, especially Nixon and Carter, have been exceptions to this rule. President Nixon supported and implemented some far-reaching changes in the federal grants-in-aid system for state and local government. He also fostered some important reorganization actions in the federal bureaucracy, including the creation of the Office of Management and Budget (OMB) from the old Bureau of the Budget, which had a much smaller mandate. The reorganization added the "M," management responsibilities, to the old bureau.

President Carter invested considerable time and prestige in a major reform of the civil service system. Dissatisfaction in the country with government management had led Carter to make such reform an important campaign promise. The reforms legislated in 1978 were the most far-reaching since the civil service system was created in the 1880s.

The Carter Reforms in Top-Level Federal Management

The newly implemented civil service plan has two major goals. One is to make the federal bureaucracy more responsive to the goals and policy initiatives of the president and the corps of political executives, while assuring even more strongly than in the past that the service is protected from the sting of partisan political activity. This is no easy task. The problem represents a fundamental dilemma in public management—efficiency and expertise on the one side versus responsiveness to the legitimate initiatives of the democratically elected leadership of the country. The second underlying goal of reform, related to the first, is to make it easier to reward managers and others who perform well and to penalize or remove those who are not performing.

The major changes mandated by the new law included the elimination of the Civil Service Commission, a semi-independent body that for nearly a century had been responsible for most of the personnel functions of the federal government.[5] The Commission was replaced by the Office of Personnel Management (OPM), an executive agency reporting to the president and responsible for most of the personnel activities of the government. A second agency, the Merit Systems Protection Board (MSPB), a semi-independent commission, is responsible for reviewing employee grievances, including dismissals. A Federal Labor Relations Authority, comparable to the National Labor Relations Board for private-sector employees, was also created.

The most important provision of the bill from a management perspective is the creation of the Senior Executive Service (SES). This is the elite corps of federal managers, the 8,400 individuals discussed above. Members of the Service have less tenure in their jobs than they did under the old scheme; they can be demoted or removed from the Executive Service. The government improved its reward structure for the SES by introducing a sizable year-end cash bonus system. Up to half of those in the larger agencies can receive a bonus of up to 20 percent of their salary. Five percent of the 8,400 could receive a "meritorius" rank, carrying a bonus of $10,000, and 1 percent could be designated "distinguished," with an award of $20,000. No person could receive more than one award in a five-year period, and no person could receive a salary of more than $66,000, the pay of a cabinet secretary. Merit pay systems were also adopted for middle-level managers.

The Carter reforms, based on private-sector models, are a fundamental change in the rewards, incentives, and penalties for government managers. There will be numerous difficulties in implementing the new law, including developing measures of performance where profit/loss and similar criteria do not apply. Yet, this system will create a new environment that could profoundly alter the way government is managed.

The Benefits of Public Employment

The salaries of those public executives in the General Service are shown in table 2.7. Those in the supergrade category, GS, 16–18, and in the Executive Schedule (ES) were frozen at $47,500 per year. This freeze was put into effect in October of 1977. For five years prior to that, the figure was frozen at $36,000 and later for a while at $37,800. The salaries of cabinet secretaries and certain other high officials are $66,000 per year. A few in the ES have salaries between the frozen level of $47,500 and $66,000.[6]

In June 1979, President Carter sent to Congress a proposal to overhaul the federal pay system. A major aim of the plan is to peg federal salaries to private-sector salaries on a regional basis. Federal pay in the past has been linked to counterparts in the private sector, but regional disparities have made the system inequitable.

A major feature of this program is the consideration of both fringe benefits and pay instead of just pay in comparing public and private salaries. The problem, of course, is mainly in lower-level management and clerical positions; top-level management salaries in government have always been less than top-level salaries in business and industry. Another problem is that federal workers tend to be underpaid in large metropolitan areas and overpaid in rural areas.

Like other plans affecting federal workers, the proposal would not lower any pay scales, but if it is passed by Congress, future raises for many white-collar and blue-collar workers would be smaller.

One major difference between the top federal executives and their subordinates is their place of work. Unlike the decentralized pattern of employment in the total federal work force, 73.4 percent of all the federal executive-level personnel worked in the Washington metropolitan area in 1976.

The average length of service for those in the nonpolitical categories is 22.4 years. This represents a substantial career in the public service. Political executives remain in the public service for less than four years. The educational level of the career executive is very high: 93.4 percent have at least a bachelor's degree, 63.4 percent have advanced degrees, and 24.4 percent have a doctorate. The younger executives have higher educational credentials than the older ones.

One interesting characteristic of federal service is the large number of executives who have law degrees: 16 percent. A law degree seems a good way to prepare for the federal Civil Service.

A recent survey asked all federal executives why they had entered the public service. Nearly one-third answered that it offered an interesting and a challenging assignment. Another 25 percent claimed that the federal service offered the best opportunity for pursuing their chosen occupational field; slightly more than 10 percent claimed it was the best offer they had had in terms of location, pay, advancement, and benefits.

One question that comes up frequently in business circles is the nature of the federal retirement system. There are several different retirement systems in the Civil Service. Law enforcement officials, members of Congress, congressional employees, air-traffic controllers, and others have slightly more liberal benefits than the standard government retirement system. And, of course, the military retirement system is quite different from all others.

Several study groups have examined the comparability of the federal retirement system with the private sector. The conclusion drawn is that the Civil Service retirement annuities are not seriously out of line with private pension plans.[7] Federal employees pay half of the cost of the retirement system, contributing 7 percent of their salaries. Benefits and retirement eligibility are calculated on the basis of a formula; employees with thirty years service are eligible to retire at fifty-five, at about 56 percent of their final salary, but most stay longer. Employees covered by the average private pension plans and Social Security with thirty years receive pensions equaling about 57 percent of their final salary, of which about 15 percent, the Social Security portion, is not taxable. Federal employees do not participate in the Social Security system, consequently 100 percent of their retirement is subject to federal income tax.

The major attraction of the federal scheme is that for the past several years federal retirement benefits have been indexed to inflation. Whenever there is a 3 percent rise in the Consumer Price Index, the retirement annuity goes up. Adjustments are made every six months. Given the substantial rise of the index in the last several years, the indexing has become a desirable feature of the federal retirement system.

The Congressional Budget Office (CBO) recently concluded that the federal retirement system is more generous than private-sector systems. However, federal employees on the whole contribute more of their salaries toward retirement than their private-sector counterparts. Some changes were suggested by CBO, including bringing federal employees under Social Security. The changes would not be dramatic, because the differences between public and private pension systems are not significant.

Separation from the Service

The number of federal civil servants terminated or fired is a controversial topic in which the public seems to have an unusually lively interest. Although published statistics suggest that very few federal employees are actually fired, this is not accurate. The misconception is caused by faults in the statistical and reporting processes.

It certainly is possible to fire federal workers. Indeed, over 17,000 federal employees were fired for cause or involuntarily separated from federal employment in 1976. This figure does not include those who saw the handwriting on the wall and left before they were asked. It also does not include the number of people laid off because of reorganizations or changes in their functions. In a bureaucracy of about 2.8 million people, yearly separations of an estimated 25,000 are not insubstantial.*

The federal bureaucracy today is a large, complex institution vulnerable to criticism. Even presidents seeking reelection find it difficult to resist the temptation to exhort the public with the wildest, worst examples of bureaucratic excesses committed, ironically enough, in a bureaucracy for which they are legally responsible. They speak of ending waste and inefficiency in government bureaucracies, of reducing the number of bureaus, offices, and agencies, and of reorganizing the bureaucracies to reduce the number of employees and increase efficiency in operations. Most of these efforts, unfortunately, fail to achieve their goals, often because the reform plans are based on erroneous assumptions.

Candidate Carter played the bureaucracy numbers game in

* The total number of federal employees dismissed in calendar year 1976 was 17,157. This figure includes:

- 226 who were separated for inefficiency based on unsatisfactory performance of duties
- 2,287 who resigned in lieu of adverse action, some of whom may have done so because of poor performance
- 4,261 who were terminated during their probationary periods
- 240 who were removed because of some condition that existed before they were hired
- 3,164 who were dismissed for some form of misconduct
- 418 who were separated for suitability reasons
- 4 who were separated under the Foreign Service system
- 6,557 who were discharged for a variety of additional reasons that the data do not differentiate.

See: *Civil Service News,* U.S. Civil Service Commission, 20 April 1978 campaigning for the presidency. One of his campaign brochures claimed that as governor of Georgia he had eliminated 278 of the 300 agencies in Georgia's bureaucracy. Later in the campaign, he promised to reduce what he said were 1,900 federal agencies to 200. Since the election, reorganization planning has been a major activity of the Carter administration. In the process of preparing for the reorganization, Carter counted 2,103 government agencies in operation. This is an exaggeration based on the inclusion of 1,185 advisory committees and 129 interagency and interdepartmental committees. Reducing the number of federal agencies can be a political maneuver. One simply counts every little commission or committee (generally these are not staffed and have little or no budget), then abolishes or consolidates them, and claims a reduction in the number of government agencies.

Public Management and the Public

The repeated attacks on the bureaucracy have made the average citizen quite skeptical about its role in society. Such public skepticism of government is healthy in a democracy, but too much skepticism can quickly grow into a dangerous condition of self-fulfilling prophecy. With the public constantly exposed to criticism of bureaucracy, it is not surprising when national polls reflect low regard for bureaucracy. A January 1978 Harris Poll indicated that only 23 percent of those polled had a great deal of confidence in the people charged with running the federal government.[8] In 1966, 41 percent of those polled had indicated confidence, and in 1976, the figure had declined to 11 percent. Incidentally, public confidence in state and local officials tends to be lower than in national officials.

Faulting public bureaucracies seems to have become a major feature of modern political life. The American public has responded positively to politicians who claim that one of our major problems is bureaucracies that lack judgment, foresight, intelligence, and management skills. Unfortunately, the charges are usually too simplistic. There are plenty of examples, some of them gross, of bureaucratic ineptitude, but public bureaucrats are easy targets. It should be remembered that bureaucrats do not create bureaucracies; they are created in response to public demands put into the form of law and funded annually by an elected legislature. What's done can be undone.

Certainly bureaucracy needs to be constantly improved and reformed. On the other hand, using bureaucracy as a scapegoat for major social ills and social difficulties opens the way for demagoguery and simplistic solutions to complex problems.

One scholar recently wrote:

> Bureaucracy is both a monstrous growth that threatens to strangle liberal democracy and a sinister force that undermines the attempt to achieve social justice. It is also the chief abetter of inefficiency, impersonality, alienation, and oppression. Sometimes even more. Thus, a well-known American columnist laid the blame for American deaths in Viet Nam on the altar of the military bureaucracy. From late-Capitalist United States to post-Maoist China, the anti-bureaucracy liturgy sounds surprisingly the same. . . .[9]

This attitude could lead to a serious deterioration of public support for government. This kind of either/or attitude—one is either for bureaucracy or against it—provides an opening for the quick-fix demagogue who argues that the nation's problems could be solved if only he or she were given the chance. Bureaucracies need to be kept under control and constantly monitored to improve their operations. Representative government can generate the pressures to bring about this reform.

A healthy and constructive approach by the business community to the problems of bureaucracy takes time and information. Time should be taken to look behind the criticisms of bureaucratic performance and determine whether or not there might be some reason for the bureaucratic behavior the business community finds so repugnant. Red tape, for example, is sometimes the result of procedural requirements forced on public bureaucracies by interest groups, sometimes by business itself. Often fairness demands that certain open, cumbersome, time-consuming procedures be followed. Public bureaucrats are usually more opposed to these requirements than anyone else—they have to live with them every day. One person's red tape or bureaucratic slowdown is another person's idea of what constitutes fairness, equity, and good government.[10] On the other hand, cumbersome, costly bureaucratic procedures that benefit no one and protect no one's rights should be fought and changed.

To fight effectively and to bring about lasting change in government, one must understand the processes and forces behind bureaucratic requirements that created the problems in the first place. It is to an examination of those forces and decision-making processes which we now turn.

Notes

1. Spencer Rich, "U.S. Payroll Exceeds Six Million," *Washington Post,* 18 July 1978. See also Daniel Guttman and Barry Willner, *The Shadow Government* (New York: Random House, 1976).

2. Alice Bonner, "OSHA: Backlog Swells While Its Staff Doesn't," *Washington Post,* 19 July 1978.

3. Michael Bell and L. Richard Gabler, "Government Growth: An Intergovernmental Concern," *Intergovernmental Perspective,* 2, no. 4 (Fall 1976): 8.

4. Hugh Heclo's study of those individuals in high-level management positions in the public bureaucracy is the most comprehensive one done in several years. See *A Government of Strangers: Executive Politics in Washington* (Washington, D.C.: The Brookings Institution, 1977).

5. Two comprehensive reports and analyses of the new program can be found in Ann Cooper, "Congress Approves Civil Service Reforms," *Congressional Quarterly,* 14 October 1978, pp. 2945–50; and Timothy B. Clark, "Senior Executive Service—Reform from the Top," *National Journal,* 30 September 1978, pp. 1542–46. The bill, S. 2640, was signed by President Carter on October 13, 1978. It became effective in January 1979. See also Bernard Rosen, "Merit and the President's Plan for Changing the Civil Service System," *Public Administration Review* 38 (July–August 1978): 301–304; and Alan Dean, "A Comprehensive Approach to Civil Service Reform," *The Bureaucrat* 7 (Summer 1978): 2–4.

6. Most of the data on federal personnel are from the most recent yearly publication of the U.S. Civil Service Commission, Bureau of Executive Personnel, titled *Executive Personnel in the Federal Service,* (November 1977).

7. See *Summary Report: The Future of Federal Retirement,* National Association of Retired Federal Employees, Washington, D.C., 24 January 1978. Most of the data on retirement in subsequent paragraphs is taken from this study.

8. *Washington Post,* 5 January 1978.

9. Stephen Miller, "Bureaucracy Baiting," *The American Scholar* Vol. 47, No. 2 (Spring 1978): 205.

10. See Herbert Kaufman, *Red Tape: Its Origins, Uses, and Abuses* (Washington, D.C.: The Brookings Institution, 1977) for a provocative, lively essay on the problems and sources of red tape.

three

Government Rules and Regulations

What, Why, and From Where

Government rules and regulations have irritated the business community for decades. The very words "rules and regulations" make business executives uneasy and resentful—and understandably so. No one likes being regulated; moreover, regulation runs counter to the free enterprise philosophy. Yet the business system cannot work without government rules and regulations to organize and monitor the marketplace. Business executives have known this for decades and have actively lobbied to shape and develop the present regulatory system.

Government regulations are the main contact and often the main source of friction between business and government. Historically, business has cooperated with government in formulating rules and regulations. The regulatory system has accommodated the business community, and that community has learned to live with it. This picture began to change about twenty years ago, however, and today the business community confronts rules and regulations markedly different in type and quantity from those in the past.

Previously, most government regulations were directed at organizing the marketplace and protecting the business environment. Licensing procedures, antimonopolistic efforts, incorporation procedures, and certain financial reporting requirements were the common forms of government intervention. Regulations made it possible for business to operate in a competitive environment. Without these regulations it would have been impossible to create the large commercial and industrial systems that exist in this country today.

Recently, government has become a more active regulator, focusing now on the internal activities of business: on safety and health in the work place, and on the race, sex, and age of the worker. Government has also become concerned with the impact of business activities on the external environment: air, water, land, and endangered species.

This emphasis is substantially different from past regulation. It has less to do with the orderly operation of enterprise than it does with the impact of enterprise on society and the quality of life in general. As a nation we have moved close to a point where government affects business as much as any externality, including the marketplace.

Further exacerbating the relationship between business and government are the often ambiguous interpretations of what constitutes necessary or valuable regulation. Disputants on each side can cite example upon example of governmental regulation to bolster their particular point of view. Furthermore, the same ambiguity arises when analysts seek to determine the advantages or disadvantages, the costs or the benefits, of any specific government regulation.

The difficulties of trying to separate truth from fiction are enormous. An interesting example of how two writers intimately involved in the politics of regulation can view the issue of governmental regulation in completely different ways was seen in the pages of *The Washington Post* on successive Sundays.

Writing with a proregulation point of view, Nader stalwart Mark Green fantasized:

> I have this recurring nightmare. Jonas Salk has just announced his cure for polio. A bill is introduced in Congress to require mandatory inoculation of school children under HEW direction. Opposition then appears. Ronald Reagan urges "free choice by parents rather than compulsion by government." Mobil runs advertisements with the headline, "From gas tanks to bloodstreams. Where will government go next?" An associate professor of economics does a study for the American Enterprise Institute demonstrating that more lives may be lost by car accidents en route to doctors' offices than will be saved by the Salk vaccine. Abbott Labs argues that its product, "Polioaide," has been effective since thousands of doctors have been prescribing it for two decades. The bill then fails in the House Commerce Committee by one vote—after the wheelchair industry, citing job losses, gives $200,000 in campaign gifts to committee members.[1]

The following week Peter Shuck, former Nader aide and former deputy assistant secretary at HEW, published his regulation fantasies.

> Like Mark Green, I have had nightmares about regulation. But mine are different. In his, you will recall, big business and its minions gang up on Congress to defeat a regulation to end polio. In one of mine, a government agency mandates that children's sleepwear be flame-retardant only to learn—many millions of dollars and perhaps many cancers later—that the chemical that the agency knew would be used to comply was carcinogenic and the sleepwear could not be used.
>
> In another, a government agency mandates that each new vehicle be armed with a costly system that prevents ignition until seat belts are fastened, only to find that consumers are disarming the systems in frustration. In another, a new government agency is created to increase the security of pensions, only to learn that its efforts have succeeded in discouraging the creation of pension plans and in helping to drive many small ones out of business.[2]

Two Classes of Government Regulation

The shift in the nature of regulation is so dramatic that the field of government regulations requires analysis from two different perspectives, for there are now two quite separate classes of regulations.

Regulation I, the traditional form can be defined as:

> Government regulation that creates the necessary institutions for competition: government money-supply management, enforcement of private contracts, protecting private property, patent and copyright protection, and so forth. The primary role of these regulations is to protect and enhance competitive forces in the economy, not to supplant them. On the other hand, when competitive forces are augmented by regulation as they often are—to limit entry into a field, such as traditional airline and trucking regulation—the results benefit specific businesses or industries.

Regulation I, the bulk of all regulation, is supported by business and usually initiated by business itself. These regulations are least susceptible to reform, because of the difficulty in generating enough public support to bring about changes. Although some segment of the business community might desire change in Regulation I, there is little possibility of achieving consensus for significant change.

Regulation II, the new type of regulation, is largely a phenomenon of the last twenty years. It grew out of broad-based political movements labeled environmental, civil rights, or consumerism. Though small by comparison with the volume of Regulation I, this fast-growing area gives corporations the most difficulty. Regulation II can be defined as:

> Regulations defining what goods should or should not be produced. They provide product specifications and procedures in industrial processes designed for industrial safety. These regulations define modes of environmentally acceptable production, types of employees who should be hired, acceptable working conditions, pay conditions, retirement systems, and similar issues.

Regulation II is directed more at *social* than *economic* policy. New and large groups, such as Common Cause, women's organizations, and a variety of consumer groups, are active in political processes to bring about social changes by requiring business to operate differently. One student of regulation has written about the new type of regulation:

> The real purpose of government regulation is not to correct the deficiencies of markets but to transcend markets altogether—which is to say, government regulation is not economic policy but social policy. It is an effort to advance a conception of the public interest apart from, and often opposed to, the outcomes of the marketplace and, indeed, the entire idea of a market economy.[3]

Most of the newer regulations apply to the nonprofit sector as well as to business. Universities, churches, state and local governments, and the federal government must meet environmental, equal employment opportunity, and other standards.

The growth of the new type of regulation has fostered a new concern in business about its relationship with government. It has led to the creation or strengthening of offices of legislative affairs. Many corporations are opening Washington offices or enlisting the support of Washington law firms or other lobbying organizations to represent them. Some corporations, such as Mobil Oil, have moved their headquarters to Washington, D.C., as have groups such as the National Association of Manufacturers.

The cry for deregulation has rallied the support of many members of the business community. Their voices have been heard at the highest levels, and both Presidents Ford and Carter proposed deregulation and regulatory reform. They both have found it easier said than done. Shortly after he assumed the presidency, President Ford created a high-level staff group in the White House which criticized the regulatory programs of several federal agencies. These statements were included in Ford's first *Economic Report* (1976). President Ford also proposed legislation to deregulate the airline, trucking, and railroad industries. None of the legislation reached the point of serious congressional consideration during his administration.

"MORE RULES AND REGULATIONS!"

In March 1978, President Carter issued Executive Order 12044 establishing procedures for the adoption of new regulations. This process is designed to ensure that the need for the regulation proposed is clearly established, meaningful alternatives to the proposed regulation are considered, and compliance costs and other burdens on those regulated are minimized. It is too soon to know whether or not the order will make a substantial difference.

Although Presidents Ford and Carter made some advances in improving regulatory procedures, a curious thing happened to them on the way to deregulation. They discovered that although business favors deregulation in principle, in practice business generally declines to support specific deregulation proposals. There is a great deal of disagreement in the business community about which regulations should stay and which should go.

The Difficult Politics of Deregulation

Ambivalence on the value of various regulations is understandable when one looks at the traditional body of regulation, Regulation I, which has been on the books for some time. A large portion of Regulation I can be labeled "private-interest generated." That is, it was put on the government's books at the request of one business or one industry to improve its position in the marketplace. For many decades students of government have criticized the regulatory agencies for responding almost exclusively to the requests of business. No conspiracy existed to bring about this situation. It was just that most of those who participated in regulatory decision-making were business representatives. Consumers and representatives of the general public were poorly organized and relatively inactive. Consequently, the regulatory books of government are crowded with provisions that make it difficult for new market entrants and also give one type of product a competitive edge over another. Until fifteen years ago, for example, these regulations made up almost the whole regulatory arsenal of the Federal Trade Commission (FTC).

The rules and regulations of the Federal Trade Commission, since its creation in 1932, were almost without exception issued at the request of business. When transistor radios became popular a few years ago, for instance, they began to appear on the shelves of discount houses and drugstores at very low prices. They were often advertised as containing twelve or fifteen transistors and sold for under ten dollars. The well-established radio manufacturers in the United States knew that it was impossible to produce and market a twelve- or fifteen-transistor radio and sell it for ten dollars.[4] They investigated and discovered that while the radios in question had the advertised number of transistors, only two or three of the transistors were part of the radio circuit; the rest were dummies wired to the chassis.

The radio manufacturers asked the Federal Trade Commission for a hearing. At the hearing, the manufacturers made their case and asked the commission to write a rule requiring that whenever radio advertisements stated the number of transistors, those transistors must be a part of the operating radio circuit. It was a very short hearing. The commissioners saw the reasonableness of the manufacturers' demand and wrote the regulation requested. Another rule was created. More red tape and more enforcement mechanisms were added. The expense, the reporting, and other aspects of regulation to which businessmen object were sought in this case. The commission had moved at the request of an industry to help straighten out a problem in the marketplace.

The Flammable Fabrics Act of 1967 provides another example of private-interest-generated regulation. In this case, the argument was presented on all sides by reputable members of the business community. In the congressional hearings on the legislation, the debate was between two segments of the clothing industry: the chemical-fiber manufacturers supported the act, while the natural-fibre manufacturers opposed it. The former group, those who manufactured and marketed fire-retardant products, won. The public, of course, also benefited, but there was almost no public participation in the legislative process. It was mostly a debate between giants in the industrial world. Once again, new regulations were promulgated, with all the accompanying paperwork and enforcement activity. Today, the bulk of government regulations are generated by private interest, and are a result of the use of government to resolve conflicts in the business community.

In the last fifteen years, Regulation II—those that apply to business as a whole—have grown in size and importance. These might be called "public-interest-generated" regulations, because they are supported by broad coalitions of civil rights, consumer, and environmental groups who do not have direct economic ties to the decisions. Phrases like *"quality of life"* and *"rights"* replace *"marketplace," "profits,"* and similar words.

Regulation II is an extremely difficult area for business, because these regulations, at least in part, reflect major social controversies. Regulations imposed on the nuclear energy industry are viewed, for example, as retardants to progress by the industry and therefore inimical to business. On the other hand, environmentalists argue that since the danger in the production of nuclear energy is so great and potentially so harmful to the environment, these regulations must not only continue but be strengthened.

Oil company exploration processes are also surrounded by numerous government regulations designed to protect the environment. Oil companies feel they are too stringent and costly, while environmental groups see them as reasonable protections to the environment. Equal employment regulations are viewed as difficult and costly for the operations of business and nonprofit organizations; civil rights and women's groups feel that they are essential to social progress. In this category of regulation one can see some of the major social issues of our time being fought out. These are reasonable debates and healthy for a dynamic, democratic society, even though the resolutions are often seen as costly and perhaps even unclear.

One result of the intense pressure from business and broader social groups has been an increase in the total number of government regulations. Many of these new rules seem unnecessary and even frivolous. Some regulatory programs are unreasonable and contradictory, and reporting requirements are expensive, perhaps even impossible. Others border on the irresponsible. Sorting out the unnecessary from the necessary is no simple task.

While engaging in the politics of regulatory reform, it is well to remember that most regulations have wide support somewhere in society—often in business itself. Otherwise, they would not have been adopted in the first place.[5] Furthermore, public support for regulation is surprisingly intense. The Consumer Product Safety Commission, created in 1972, is generally most unpopular with business, yet the legislation creating the commission passed the Senate by a vote of 69–10; the House by 318–50. Congressional analysts would call that vote close to unanimous. This show of support for regulation demonstrates that the politics of regulation have changed and that the roots of this change run deep. In dealing with Regulation II, business must recognize that these regulations are government's response to large, politically active segments of the population. These groups are using regulatory processes to attain goals they perceive as important, just as business interests have used regulatory processes for decades to achieve business goals.

Public support for environmental regulations apparently has not been eroded by concern over the costs of regulation, levels of government spending, or rates of inflation. A Louis Harris poll, taken in March 1978, showed the public strongly opposed to slowing environmental cleanup to produce more energy: 65 percent against to 22 percent for. A survey done in 1977 found 55 percent agreeing with the following statement: "Protecting the environment is so important that requirements should be continued *regardless* of the cost." Also, the day Proposition 13 passed in California, voters also approved a $374 million bond issue for water pollution control.[6]

Increasingly, business leaders are making distinctions between types of regulations and showing greater sophistication in dealing with them. One hears fewer blanket indictments of government regulation and more selective criticisms of regulations that hurt industries greatly and seem to offer marginal benefit to the public. Alec Flamm, senior vice-president of Union Carbide Corporation, made the following comments in an address before a group of business executives:

> For a start, we can make it clear that we understand the need for regulations; that while we may seek to modify the shape and thrust of regulation, we know that in the complex society and economy, in which we are all living downstream from someone

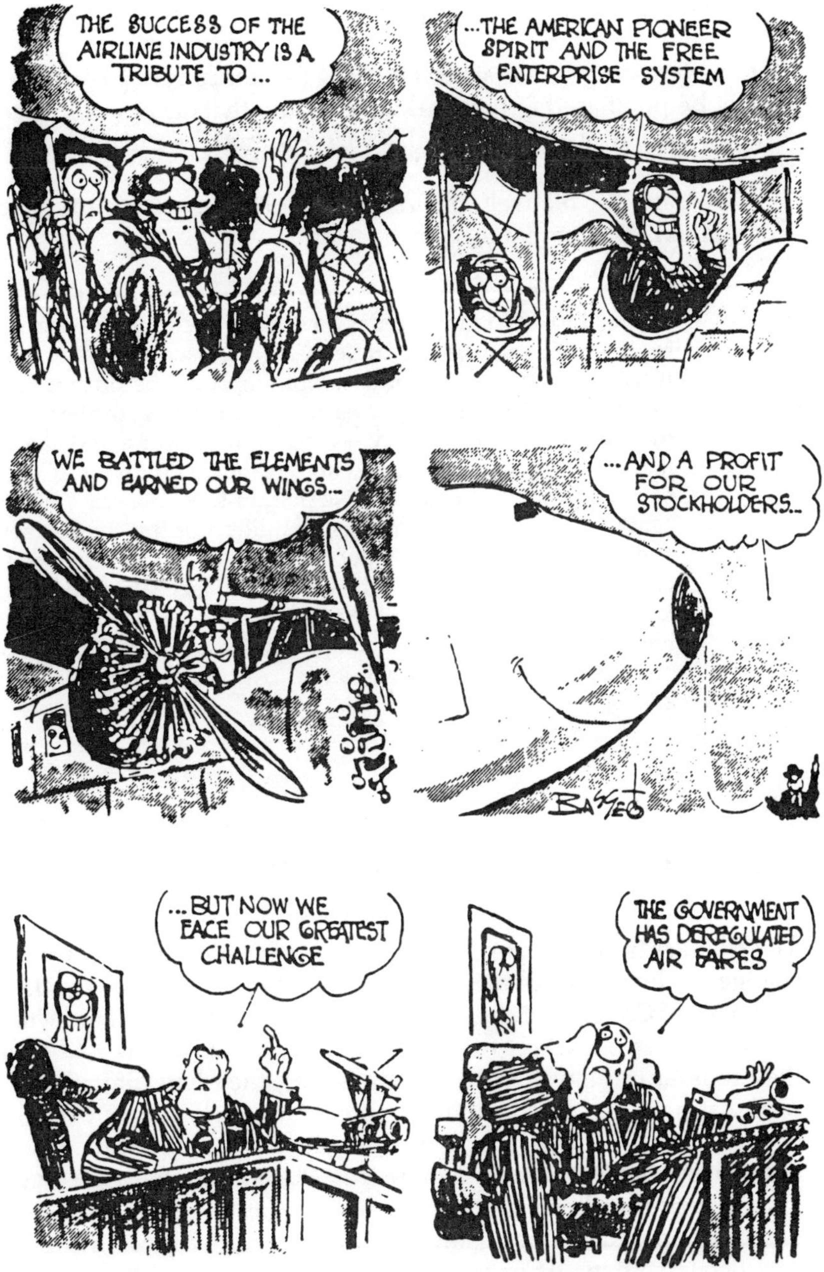
THE SUCCESS OF THE AIRLINE INDUSTRY IS A TRIBUTE TO...
...THE AMERICAN PIONEER SPIRIT AND THE FREE ENTERPRISE SYSTEM
WE BATTLED THE ELEMENTS AND EARNED OUR WINGS...
...AND A PROFIT FOR OUR STOCKHOLDERS...
...BUT NOW WE FACE OUR GREATEST CHALLENGE
THE GOVERNMENT HAS DEREGULATED AIR FARES

> else, business autonomy is bound to be at least partly circumscribed by government.

Flamm went on to say that certain things Americans need and want cannot be purchased in the marketplace, and that clean water, clean air, and similar goals and social objectives must be articulated and implemented by government.

Howard W. Blauvelt, chairman and chief executive officer of Continental Oil Company, said:

> From my comments so far, you may have concluded that I am opposed to any kind of federal regulation—that I am yearning for the good old days of a laissez faire approach to business regulations by federal authorities. Nothing could be further from the truth. I think that only government can express the wishes of the people on major policy issues. Government alone can set national targets for growth in Gross National Product and levels of employment. In a competitive market-type economy, significant advances in such things as cleanliness of the environment and greater employment opportunities for the disadvantaged can only be achieved through government legislation and regulation. Otherwise, under a voluntary system, the least responsible company would have a competitive cost advantage over the company trying in good conscience to achieve progress in these areas.

Business Lobbying in Washington

The changes in the nature of government regulation have fostered a change in business lobbying in Washington. For years the U.S. Chamber of Commerce and the National Association of Manufacturers were the major voices for business in the United States. Although they took strong positions on many issues, they had difficulties in formulating a business or industry position on government regulation because of the lack of consensus in the membership. It was nearly impossible to generate more than 20 or 30 percent agreement among their membership on any position regarding regulation. Regulations opposed by one business or industry were almost invariably beneficial to others. As most major corporations (as well as hundreds of small ones) belong to these groups, they found themselves on both sides of a regulatory issue at the same time. It is not possible to lobby effectively while so divided.

Airline deregulation posed problems for the Chamber of Commerce. The trunk carriers opposed deregulation, but the feeder carriers and many of the businessmen in the smaller cities that the feeders service favored deregulation. The Chamber was frozen into silence between these competing business interests. This dilemma is a reflection of the conflict within the business community on government regulation and is typical of the political patterns associated with Regulation I.

In 1972, the Business Roundtable was founded. This unique and potentially powerful group is composed of the chief executive officers of the 180 largest corporations in the country. The group has a very small Washington staff, and the chief executive officers themselves decide on an agenda and do much of the representational work, using their own corporate staffs for support.

Although the Roundtable examines a variety of public issues from accounting principles to wage and price controls, its major concern is with the impact of Regulation II on U.S. business. The emergence of Regulation II provided an opportunity for the major corporations to come together to present to government business positions or viewpoints on the important issues involved in these newer areas of regulation. The industrywide impact of these regulations makes it easier for the business community to present a united front.

Real problems remain, however, in developing industrywide or businesswide positions on regulation. Regulation II involves complex and controversial issues of policy without easy solution. H. L. Mencken once said that all major social problems have easy solutions that are "neat, plausible and wrong." As the Roundtable works on environmental and energy policy and other issues included in Regulation II, it is encountering the same difficulties that Congress and the public have encountered in developing policy in these areas. Its members are also struggling to reach agreement on these major issues. Business executives should realize that if the 180 corporations in the Roundtable cannot agree on major policy issues, it is infinitely more difficult for government, which represents a much more diverse constituency, to develop meaningful policy.

Few government regulations in any category do not benefit some segment of business or industry. Although many corporations find air-pollution control requirements burdensome, new corporations are being created and joining established ones like Boeing to develop new lines of air-pollution-control equipment.[7] Over the past five years, the pollution control industry has grown at the rate of 20 percent per year compared with a 9 percent annual growth rate for all manufacturing companies (figure 3.1).[8] A study by Arthur D. Little, Inc., predicted that demand for pollution control equipment would grow from $1.8 billion in 1977 to $3.5 billion in 1983, a growth from 35,850 to 43,900 jobs.[9]

The pollution control industry is not alone. Higher mileage standards on automobiles have created a whole new technology and

Figure 3.1

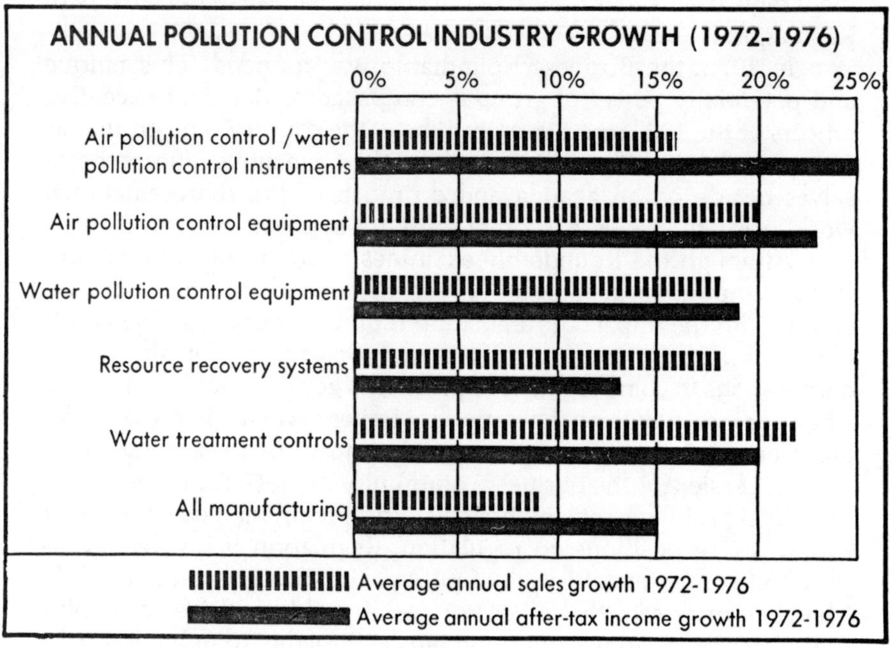

Source: Hal Hoover, Washington Post, 15 October 1978. Data from Arthur D. Little, Inc.

a market for new equipment. Air-bag devices in automobiles are opposed by the auto industry and controversial with the public, but the insurance industry has supported a regulation requiring them for some time. Even in the area of Regulation II, it is difficult to identify a regulation that does not have some important industrial backers. The longer a regulation is on the books, the more business support it gathers.

The subcommittee on government regulation of the Business Roundtable has identified five major areas for consideration. One area of concern is suggestions on improving management practices in government. Another area is the quality of government personnel working on regulatory programs. They are also looking for possible improvements in individual regulatory agencies and studying civil service reform and the cost of government regulation. The work of the Roundtable is high quality and well informed, and has the potential to make a significant contribution to public policy-making processes.

To deal successfully with government regulations, executives must understand the process by which regulatory decisions are made. First they need to understand where the government rules and regulations come from, who supports particular regulations and who opposes them. Once it is recognized that most rules and regulations are supported by some portion of the business community, changing that policy requires a change in rhetoric and political approach.

Government regulations can provide certain industries with added credibility. The mobile home industry was plagued by fly-by-night companies that were giving the whole industry a bad name. In June 1976, the Department of Housing and Urban Development set uniform building regulations and strict inspection codes for the industry. As the number of complaints about mobile homes has dropped, the industry has become a strong supporter of government regulation.[10]

Consider also the Occupational Safety and Health Administration (OSHA), popular target in speeches, books, and articles attacking regulatory excesses. Although it is difficult to find support for the frivolous rules and regulations that emanated from that agency in the first years of its existence, the agency has friends in the business community. Responsible organizations in American industry, which go to great expense to provide safe work places, support OSHA, for it requires their competitors to provide similarly safe conditions. The defense of OSHA is a classic one for government regulation. OSHA's rules and regulations help to structure the marketplace in such a way that no single company can take unfair competitive cost advantage of an entire industry by using shoddy standards for industrial safety.[11]

Of course, some of the rules and regulations issued by OSHA are overly detailed, nit picking, and costly to business; however, things change in the regulatory field. In the last two years a regulatory housecleaning has gone on at OSHA. In 1977, OSHA exempted almost all of the nation's 3.5 million smallest businesses from its annual reporting system. In the summer of 1978, the agency exempted an additional 110,000 small businesses. In two years, the number of businesses required to fill out OSHA's annual reporting requirements went from 4 million to about 70,000.[12]

The changes at OSHA are an indication that a careful presentation of problems created by regulations for business can yield some changes helpful to business. Recently, the Environmental Protection Agency, responding to a request from the Caterpillar Tractor Company, changed its permit-issuing procedure to allow for approval of all permits simultaneously before construction begins. An executive of the corporation called the deputy administrator of the Agency and asked for the change. Barbara Blum, the deputy administrator was quoted in the press, "Dodge was right. They could sink millions into the design, construction and occupancy of a large industrial manufacturing system and then arrive at a new hurdle."[13] Reasonable requests are responded to reasonably, sometimes to the surprise of both business and government officials.

Some observers of national trends have noted a public shift in the direction of more support for business, especially on regulatory issues. The evidence is fragmentary and inconclusive. Robert J. Samuelson, a reporter on economic affairs for the *National Journal,* cites liberal journals that increasingly support business positions on regulatory questions.[14]

These changes are likely to be seen in the specific areas of trade policy, tax policy, and in those instances when convincing specific cases can be made that show either that a regulation is unnecessary or too costly. The large social concerns of consumer groups, environmental groups, and labor unions are not likely to change dramatically. These groups will continue to support many of the regulatory programs that business finds onerous. This is a classic confrontation and an important one in American life. Recognizing this and learning to deal with regulations of all types effectively is one of the management skills expected of the modern corporation executive.

Political Action Committees

A recent change in the campaign-financing laws has opened up a significant opportunity for corporations and business associations to participate more directly in the electoral process. These changes make it easier for business organizations to organize Political Action Committees (PACs). PACs raise funds from corporate employees and even stockholders for contributions to individual political campaigns and to political parties. (For information on how to organize a corporate PAC see Appendix F.) The changes are too recent for anyone to judge how financial support to candidates favoring corporate positions might change policy in the regulatory area. The conflicting corporate positions on regulation mitigate against dramatic changes. However, PACs provide corporations with an important opportunity.

PACs began to emerge in the 1940s in the major industrial and trade unions in this country after the Smith-Connally Act of 1943 made it illegal for unions to use dues for campaign contributions. PACs were created as separate organizations collecting dues on their own from union members and then passing them on to favorite candidates. Several large union PACs were set up in the 1940s, 1950s, and 1960s. The largest one, created in 1955 by the AFL-CIO, is COPE, the Committee on Political Education.

Business executives and business organizations did not follow the lead of the unions. There were some small-business PACs, but most business contributions were given individually by leading members of business organizations directly. It was, of course, illegal to donate from corporate treasuries. The earliest important corporate PAC was BIPAC, the Business-Industrial Political Action Committee, founded by the National Association of Manufacturers in the 1960s. It was similar to COPE in its organization. Not until the 1970s did business begin actively to organize political action committees.

There are two reasons why PACs became more feasible and attractive to business in the 1970s. One was change in the federal elections laws that greatly restricted the amount of money an individual could give to a single candidate or national political party. The Watergate scandals brought many violations in corporate giving practices to public attention. The second major encouragement to corporate PACs was the Federal Election Campaign Act of 1971, which specifically sanctioned corporate PACs. There was, however, one stumbling block left. The 1971 act still prohibited organizations with government contracts to participate in campaign-support activities. A 1974 amendment to the act eliminated that barrier.[15]

The changes in the federal election laws led to an explosion in the number of political action committees, from about 450 in 1976 to almost 2,000 in 1978. In the 1977–78 state, local, and national elections, the political action committees spent $76.3 million. Among the leading corporate PACs in 1977, ranked by the dollar amount of contributions raised, were the PACs of the General Electric Company, Southern Railway Company, International Paper, LTV/Vought, Hughes Aircraft, Standard Oil of Indiana, Lockheed Aircraft, and Coca-Cola.

PACs are allowed to solicit contributions from employees, and some corporations even use payroll withholding plans for contributions. Often employees are allowed to indicate to which candidate or party they want their contribution to go. A corporate committee decides to whom funds not earmarked will be contributed. The recent changes in campaign finance laws result in more flexibility for PACs than for individual givers. An individual can contribute only $1,000 per election for any candidate, with a $25,000 annual limit. Individuals also may give $20,000 to the national party committee and $5,000 to other political committees. But the annual limit is still $25,000. PACs, on the other hand, may give $5,000 per election to any candidate, with no annual limit on total contributions. Furthermore, PACs may give $15,000 a year to a national party committee and $5,000 to other election committees.

Most candidates' funds still come from individual donors, but the dollar impact of PACs is growing more substantial every year. In the 1978 congressional campaigns, 18 percent of the $199 million spent by candidates came from PACs.[16] One of the results of the increasing importance of PACs is more vocal demands for public financing of congressional elections. In 1976, the presidential campaign was in part funded through public funds. As PACs become more influential, there will be more pressure to reduce their importance by putting more of the burden for congressional campaigns on the public treasury.

PACs are important mechanisms for corporate support of candidates, but their effectiveness in influencing candidates is undetermined. Even their impact on one party or another is not entirely clear. Corporate and business-related PACs favored Democratic *incumbents* over Republican challengers by a margin of more than two to one in the 1976 general elections. On the other hand, nearly 59 percent of the corporate PACs directed their contributions to Republican *candidates,* while nearly 97 percent of union PAC contributions went to Democrats.[17]

Notes

1. Mark Green, "The Faked Case Against Regulation," *Washington Post,* 21 January 1979.

2. Peter H. Schuck, "On the Chicken Little School of Regulation," *Washington Post,* 28 January 1979.

3. Paul H. Weaver, "Regulation, Social Policy and Class Conflict," *The Public Interest,* 50 (Winter 1978): 45.

4. Federal Trade Commission Rule, Relating to Deception as to Transistor Count of Radio Receiving Sets, Including Transceivers, 10 December 1968.

5. See Sylvia Porter, "Business May be Staunchest Supporters of Regulations," *Washington Star,* 7 January 1979, for an interesting commentary on business support for government regulations.

6. These polls are summarized in "Polls are Consistent in Backing Environmental Cleanup Plans," *Washington Post,* 2 January 1979.

7. A summary article in *The Washington Post* indicated that more than six hundred

companies are involved in producing equipment associated with environmental cleanup. Environmental control equipment is a multibillion dollar industry at this time. Wall Street analysts call it a growth industry with an extremely bright future. See "Major U.S. Industries Discover Profits Fighting Pollution," *Washington Post,* 3 April 1978.

8. Larry Kramer, "Pollution-Control Industry is Cleaning Up," *Washington Post,* 15 October 1978.

9. "Pollution Control Business Grows," *Washington Star,* 29 November 1978.

10. "Mobile Home Industry Likes U.S. Regulation," *Washington Post,* 19 April 1979.

11. See Robert A. Leone, "The Real Costs of Regulation," *Harvard Business Review* 55, no. 6 (November–December 1977): 57.

12. "OSHA Plans Exemptions for 40,000 Firms," *Washington Post,* 28 June 1978.

13. Larry Kramer, "EPA Changes Rules at Business Request," *Washington Post,* 21 September 1978.

14. Robert J. Samuelson, "Softening Attitudes Toward Business," *Washington Post,* 11 November 1978.

15. A complete description of the development of PACs and much of the data used in this section of the book are from Charles W. Hucker, "Corporate Political Action Committees," *Practical Politics* (May–June 1978): 21–25. An unpublished colloquium paper written by Edwin M. Epstein, "The Rise of Political Action Committees" (Washington, D.C.: Woodrow Wilson International Center for Scholars), contains an excellent historical perspective on the development of both union and corporate PACs.

16. For a discussion of the impact of PACs on congressional campaigns, see Edwin M. Epstein, "The Irony of Electoral Reform," *Regulation* 3 (May–June, 1979): 35–41.

17. Hucker, p. 21.

four

The Management of Government Regulations

The main contact point between business and government is the civil servant who enforces and interprets regulations. These individuals are career officials; only a few are political or presidential appointees.

After Congress establishes a regulatory program, it delegates authority to the appropriate executive branch agency or regulatory commission to carry out the program. (The processes of delegation and congressional oversight are examined in the next chapter.) These processes give a considerable amount of authority to administrative agencies to interpret, develop, and enforce the regulatory programs legislated on Capitol Hill. It is important to note that regulations are born in Congress, although they are nurtured and shaped by the bureaucracy. At times the bureaucracy expresses some consternation with the mandates of Congress and sometimes with those of the courts. Douglas Costle, the administrator of the Environmental Protection Agency (EPA), told a reporter:

> People often think of regulators as entrepreneurs who have to figure out a way to make everybody's life miserable. It's just not so. . . . Eighty percent of the regulations that came to me in the first 90 days I was here came because the statute [Congress] said the agency shall promulgate or a court ordered the rule by a certain date.[1]

Who are these people who write the rules and regulations in the regulatory area? How many are there? And what are their backgrounds and interests?

Determining the number of federal employees involved directly in government regulations is difficult, because definitions of regulation can vary widely. In 1976, the Congressional Budget Office

(CBO) completed a study of the number of federal regulators. It defined regulatory activities as those that:

> impact on the operating business environment of broad sectors of private enterprise, including market entry and exit, rate, price and profit structures, and competition;
>
> impact on specific commodities, products or services through permit, certification, or licensing requirements; and
>
> involve the development, administration and enforcement of national standards, violations of which could result in civil or criminal penalties or which result in the types of impact described above.[2]

Using this definition, the CBO report estimated that during fiscal 1976, thirty-three departments and agencies devoted 92,172 person-years to regulatory activities. When certain administrative and program support positions—involving public information, complaint processing, business and consumer assistance, data gathering, and economic analysis activities—are excluded from the definition, the figure drops to 84,773 person-years. This leaves about 3 percent of the federal government's 2.8 million employees engaged in what the Congressional Budget Office considers regulatory activities. This may be a conservative estimate but not an unreasonable one. If the tax code were considered a regulatory mechanism, the number of regulators in the federal service would grow substantially, and if procurement and contracts management people were included, as regulators, the number would leap again.

The congressional study identified four categories of government regulation:

1. economic regulation of commerce, transportation, agriculture, and communications (16.7 percent of the total regulatory person-years);
2. health, safety, environmental, and consumer protection regulation (58.3 percent);
3. regulation of banking and financial activities (14.3 percent); and
4. employment and civil rights regulation (10.7 percent).

The first category, economic regulation, covers the activities of many of the traditional independent regulatory commissions, such as the Interstate Commerce Commission (ICC), the Federal Trade Commission (FTC), and the Federal Communications Commission (FCC). These independent agencies perform a variety of licensing, certification, antitrust, rate-setting, and rule-enforcement activities. However, more than one-third of the regulatory activity in this category is performed by two cabinet-level departments: Agriculture and Commerce. Agriculture, incidentally, employs more regulatory personnel than any other federal agency. Its employees inspect, grade, classify, and standardize various agricultural products and administer acreage allotments and market quotas.

A clear majority of the person-years devoted to regulatory activities are in the second category, health, safety, environment, and consumer protection. The Department of Agriculture also plays a dominant role in this category, with its meat and poultry inspection, animal, and plant disease programs, and pest control activities. These activities account for almost one-third of the person-years in this regulatory category. Aviation safety and water safety programs account for another 17.3 percent. These programs are administered by the Federal Aviation Administration and the U.S. Coast Guard, both of which are in the Department of Transportation. The Food and Drug Administration contributes 15 percent of the activities in this category. Other significant agencies working in this area include the Environmental Protection Agency, the Department of Labor's Occupational Safety and Health Administration, the Department of the Interior's Mine Safety Program, and the Nuclear Regulatory Commission.

The third category consists primarily (61 percent) of federal chartering, deposit insurance, and financial oversight of banks, credit unions, and savings and loan institutions. Regulation of securities and commodity futures trading and employee pension plans are also included.

Among the major activities covered by the fourth category are enforcement of equal employment opportunity laws, regulation of labor relations, and administration of federal laws pertaining to compensation.

Characteristics of the Regulators

The training, educational, and social backgrounds of those involved in regulation are important factors for business executives to understand. Unfortunately, it is difficult to generalize on this subject, and few studies of the backgrounds of public administrators have been done.

One characteristic of regulators most often noted is that they are "in-and-outers." A study by Common Cause, a public-interest group based in Washington, showed that several high-level employees of the regulatory commissions had major stock holdings in the corporations they were charged with regulating.[3] Furthermore, in the view of Common Cause, a disproportionate number of government officials were recruited from the industries their agencies are mandated to regulate. The door revolves in the other direction, too; many middle-level and upper-level government employees leave government and go directly to work in the industry they were regulating.

The Common Cause study found that 518 employees in eleven regulatory agencies had financial interests that conflicted or appeared to conflict with their official duties. It also found that 52 percent, or 22 of the 42 regulatory commissioners appointed during fiscal years 1971 through 1975, came from companies regulated by their agency or from law firms representing those companies. And 48 percent, or 17 of the 36 commissioners who left during the five-year period, went to work for companies they had regulated or their law firms. Another interesting statistic: 53 percent, or 73 of the top 139 employees of the Energy Research and Development Administration, used to work for private enterprise in the energy field.

It is apparent that many people working at the top of the major regulatory agencies in government have had, or are likely to have, careers in the private sector. The prevailing belief among many corporate executives is that these agencies are hostile to industry and ignorant of its needs. It is difficult to argue that the government regulatory agencies overseeing specific industries are staffed by people who do not understand the industry and who are unsympathetic with it. A large proportion of those in high-level policy jobs in the regulatory agencies have experience in the industries they are charged with regulating. However, officials of the newer social regulatory agencies, like the Equal Employment Opportunity Commission and the Environmental Protection Agency (those responsible for Regulation II), are not likely to be as closely associated with business.

The career patterns and backgrounds of the higher civil servants as a whole are somewhat different than the characteristics of those in the regulatory commissions. In the top ranks of the civil service, there is little job mobility. Over the past several years, 90 percent or more of the top positions were filled from within the agency involved, 4 to 5 percent of the positions were filled from other agencies, and less than 5 percent were filled from outside government. The highest rate of interchange between business and government occurs in the regulatory commissions.[4]

The revolving door is likely to be slowed but not stopped by the provisions of the Ethics in Government Act of 1978. This stringent legislation took effect on July 1, 1979. It strengthens the two-year ban against former federal employees working for organizations involved in cases before agencies that previously employed them. The new law also prohibits top-level executives and military officers from having professional relationships of any kind with the former agency for twelve months. The most vexing requirement prohibits top officials, for two years after leaving office, from aiding, assisting, counseling, advising, or representing anyone before the government on matters for which they have had direct or indirect responsibility. This last provision could make top-level government employees virtually unemployable in any meaningful job for two years after government service.[5] The provision is so severe it probably will not stand a strong court or legislative challenge. The 1978 law illustrates the practical problems of dealing with conflict-of-interest situations through general legislation. Although the law will be difficult to enforce and will probably be amended, it is likely to have a chilling effect on those who seek high-level federal jobs and discourage some talented people from seeking public employment.

Some Problems in Regulatory Management

If there is anything worse from a business executive's point of view than regulation, it is poorly managed regulation. Management of the regulatory system is one of the major problems facing government today. The areas of actual or potential conflict are numerous. Problems of coordinating programs that seem in conflict with each other and difficulties in the operational definitions and enforcement of regulations in complicated areas of health, safety, and environment are beginning to plague the regulatory system. Modern government regulatory programs take us into uncharted waters. It is difficult for science to tell us, for example, what the impact of certain toxic substances might be on any individual. Furthermore, there are at least two ways of measuring the extent of toxicity: its cumulative effects over a period of several months or years or its immediate impact on workers in a given location.

Coping with government regulations can be enormously time-consuming and expensive. In the case of offshore oil drilling leases, for example, managers must deal with the Bureau of Land Management, the Environmental Protection Agency, The Army Corps of Engineers, the Department of Energy, the Federal Trade Commission, the Fish and Wildlife Service, the Interstate Commerce Commission, the National Oceanic and Atmospheric Administration, the Coast

Guard, and the Geological Survey, among others. Many state agencies also have to be consulted, along with legislatures, courts, and citizen's groups. The reason for involvement of each of these agencies and groupings is likely to be legitimate. Offshore oil and gas drilling can have enormous impact on the economic and social well-being of large segments of the population. The difficulty is that the process is so convoluted that drilling may be delayed for years to the detriment of our energy needs and our own wallets. One could argue that each clearance or stop in this licensing process is reasonable and could stand on its merits. There certainly are major state concerns, environmental questions, economic impact questions, and fish and wildlife considerations whenever drilling occurs. Although each single requirement can be defended reasonably, there is no good defense for the process taken as a whole. Overlap, duplication, and expensive paperwork are a noxious byproduct of the regulatory system. The sum of the regulatory process in this case and others is many times worse than its parts.

It's either "Gordian Knot" or "Government Regulations."

As a partial response to these problems, President Carter has moved to establish a new discipline within the bureaucracy for the management of regulation. There are three major components of the Carter program. One is the requirement that regulatory impact analysis be done within each agency when it proposes new regulations. The analysis must include an assessment of the proposed regulation's impact on inflation. This policy is monitored by the Office of Management and Budget (OMB).

A second component is the establishment of a high-level group called the Regulatory Analysis Review Group, whose members include some of the closest advisors to the president. They undertake studies of specific important regulations to determine whether or not they might be eliminated or improved.

A third component of the Carter program is the Regulatory Council. The Council is charged with coordinating regulatory activities among agencies. Thirty-five agencies are members of the Council. President Carter stated that the Regulatory Council "will help inform me, the public, and the Congress about the cumulative impact of regulation on the economy."

One of the most important functions of the Council is to publish a regulatory calendar, which is a comprehensive catalogue of federal regulations at an early stage in their development. This preview focuses on the objectives and benefits of the regulations being considered, the sectors of the economy that they affect, their economic implications, and major alternatives under study. According to Douglas M. Costle, the chairman of the Council and the administrator of the Environmental Protection Agency, the calendar will help Council members to:

> 1. identify areas of potential duplication, overlap, or inconsistency among regulations under development in different agencies and find ways to minimize such problems;
> 2. identify selected economic sectors facing multiple regulatory activity and analyze the extent and nature of the impacts upon them;
> 3. develop consistent analytical and decision-making methods to aid agencies in dealing with the same or similar problems under different laws; and
> 4. better assess the benefits of regulation.

The first "Calendar of Federal Regulations" was published on February 28, 1979.[6]

The difficulties of coordinating regulatory programs are enormous. The government decision-making processes discussed in the next chapter will give the reader a heightened appreciation of the size and complexity of the problems of regulatory management and reform. One of the early efforts to coordinate agencies' regulatory programs is in the area of toxic chemicals. The control of toxic substances is typical of many of the newer regulatory programs. It crosscuts the responsibilities of at least four regulatory agencies: The Consumer Product Safety Commission, the Environmental Protection Agency, the Food and Drug Administration, and the Occupational Safety and Health Administration. In the spring of 1977, the directors of those four agencies formed a group called the Interagency Regulatory Liaison Group. That summer the group announced they had developed cooperative mechanisms in the following areas:

1. development of compatible testing standards and guidelines;
2. risk and safety and health assessments;
3. information sharing;
4. research planning;
5. regulation development;
6. compliance and enforcement; and
7. interagency communication and public education on the regulation of toxic substances.

In a letter to President Carter, the group said:

> We have concluded that within our collective legislative mandates there are significant and exciting opportunities—acting as a team—to effectively control hazardous materials for the protection of public health. . . . Our goal is to make the regulatory processes more efficient for our agencies, for industry and for the public.

Whether or not the four agency heads succeed in making progress, the fact that they are now meeting and working jointly is a significant development.

What Does Regulation Cost?

The cost of government regulation and its impact on inflation has become a major economic and political issue in the United States. Measuring the cost of regulation is, of course, very difficult. Measuring the benefits of regulation is even more difficult. And determining the impact of these costs and benefits on the economy is more difficult still.

Looking only at the budgeted costs of administering regulatory programs, one is confronted with a wide range of estimates on what the federal government spends on regulatory programs. The Congressional Budget Office reports that the total outlays of the regulatory agencies as they define them and partial outlays of other agencies involved in regulation were almost $3 billion dollars for fiscal 1976. Two former high-level officials of the Council on Wage and Price Stability give a much higher estimate of $6.8 billion for the preceding fiscal year. The higher figure amounts to about 1 percent of the total federal budget.[7] This figure would have to be multiplied by a large factor to include the expenditures of state and local government on the administration of regulatory programs. Even so, this figure is only a small part of the story.

The real costs of regulation come in the additions to the costs of manufacturing, sales, and management in the private sector. Professor Murray Weidenbaum has compiled a list of these extra costs imposed by regulatory programs. His list includes:

> 1. higher production costs due to Consumer Protection Safety Commission, Environmental Protection Agency, Occupational Safety and Health Administration, and other federal agency requirements;
> 2. higher personnel costs resulting from federally mandated fringe benefits such as Social Security, unemployment insurance, and workman's compensation;
> 3. higher interest rates as financial markets react to increased demand generated by various federal loan guarantee programs; and
> 4. higher government procurement costs because of federal contracting regulations which require suppliers to hire on a nondiscriminatory basis, provide safe working conditions, pay prevailing wages, and give preference to U.S. products in their purchases.[8]

Weidenbaum is attempting to measure the wider impact of government activities on the economy. Others make a similar argument. A Council on Environmental Quality document predicts that the Environmental Protection Agency regulations will cost the economy an additional $40 billion per year by 1984. An OSHA report predicts capital costs of $18.5 billion as a result of proposed noise-control regulations.[9] These researchers are primarily concerned with the cost effects of the new social regulations (Regulation II). Other writers have concentrated on traditional economic regulations and have found similar high costs associated with them.

The Business Roundtable study of costs of government regulation showed a wide variation in these costs. The study examined six regulatory agencies and forty-eight corporations. The Environmental Protection Agency accounted for 77 percent of the total cost of regulation for these companies, while the Federal Trade Commission accounted for only 1 percent. The most important aspect of this study was the methodology for assessing regulatory costs more accurately. Future studies will build on the work of the Roundtable.[10]

The more traditional economic regulation includes such activities as certifying forms for entry into a given industry, rate setting for public utilities and other national monopolies, rate regulation for natural oligopolies such as airlines, and approving mergers within industries. Businesses subjected to such controls generally find them less offensive and less expensive than social regulations, because they have had several decades to adapt to them. Many economic regulations also provide substantial benefits to the industry they regulate. Paramount among these benefits is stability. For example, the Civil Aeronautics Act of 1938 was passed in response to the young airline industry's desire to protect its members from cut-throat competition.[11] In the forty years since its creation, the Civil Aeronautics Board (CAB) has not certified any new trunk carriers. This lack of competition was the rallying point for the critics of the board, who successfully brought about major changes during 1977 and 1978, including legislation that will eventually abolish the board. The Interstate Commerce Commission cannot match the CAB's perfect record in this respect, but its general orientation has been similar. It has also restricted entry into an industry, trucking, which because of its lower capital requirements is potentially more competitive than the air transportation industry.

Mark Green, citing the work of various regulatory economists and lawyers, estimates that the annual economic waste through higher prices and inefficient resource use from four regulatory agencies (ICC, CAB, Maritime Administration, and FCC) is $16 to $24 billion.[12]

What Are the Benefits of Regulation?

When the government mandates certain activities by industry, it can cost the public a great deal through increased production and management costs. At the same time, the government regulation can make some industries less competitive, thereby increasing the possibility that consumers will pay more than they would in an openly competitive system.

It is hard to argue with the claim that the nonsocially oriented regulations (Regulation I) cost the consumer a considerable amount of money, while producing few benefits to the general public. The newer regulations (Regulation II) are the result of the demands of the public for a safer work environment and a generally cleaner and healthier living environment. If these regulations accomplish what they promise, their costs might well be worth it. It must be realized, however, that those costs are likely to be high. These regulations often alter the structure and nature of doing business.[13] The costs must be evaluated against the benefits deriving from the regulations. One of the difficulties the government policy-maker encounters is developing an acceptable method for measuring benefits. If the cost of government regulations are difficult to pin down, it is often impossible to gain consensus on a measure of the benefits. In 1971, for example, the National Highway Traffic Safety Administration estimated that the cost to society of one traffic fatality was $200,725. This figure includes consideration of future productivity losses (direct losses were estimated at $132,000, indirect costs at $41,300), victim's pain and suffering ($10,000), and a variety of lesser costs. Thus, the prevention of one death produces a benefit of $200,000, and by extension, the prevention of 50,000 highway deaths would benefit a society by $10 billion dollars.[14] It is not difficult to develop an argument that the cost of shoulder belts, airbags, and generally safer automobiles and highways is low compared to the cost of keeping more automobile drivers and riders alive. But perhaps the Highway Safety Administration's estimates are too narrow and too low. What value would you put on a human life? On the other hand, what opportunity costs are involved? Perhaps the money spent on automotive safety would produce even greater benefits if it were spent for some other purpose, like mass transit.

Alternative Approaches to Regulation

The government's approach to regulation might be called "the command and control approach." The government determines what regulations are needed in a given area, promulgates them, and then seeks to bring all producers into conformity with them. There are alternatives to this approach. Most of them rely on greater use of the economic forces of a free marketplace. One of the most frequently discussed types of market-oriented regulation is the "effluent fee." The fee charged a given factory would be determined by the amount of air or water pollution that factory produces. The reasoning behind this is that if government makes it expensive to pollute, industry will find ways to reduce the amount of pollution in order to lower its production prices and be more competitive.[15]

Taxes based on the rate of worker injury are another example of this kind of regulation. Companies with high injury rates would be taxed more than companies with lower rates. If the tax based on worker injury were set high enough, there would be a real economic incentive for the industrialist to provide a safer working environment.[16]

One of the problems with approaches based on economic incentives is that they rely heavily on the tax structure for their management. The tax structure is already overburdened with complications. Perhaps it would be too much to ask it to take on the added burden of regulatory management.

Alfred Kahn, the president's chief inflation fighter, proposed an "easy" tax-based solution to encourage the use and production of nonleaded gasoline. Consumers are tempted to use leaded gasoline, thus damaging auto air-pollution-control systems, because it is cheaper than unleaded gasoline. Why not raise the tax on leaded and lower it on unleaded, thereby making it a sound economic choice for the consumer to buy unleaded? This proposal seems on the surface to be the essence of reasonableness. A *Washington Post* editorial, however, explains what can happen to single proposals when exposed to the machinations of tax policy-making. The editorial also says a great deal about government decision-making processes.

> The effervescent Alfred E. Kahn has an answer to the question about unleaded gasoline. As you may recall from our last exciting installment, the price gap between leaded and unleaded gasoline is widening steadily. That tempts people with new cars to use the cheaper leaded gas, and the lead destroys the catalyst that controls the pollution in the cars' exhaust. Mr. Kahn's solution is simplicity itself. He suggests raising the tax on leaded gasoline and lowering it on unleaded gasoline. Mr. Kahn is more rational than a man in his position, as adviser to a president, can safely afford to be.
>
> Perhaps he was not following the energy bill or the tax-reform bill in the past Congress. If the administration adopts the Kahn plan, recent history offers a pretty clear view of the rest of the story.
>
> Mr. Kahn will draft a one-page bill to raise the tax on the one kind of gas and lower it on the other. But the White House political staff will immediately point out that his draft fails to address profound questions of social equity. What about the poor, who buy unleaded gas because it's cheaper? What about young people driving old cars? What about the inhabitants of lower Louisiana, who need their outboard motors to get around

the swamps and bayous? There will have to be a rebate formula. It will take into account each family's income, the number and ages of its various automobiles and the distance from its front doorstep to the bus stop. The legislative draftsmen at the Energy Department have had a lot of experience with that kind of formula, and eventually the 53-page bill will be sent to Congress.

The House will receive the bill without much warmth, remembering the exceedingly modest support the Carter administration gave its own gasoline tax the last time. But the members of the Ways and Means Committee are good sports, and they will move it along in due course. The real fun will start when it arrives at the Senate Finance Committee. First the committee will add tuition tax credits for families with children in private schools. Then, warming to its work, it will vote import quotas on straw hats from Hong Kong, beef from Argentina and automobiles from Japan. At that point Chairman Russell Long (D-La.) will complain publicly that the committee is running out of control. As if to prove the accusation, it will then add several obscure but pregnant provisions that seem to refer to the tax treatment of certain oil wells in the Gulf states. When the 268-page bill comes to the Senate floor, the administration will narrowly manage to defeat an amendment to improve business confidence by repealing the capital-gains tax and returning to the gold standard.

When the bill gets back to the House, liberal Democrats will denounce it as an outrage and declare all-out war. They will succeed in getting all references to gasoline taxes and the environment stricken—but not, unfortunately, the import quotas or the obscure tax changes for the oil wells. By the time the staff of the Joint Committee on Taxation has straightened out a few technical difficulties, the bill will run to 417 pages and Ralph Nader will be calling on President Carter to veto it. But the feeling at the White House will be that Congress has worked so long and hard on the bill that he has no choice but to sign it. By the time the bill is finally enacted, late in the autumn of 1980, Mr. Kahn might well wish he had chosen some other instrument of policy.

It's a pity that things will work out that way, because a 10-cent increase in the tax on leaded gas is the quickest and most effective way to discourage people from using it. But fiddling with taxes to influence social behavior is a device that has been overused in recent years. The administration could afford to try it again this winter only if it had assurance of a wide consensus in Congress to support it, move it quickly, keep it simple and exclude any amendments. Since there is no sign of anything close to a consensus, the country is evidently going to have to

> live for a while with a wide spread between leaded and unleaded fuel prices. Perhaps it's a public risk that is, on balance, less risky than the solution.[17]

Another alternative would be simply to rely on fines. Government could set health and safety standards, and if a company did not meet these standards, a system of fines could be applied. Those industries in compliance with the standards would have many of their reporting requirements eliminated, thus lowering their operating costs and improving their competitive position. There is much merit in this approach. One major difficulty, however, is the problem of administering a system of inspections and imposing large fines. Furthermore, fines are always administered after the event. A major industrial accident taking lives might have been averted through preinspection and mandated compliance with safety regulations. After the accident occurs, lives are gone and no fine can bring the dead back or restore a permanently crippled worker's ability to work.

A third approach involves setting standards for a whole geographic region and then letting industry and government in that region decide how they will comply with those standards. A new company, even a relatively large pollution source, may locate in a region if it is *offset* by reductions in emissions from other sources in the region. Local public-sector and private-sector officials, with citizen input, decide on the types of pollution to be allowed and on the trade-offs to be made to meet the clean air and water standards. Cutting auto emissions, for example, through increased reliance on mass transit, might allow for more industrial air pollutants. At the individual firm level, it might be posssible to auction off the rights to pollute, within certain set limits, to the highest bidder. This would mean that the industrialist who found it most expensive and most difficult to convert to pollution-control equipment would pay for the right to emit pollutants into the environment, while those industrialists who could convert more easily would do just that. The level of pollutants in the environment would be reduced, and the marketplace would have decided which company reduces.

Almost certainly, new attempts will be made to make the regulatory system more efficient and cost effective. The high costs of government are a major concern to the voting population, and inflation is the primary domestic concern. Questions of whether new regulatory initiatives can be borne by the government and by the taxpayer will be more frequent. It is also safe to predict there will be greater reliance on the marketplace for enforcement of regulations when it can be demonstrated that safety and health standards can be achieved at lower enforcement costs.

Regulatory policy, like all other government policy, is made in decision-making systems. Understanding the process by which these policies are made is the key to becoming effective in developing and changing government policy. To begin to understand these processes, business executives need a map or systematic guide to the operations of the decision-making systems of government.

Notes

1. Margot Hornblower, "Decade-Long Regulation vs. Inflation Fight Continues," *Washington Post,* 2 January 1979.

2. *The Number of Federal Employees Engaged in Regulatory Activities,* staff paper prepared for the Subcommittee on Oversight and Investigations of the Committee on Interstate and Foreign Commerce, House of Representatives by the Congressional Budget Office (Washington, D.C.: U.S. Government Printing Office, August 1976), p. v.

3. *Serving Two Masters: A Common Cause Study of Conflicts of Interest in the Executive Branch* (Washington, D.C.: Common Cause, October 1976).

4. Hugh Heclo, *A Government of Strangers: Executive Politics in Washington* (Washington, D.C.: The Brookings Institution, 1977), p. 114. The whole interesting issue of the demographic and social characteristics of the civil service is discussed in Harry Kranz, *The Participatory Bureaucracy* (Lexington, Mass.: Lexington Books, 1976).

5. "Thou Shalt Not—What?" 2 February 1979, *Washington Post* editorial. Also see *OPM NEWS* U.S. Office of Personnel Management, Washington, D.C., 31 March 1979.

6. "The Regulatory Council: Calendar of Federal Regulations," *Federal Register* 44 (28 February 1979).

7. William Lilley III and James C. Miller III, "The New Social Regulation," *The Public Interest* 47 (Spring 1977): 50.

8. Murray L. Weidenbaum, *Government Mandated Price Increases: A Neglected Aspect of Inflation* (Washington, D.C., American Enterprise Institute for Public Policy Research, 1975).

9. Lilley and Miller, "The New Social Regulation."

10. See "Regulation Cost 2.6 Billion for 48 Companies," *Washington Post,* 15 March 1979; and "A Start at Auditing the Costs of Regulation," *Business Week,* 26 March 1979, p. 30.

11. Lee Roger Teal and Alan Altshuler, "Economic Regulation: The Case of Aviation," *Policy Studies Journal* 6, no. 1 (Autumn, 1977): 50–60.

12. Mark J. Green, ed., *The Monopoly Makers: Ralph Nader's Study Group Report on Regulation and Competition* (New York: Grossman, 1973), p. 24.

13. See Robert A. Leone, "The Real Costs of Regulation," p. 57, for a very

careful and interesting discussion of the impact of contemporary regulation on the modern corporation.

14. In a 1978 report, the National Highway Traffic Safety Administration put the cost to society of traffic injuries and death at $43 billion. It also claimed that costs of new, required safety equipment were about $250 per car, less than half what auto-makers claim. The agency also argues that fuel-efficiency requirements save consumers about $500 in gasoline costs over the life of an auto. Arguments using data in the regulatory area could go on forever.

15. See Larry Ruff, "The Economic Common Sense of Pollution," *The Public Interest* 19, (Spring, 1970): 69–85, for an argument supporting the use of effluent fees.

16. See Charles L. Shultze, *The Public Use of Private Interest* (Washington, D.C.: Brookings Institution, 1977), for an interesting argument on the virtues of the market as a regulatory mechanism.

17. "Dangerously Reasonable," 26 December 1978, *Washington Post* editorial.

five

Mapping the Decision-Making Processes of Government

The government decision-making structure is large and complex. While it is open and visible, to the untutored eye it can be confusing without a guide or a roadmap to the centers of decision-making power. Government becomes less confusing when one realizes that the government as a whole seldom acts on any one specific issue. The important decisions of Congress, for example, are made by small groups of that body. The votes on the floor of the Senate and the House usually ratify decisions made at lower levels in Congress. Also, the executive branch seldom operates in a coordinated way. Important decisions are made in the hundreds of bureaus and agencies that make up the executive branch.

The decision-making systems described in this chapter are the power centers, the action centers, for most government decisions on both domestic and foreign policy. Some decisions not made in these systems will be discussed later. They tend to be the larger, nonroutine decisions one reads about in the press. However, 80 to 90 percent of the operational decisions that governments make—decisions directly affecting the private sector—are made through the types of systems analyzed in this chapter.[1]

The Early Steps: Define Program Interests with Precision

The first step in understanding the decision-making process of government is to locate the centers of power and the level at which decisions are made. Decision-makers are located throughout the process, but their locations are not always obvious. Key decision-makers are seldom located in the top positions of government organizations. The president, the leadership of Congress, and the cabinet have very special roles in government, but they are usually *not* the people who make the bulk of the policy decisions important to business executives.

To locate a decision-making system, start by carefully identifying and defining the program or issue to be tracked, supported, or changed. This must be done with precision. Decision-making systems in Washington, and in other governments in this country, are organized around programs. These programs are specifically defined in law.

Government decision-making is not focused on abstractions. There is no real decision-making system for something as broad or vague as "foreign affairs" or "commercial policy" or "agriculture policy." These are debatable political abstractions with little or no operational meaning. Instead, commercial or agricultural policies of the United States government are the sum of dozens of specific programs that are defined in specific terms in statutes and agency regulations. For example, health policy is the sum of hospital construction, cancer research, medical school education, drug licensing, communicable disease control, and dozens of other specific programs. Rather than looking for operational decision-making systems for "agricultural policy," business executives should look for decision systems organized around specific agricultural programs, like price supports for various commodities, soil conservation, meat and grain inspection, and food stamps.

The decision-making system comprises a set of institutions and individuals that handle more than one program, but all those programs are closely related. Incidentally, the word *system* is chosen carefully, for they have several of the formal characteristics of a system: a high level of interaction, feedback, and predictability. Figure 5.1 is an illustration of a government decision-making system.

There are nearly as many of these systems as there are groups of closely related legislated and funded programs in national government; a reasonable estimate would be in the neighborhood of 800 to 1,000.

Components of Decision-Making Systems

Each decision-making system consists of several sets of actors. In Congress, *two* subcommittees are responsible for each government program: one in the House and one in the Senate (figure I). These are the authorization committees of those bodies, responsible for the

Figure 5.1

A government decision-making system

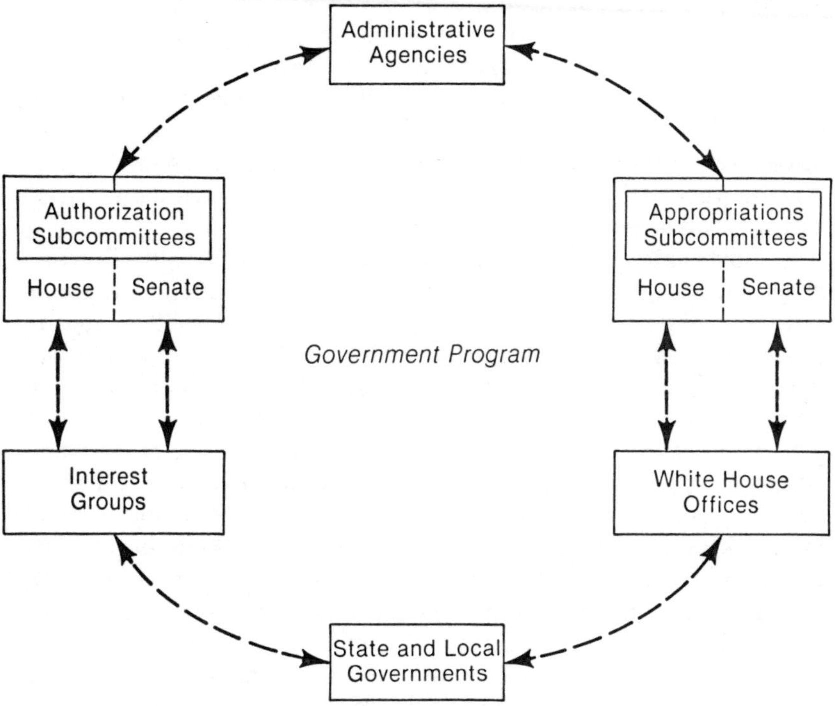

legislation that creates the program. They also exercise oversight functions as the program becomes operational.

Another set of subcommittees on the Hill is also a part of the decision system: the appropriations subcommittees. Before the work of the authorization committee can be implemented, the appropriations committees must allocate funds for each authorized program. It is important to remember that in any given program of the federal government, the whole legislative cycle, including presidential signature, must be completed twice. One cycle authorizes or creates the program. Depending upon the program, this must happen once every one, two, or three years. Often an expenditure ceiling is set in the authorizing legislation. However, no money can be spent from the U.S. Treasury until the legislative wheel turns again and a second bill becomes law—an appropriations bill. The second legislative cycle is the yearly appropriations and budget cycle.

Very few programs become operational in a hurried or haphazard fashion, because the legislative wheel must turn twice, each turn marked by numerous checkpoints or potential hazards. It takes a considerable amount of effort, pressure, and time by those inside and outside of government to make a program operational. Government programs can be weak, ineffective, inappropriate, misguided, and costly, but major forces in society have been instrumental in pushing them through the process that converts an idea or a proposal into law. The assumption that a bad program—that is, one with which we disagree—is the product of a few misguided government officials acting alone is generally wrong.

Government officials, whether in Congress or in the bureaucracy, are crucial to the development and operations of programs, but they seldom act without the guidance and pressure exerted by powerful political groups and social forces. This is a major reason why a program, once started, is so difficult to stop. There are many people supporting a program initially, and as time passes these programs increase and solidify their support. In the few cases where support is not impressive to begin with and fails to develop, the program or regulation usually disappears in a hurry. The auto seatbelt interlock system regulation, which required that belts be fastened before auto engines could be started, was promulgated and withdrawn within one model year. There was little support for it anywhere after the initial surge.

Another important factor in the decision-making system is the White House. The president is seldom involved in these decision-making structures, but his staff is. The personnel of the Office of Management and Budget (OMB) are regularly involved in the decision systems, as are the people who work for the Domestic Policy Staff. In addition, special assistants to the president also involve themselves in the process by monitoring most legislation for the president.

Interest groups are active participants in each of the decision-making systems. The number of groups varies according to the issue and its intensity. If the issue is topical, there will be many active groups; if the issue is not a high priority on the public agenda, less participation is likely.

A very important component is the agency or bureau of the federal bureaucracy. The bureaucracy can be viewed as the quarterback of the decision-making system; power tends to be exerted more consistently and skillfully by the bureaucracy than by other actors in the process. But it is important to remember that some quarterbacks are more effective than others. A good quarterback orchestrates the game. He knows the capability of all the players and uses them to best advantage. A good agency or bureau chief does the same thing. Just as it would be an unusual football game with only the quarterback on the field, it would be a bizarre decision-making system with only the bureaucracy operating. Any one or any group of actors in the system can bring about major changes in decision-making, and they often do. The agency is an important actor, some would say "first among equals," but there is no guarantee that the agency will be able to control the system well or for long if it is not sensitive to where power is located elsewhere in the system and how that power is being exercised.

Since most domestic programs of the federal government are administered by state and local governments, the diagram of any decision-making system must include state and local legislatures and bureaucracies. It is extremely difficult to draw up a list of domestic programs funded and administered exclusively by the federal government. Housing, welfare, education, highway, mass transit, airport programs, for example, are funded in part by Washington but run almost wholly by state and local governments. The Postal Service, veterans programs, and the federal regulatory programs are exceptions to this rule. They are programs with little state or local government participation in their management. The high degree of state and local involvement in most federal programs necessitates their inclusion in the map of almost any decision-making system. The implications of state and local involvement are explored further in a later chapter.

These decision-making systems are the key to understanding how government works in this country. It is important to have a picture of these systems in mind throughout this book.

Important Characteristics of Decision-Making Systems

The decision systems of government are not readily visible to the general public; one must know where to look and one must learn how to participate in them. The mass media generally does not cover the federal government by program. Instead, it covers government by institution. The television and radio networks, for example, assign White House, Capitol Hill, and Pentagon correspondents. This approach can be misleading and is one of the reasons why the general public does not focus on the decision-making structures as they actually operate. Those who want to work with government decision-makers must focus on the systems that control the programs to be influenced. It is relatively easy to find them. The next chapter will deal with the process of identification in some detail, but first some of the special characteristics of the decision-making centers have to be identified.

One surprising characteristic is the breadth and depth of the systems' control over the program for which they are responsible. The actors in the systems create the program through the authorizing legislation, fund it through the appropriating legislation, manage it in the federal agencies, and review it in Congress through oversight hearings. There are, of course, review points outside of the decision-making system. The press, the public, the General Accounting Office (an agency of Congress), and other competing decision-making systems with a direct interest in the program, all act as overseers. At times the courts become involved, but only after the issue has been processed by the system and someone has filed suit challenging the decision. All of these institutions affect the decision-making structure. But the system in control is the key body in processing policy-making on any given program from beginning to end. To initiate, change, revise, fine tune, or eliminate a program, one has to contend with the people in the appropriate decision system.

One important characteristic of the system is that the components are at a low level in the organizational hierarchies. Congress as a whole is not involved in the decision-making process on most programs. Neither is the whole House or Senate or even the full committees. Power on Capitol Hill is organized like a pyramid, with the subcommittees at the base. In perhaps 95 percent of all cases, actions of subcommittees are upheld by full committees. Actions of a full committee are upheld about 90 percent of the time on the floor of the House or Senate. This means that one has about a 90 percent chance of predicting the outcome of a decision on any aspect of a program if one knows how a subcommittee is likely to vote.[2]

The bureau or agency involved in the decision-making system is located at the bottom of the executive branch hierarchy. There are 150 bureaus within the Department of Health, Education, and Welfare alone. Seldom would a cabinet secretary or his immediate deputies be involved in any of the decision-making systems. Their roles are centered on coordination, development, and innovation, rather than on specific program activity. Active participation of interest or lobbying groups is common and important, but seldom do the presidents or boards of the groups involve themselves directly; it is the

"Here's the latest, Mr. President. The people like you better this afternoon than they did this morning but not as well as yesterday."

Washington representatives of the interest groups who participate on a continuing, daily basis.

Like members of his cabinet and their deputies, the president is an outsider—albeit a powerful one—in the program decision-making systems. Presidents have little incentive to become involved in most programs. Almost all of them are controversial and fraught with political minefields. Unless a program becomes a major issue—like energy, for example—most presidents will keep their hands off, for the costs of defeat appear much greater than the rewards of victory. Presidents are often better advised to deal with matters of foreign policy. After two years in office, President Carter looked quite weak, as evidenced by his plummeting ratings in the polls. His lack of success in a variety of domestic areas was bringing into question his viability as a candidate for reelection. The Middle East summit breakthrough at Camp David in September 1978 changed everything. Carter became an effective statesman and a powerful president overnight, and his ratings in the opinion polls soared. Presidents are reluctant to get involved in the controversial operations of hundreds, even thousands, of government programs when other, more dramatic activities can prove of greater public and political significance.

The actual number of participants in the decision-making process is quite small. Looking at Congress once again, it is the chairperson of the subcommittees, two or three other subcommittee members, and a handful of staff who are important. Other members have competing interests which usually are determined by the subcommittees they chair. About half a dozen people on each subcommittee, or twenty-five people—members and staff—on the Hill altogether, are directly involved in a specific decision-making system.

In the agencies, the number of important, involved actors is even smaller. It was noted that 90 percent of the federal bureaucracy is located outside of the Washington metropolitan area. This leaves very few people to staff the programmatic bureaus in Washington. Consequently, about six to ten people near the top of the bureaus, usually including the bureau chiefs themselves—are the knowledgeable, active participants. Also, the White House staff is a relatively small organization. There might be two or three people in the Office of Management and Budget assigned to a specific program area, and two or three on the Domestic Policy Staff. There are seldom more than six participants from the White House.

The number of participants from the interest groups varies according to the issue, and the variety at times can be dramatic. Even here, however, the number of participants is not large.

Consequently, ongoing responsibility for any given public policy issue in this country rests in the hands of thirty to fifty key people. There is considerable participation of outsiders in decision processes, and public scrutiny of programs is constant. Yet, the number of key people on the inside is surprisingly small, for the many members of the federal bureaucracy, the Washington lobbyist corps, and the Capitol Hill staff are spread rather thinly over a large number of programs. And, of course, the federal bureaucracy itself is widely dispersed geographically.

Several other important characteristics follow from the small number of key actors in each system. The people in the decision-making system know each other well; they interact almost on a daily basis, and in all likelihood, most of them have been working together for a number of years. They not only know each other well, they also know each other's views on policies affecting the program. Since the group is small and well known to each other, the decisions taken on the program are rarely surprising. Of course, change in these decision-making systems occurs regularly, but it is usually incremental and seldom dramatic. This gives government programs some stability and some predictability in a potentially volatile political environment.

There is characteristically a high level of expertise in the decision-making systems. Not only are participants usually experts in their field or program area, these systems also draw testimony and support from a larger number of outside experts. The formal procedures for hearings of congressional committees are designed to tap knowledgeable witnesses from across the country. Interest groups are also expert in their fields. There is a close relationship in the decision-making systems between interest groups and those appointed to the top jobs in the agencies. Consequently, the person who runs the National Cancer Institute is almost always a research scientist or physician. The people who run the major education programs for the federal government usually have their doctorates in education. Those who work for the various bureaus in the Department of Agriculture come out of the agricultural community.

Expertise does not guarantee wise decisions. Experts sometimes are true believers; they might exercise sound judgments in their specialities, but can see the bigger picture only with great difficulty. Developing priorities among conflicting programs is a difficult process for policy experts. Furthermore, the existence of high levels of expertise does not mean that a decision-making system uses its information well. Poor use of information is at times more of a problem than not having adequate information in the first place.

An additional characteristic of the system is stability; it is almost a perfectly balanced system. Everybody in a decision-making system knows everybody else. In fact, many of them work over the course of their careers in more than one of the institutions in the system. If an opening comes up in one of the program offices of the Department of Housing and Urban Development and a dozen people apply, it is a real advantage to have worked on the subcommittee dealing with housing and urban legislation on the Hill. A number of people move around the sytem, which helps to fuse stronger bonds between decision-makers.

A closer look at the four major components of the federal decision-making system—Congress, the bureaucracy, interest groups, and the Executive Office of the President—will help to sharpen the detail and the relationships in the decision-making map. Not only do each of the components wield power and exert influence on each issue, but this power and influence will vary in intensity and effectiveness depending upon the power and influence exercised by the other components of the system. The system must reach certain accommodations if an issue is to be processed. In most cases, failure to do so means that the program will not materialize in legislation.

Role of Congress in Decision-Making

Several observers have noted that Congress at work is Congress in committees and subcommittees. Presently there are fifteen standing committees in the Senate and twenty-two in the House. These are the regular legislative committees which do the bulk of all congressional business. Membership on these committees is determined by political party; the party with a majority has the majority of seats in committee. The Republican and Democrat party caucuses decide committee assignments. Once assigned to committees, members usually stay there to work their way up the seniority ladder. There is very little shifting around of committee assignments for reelected members. Should members take a reassignment, they go to the bottom of the committee seniority list. In the House each member is assigned to only one standing committee, while in the Senate a member can serve on three committees. Members in either body may be assigned to additional select, special, or joint committees.

Committees are divided into subcommittees so that there can be a reasonable delegation of the work load. The jurisdictions of the subcommittees mirror the organization of the bureaucracy. They are responsible for authorizing programs and overseeing the bureaus and agencies that implement them. At times the committee jurisdictions fail to match the bureaucracy because of the reorganization activities in both Congress and the executive branch. Members of Congress remain on subcommittees once they are assigned to them, because seniority usually determines the power structure of the subcommittee. Over a period of years, members develop expertise and become knowledgeable about their subcommittees' activities. The longer they remain on the subcommittee, the more probable it is they will become chairperson, with power to appoint subcommittee staff, schedule hearings, and, to a large extent, dominate the decision-making system. The subcommittees are centers of power presided over by potentially powerful people whose importance cannot be minimized. Some chairpersons are more influential than others, however. Carl Vinson of Georgia dominated armed services activities from his chairmanship, and Daniel Flood of Pennsylvania was extremely influential in even the routine management of the Office of Education. The powerful committee and subcommittee chairmen make it difficult for the overall leadership in the House and Senate to organize and run those bodies. The Speaker of the House and the majority leader of the senate operate through, rather than around, the committee and subcommittee chairmen.

The principle tasks of the congressional leaders are organizing the party to conduct its legislative business, scheduling legislation for floor debate, collecting and distributing relevant information, promoting attendance for votes, and serving as a liaison with the White House on some of the key policy issues being considered by the president.[3]

In 1946, Congress authorized staff for all its subcommittees. During the next three decades this staff grew in number, quality, and professionalism. Some observers feel the staff is too influential in the policy-making process.[4] Whether they are or not, one must remember that Capitol Hill staff serve at the pleasure of the member for whom they work. There is no civil service protection, no seniority provisions, and no appeals process for dismissals. When a staff member speaks, one can be quite certain that he or she speaks with the certain knowledge that the member of Congress in question agrees.[5]

Just as congressmen develop expertise by serving for a number of years on a committee or a subcommittee, so do staff members who work on these committees. However, staff members work full time on their legislative and program concerns whereas congressmen are distracted by reelection compaigns, constituent service, party issues, travel, and other assignments.

The major functions performed by staff members include: organizing hearings by identifying witnesses and setting times and dates; conducting research relevant to the issues confronting the committee; drafting bills and amendments; preparing committee reports; helping members prepare for floor debate; acting as a liason with interest groups; and occasionally working in election campaigns. The major characteristics of the committee staff members are limited advocacy and partisanship, loyalty to the chairman, anonymity, and program specialization.[6]

Relationships between Congress and the bureaucracy are sometimes characterized by fiery hearings where representatives and senators sharply cross-examine cowed witnesses. These flamboyant, televised hearings are rare exceptions rather than the rule. Most hearings are quiet with few people in attendance. Often only one subcommittee member represents the entire committee. People from all walks of life testify.

Agency officials and committee staff members are in constant touch with each other. Policy decisions therefore are made in a spirit of cooperation and compromise. When deadlocks occur, only the ability to bargain and negotiate in good faith can guarantee that the issue debated will move forward. Much of this bargaining is carried out by mid-level bureaucrats, committee staff members, and interested lobbyists. Failure to achieve a negotiated compromise means the issue will die, an outcome most participants in the process do not want.

Congress exercises its function of overseeing the bureaucracy in routine, quiet ways. Congress is responsible for passage of legislation, the implementation of legislation, and the impact programs have on society. The oversight function is taken seriously. It is exercised by subcommittees when they evaluate the performance of agency or bureau personnel every one, two, or three years when the program in question is due for reauthorization, and yearly when funds are appropriated for programs.

With hundreds of programs, numerous bureaus and agencies, large numbers of employees, and billions of dollars being spent by the executive branch, congressional oversight functions are necessarily limited. Critics view these oversight activities as weak and ineffective. Congress does not have enough personnel to work on new legislation, satisfy constituent requests, and monitor the activities of the federal bureaucracy. Moreover, there are few incentives for individual congressmen to pursue oversight activities, which are time-consuming and usually do not enhance reelection chances.

To assist in its oversight and investigative functions, Congress uses the Office of Technology Assessment (OTA), Congressional Research Service (CRS), Congressional Budget Office (CBO), and the General Accounting Office (GAO), which conduct hundreds of studies each year at the request of committee members seeking to monitor and evaluate programs of interest to them.[7]

The greatest hindrance to effective oversight by Congress is the extreme difficulty of trying to devise measurable objectives for human services and social programs. Given the problems of developing firm and uniform standards, it is understandable why oversight and auditing in government can be so controversial.[8]

Congress is the most colorful, and in some respects the most powerful, component of the decision-making system. It is open to public view and watched closely by the press and lobbyists. It has a decentralized power structure, which tends to reinforce controversy and intensify debate. Congress is a collection of elected officials representing a great number of diverse interests—regional, economic, urban, ethnic, agricultural, banking, manufacturing, consumer, and senior citizens. Accommodating these diverse interests requires great skill and patience. But Congress does not work alone. Other institutions in the decision-making system have roles that often challenge and compete with the functions of Congress.

Washington Lobbyists

Interest groups, or lobbies, have a bad reputation with the general public. Stereotypes often depict them as engaging in covert, even illegal activities and wielding undue influence in the policy-making process by means of bribes, illegal campaign contributions, and expensive gifts. While some of this occurs in both political and administrative life, the overwhelming number of lobbyists operating in Washington do not participate in these influence-peddling activities.

Recently, the number of lobbyists in Washington has grown enormously. Precise numbers are hard to determine, but a recent cover story in *Time* claimed that lobbyists had increased from 8,000 to 15,000 in the past five years. The largest growth area has been in representatives of major corporations. Ford Motor Company has a Washington staff of over forty people, and seventy-seven airlines have their own staff there. *Time* claims that more than five hundred corporations support Washington lobbies; that number is up from roughly one hundred corporations ten years ago.[9]

The right of the people to petition government is guaranteed by the First Amendment to the Constitution. This provision assures that control of lobbying must be minimal, because petitioning and representing one's view to government officials is fundamental to democratic government. Under great pressure to "control" lobbies, Congress inserted a section in the Legislative Reorganization Act of 1946 which required that groups spending money principally for the purpose of influencing legislation must register with the clerk of the House and file quarterly financial statements. (See Appendix E for information on registering as a lobbyist.) The amount spent by each group is public information. Each quarter, *Congressional Quarterly* publishes a list of the groups that spent the most on lobbying and how much they spent. A complete list is published in the *Congressional Record.*

Individuals and organizations engaged in lobbying must keep detailed records of all contributions they receive as well as the name

"There's Getting To Be A Lot Of Dangerous Talk About The Public Interest"

and address of each person contributing over $500. A record must also be kept of all expenditures made by or on behalf of the organization and the name and address of every person to whom the expenditure is made. The law requires written receipts to be kept for at least two years after filing the statement with the clerk of the House and the secretary of the Senate.

The penalties for violating the provisions of the act are a fine of not more than $5,000, or imprisonment for not more than one year, or both. Persons convicted of violating this act may not attempt to influence the passage or defeat of any legislation for a period of three years. The penalty for committing this felony is a fine of not more than $10,000, imprisonment for not more than five years, or both.[10]

The registration law has proved difficult to enforce because the scope of activity it covers is difficult to define with precision. Furthermore, most lobbyists do not spend all or even a high percentage of their time lobbying. They educate, they write, they do research, they plan strategy, they discuss, and they serve as transmitters of information between government decision-making systems and their employers. This is a standard democratic practice protected by the First Amendment; consequently, it is very difficult to regulate by legislation. Some states have gone further than the federal government in regulating lobbyists. In a few states, even those who sell to government must register as lobbyists. This is an uncertain area of the law and susceptible to challenge. Thus far, no single national standard has been established on excactly who must register and what must be reported. There is enormous variation among governmental units in this country on the subject.[11]

There is also substantial disagreement about the effectiveness of the registration requirement as a control mechanism. It is difficult to determine if the reports of lobbyists are complete and accurate. In Washington, there is almost no auditing or investigation of filed reports. In fact, some claim that there are so few teeth in the lobby registration requirements that they do not regulate lobbying in any significant way. The unintended result of the regulations is the creation of a new, registered profession. Young lawyers, public-relations specialists, and other free-lance types can register as lobbyists, then promote themselves to small business and large corporations around the nation as "Registered Lobbyist, Congress of the United States." This is a quick and easy way to establish credentials that often attract a rather large clientele. The development of this new, registered profession is one of the ironies of trying to control and regulate a function so basic to democratic government that the Constitution itself protects lobbying as a right available to all citizens.

Lobbyists as integrators of the system

Interest groups can be categorized in many different ways. There are interest groups such as the AFL-CIO, church-related groups, farm interests, and business organizations. Some interest groups represent more narrow concerns and focus on ethnic or minority issues, defense spending or weaponry, environmental concerns, or issues of interest to specific foreign governments. Professional associations representing the interests of social workers, doctors, and educators are all located in Washington for the purpose of trying to influence policy-makers on issues pertinent to their members. There are also organizations representing veterans, children, the handicapped, gays, motorcyclists, airline pilots, and marijuana smokers.[12]

Whether general purpose or specific, national or local, these groups all have one thing in common: access to the decision-making system. The decision-making system is a deliberative one with many checks and balances. Knowledgeable lobbyists know this and have learned that there are numerous points in the process where legislation unfavorable to their clients can be stalled, modified, or defeated.

Access to the system involves a number of techniques that vary in both intensity and effectiveness depending upon such factors as the issue, the groups favoring and opposing it, public opinion, upcoming elections, the position of the president, and many more. Some of the most common techniques are: contacting members of the decision-making system or their staff; encouraging influential constituents to pressure a representative or a senator; promoting a mail campaign favorable to a specific point of view; and providing mony, manpower, or other services in an election campaign.[13]

Interest groups spend most of their time in "fire-fighting" activities, which are usually defensive in nature. This could involve: convincing a representative that a proposed amendment is expensive, inconsequential, or detrimental to the national interest; suggesting funding cutbacks to an appropriations subcommittee staff member; or recommending work changes in the rules and regulations governing a new program. Most of the lobbyist's time is spent working with members of Congress and their staffs, reassuring them of the validity of their positions. A lobbyist's time is much better spent building a trust among the faithful than in trying to make converts.

Information is the greatest asset an interest group has at its disposal in trying to sway staff members and elected representatives. Lobbyists have access to specialists and other resources necessary to amass important and accurate information on issues being discussed in the decision-making system. This information is a tool of the lobbyist, for many policy-makers often actively seek out lobbyists for a thorough briefing on an issue of current legislative interest.

Lobbyists who understand the decision-making system appreciate the importance of the bureaucrat's role in this process. Consequently, a sizable percentage of a lobbyist's time is spent with mid-level agency personnel in the bargaining and negotiating necessary to process issues through the system.

Lobbyists talk with bureaucrats on a regular basis to determine what the legislative agenda is and how lobbyists can favorably influence that agenda. Placement and timing of an issue on the legislative agenda is often the most important step in the process, for Congress has more issues before it than time to deal with them. In some cases, conversations with agency officials involve nothing more than an exchange of information. In other cases, lobbyists try to introduce information so that bureaucrats have it available in agenda-setting meetings.

Lobbyists and agency personnel occasionally rely upon each other to exert pressure on people in Congress. Where a direct approach appears imprudent or possibly ineffective, the bureaucrat or the lobbyist might ask each other to talk with a personal friend of a committee staff member. In such cases, favors are done with a full understanding that they will be reciprocated at a later date.[14]

Not all lobbyist-bureaucrat interaction takes place in the legislative development stages. Once legislation is passed, bureaucrats are charged with the responsibility of drafting rules and regulations to guide the implementation process. Lobbyists know that decisions made at this stage can often be as important as decisions made during the legislative drafting process. By monitoring agency activities in the aftermath of the bill-signing, lobbyists seek to insure that their constituents views are well represented in the administrative guidelines.[15]

Resources of lobbyists

The information possessed by a lobbyist is, in the long run, often more important than skills, training, or special access to a member, but the information must be reasonably accurate. Bureaucrats, committee staff, elected officials, and White House personnel frequently use this information in formulating policy proposals or in making decisions about pending legislation. A lobbyist who seeks a permanent voice in a specific decision-making system cannot afford to provide that system with false or misleading information. There are too many competing sources of information. Misleading data is usually quickly exposed by other lobbyists and the misled become skeptical of the purveyors of such information. Credibility is essential if a lobbyist is to be effective in the long run.

Several other factors contribute to the success or failure of interest groups in the system. One is the proper budgeting of the amount of influence an interest group has to expend to achieve a given policy goal. If a group uses all of its resources on one issue, it is likely to find itself unable to modify decisions on issues that arise a few months later. In other words, an interest group must plan its strategy on each issue so as to maximize the impact of its limited resources, thereby retaining enough reserves to cope with future problems. The analogy is not unlike that of an army going into battle.

Having resources and knowing how to spend them is one factor. Another is knowing when to use those resources. Timing is a critical factor in the success or failure of any interest group's campaign for or against an issue. Resources expended before the system is ready to process the issue are wasted and lost forever. If the resources are held back too long, until the important decisions have been made, then they are no factor in the outcome. Interest groups try to minimize timing errors by constantly monitoring and involving themselves in the daily activities of the relevant decision-making systems. In this way, they know what all the actors in the system are thinking and which issues are scheduled for final debate and decision. This gives all the interested parties an opportunity to plan their own campaigns for participation in the debates and to influence the final decision.

Few interest groups have the time, money, or staff to wage a long and expensive campaign for or against an issue. To minimize their risks and to increase their clout, many interest groups form coalitions and pool resources. Coordinating the strategy for diverse groups is not an easy task, but the anticipated impact on the system outweighs the organizational headaches. On some issues, coalitions make for strange bedfellows. Labor and business, which oppose each other regularly, have occasionally joined forces on key votes involving the Vietnam War and wage and price controls. In politics, today's enemy can be tomorrow's ally, so interest groups rarely develop a network of permanent allies or enemies, for different issues demand different strategies.[16]

Interest groups play an important role in helping to process issues through the decision-making system. They provide timely and accurate information to Congress, the media, the bureaucracy, and the White House. They coordinate the activities of like-minded groups so that the views of a maximum number of people are represented in the decision-making system. They also provide a conduit for interest-group members to learn about the major issues of public policy by reporting on the activities of Congress, the bureaucracy, and the Executive Office of the President.

The typical lobbyist devotes much time to watching decision processes and informing allies and supporters of the time and place when important issues will be discussed or even voted on. It is not unusual for a lobbyist to inform members of Congress of the moment a crucial vote (for the lobbyist) is about to be taken in a committee. Sometimes lobbyists work to make certain that a member of the House receives a timely call from a senator, the White House, other lobbyists, or important constituents. The expert lobbyist has a highly developed sense of what should be said to whom, by whom, and when. This timely bringing together of the forces in the decision-making systems is an important contribution to government.

Notes

1. The approaches to government decision-making elaborated upon in this chapter are discussed at greater length in: Ernest S. Griffith, *Congress: Its Contemporary Role* (New York: New York University Press, 1961); Douglas Cater, *Power in Washington* (New York: Random House, 1964); J. Leiper Freeman, *The Political Process,* rev. ed. (New York: Random House, 1965); and A. Lee Fritschler, *Smoking and Politics: Policymaking and the Federal Bureaucracy,* 2nd ed. (Englewood Cliffs, N.J.: Prentice-Hall, 1975.)

2. See Randall B. Ripley, *Congress: Process and Policy,* 2nd ed. (New York: W. W. Norton and Company, 1975), pp. 190–93, for an analysis of committee and floor votes in Congress over several years.

3. For a more detailed discussion of the role of party leaders, see Ripley, *Congress: Process and Policy,* chapter 6.

4. See Michael J. Malbin, "Congressional Committee Staffs: Who's in Charge Here?" *The Public Interest* 47 (Spring 1977): 16–40.

5. For a useful and interesting analysis of congressional staff, see Harrison W. Fox, Jr. and Susan Webb Hammond, *Congressional Staff: The Invisible Force in American Lawmaking* (New York: The Free Press, 1975).

6. Ripley, *Congress: Process and Policy,* pp. 244–51.

7. For a critical discussion of the functions of these four analytical support agencies, see James A. Thurber, "Policy Analysis of Capitol Hill: Issues Facing the Four Analytical Support Agencies of Congress," *Policy Studies Journal* 6, no. 1 (Autumn 1977): 101–11.

8. For a discussion of the techniques and limitations of congressional oversight, see Walter J. Oleszek, *Congressional Procedures and the Policy Process* (Washington, D.C.: Congressional Quarterly Press, 1978), pp. 202–12.

9. "The Swarming Lobbyists," *Time,* 7 August 1978, pp. 14–22.

10. Details of the law can be found in the Legislative Reorganization Act of 1946 (Public Law Md. 601; 2 U.S.C. 261–270). Also see *Federal Regulation of Lobbying Act: Outline of Instructions for Filing Reports* (Washington, D.C.: U.S. Government Printing Office, 1976).

11. For a discussion of the history and some current efforts to expand the regulation of lobbyists, see Norman J. Ornstein and Shirley Elder, *Interest Groups, Lobbying and Policymaking* (Washington, D.C.: Congressional Quarterly Press, 1978), pp. 101–14.

12. One interesting way of classifying interest groups is used by Lewis Anthony Dexter in *How Organizations Are Represented in Washington* (Indianapolis: Bobbs-Merrill, 1969), chapter 2. Another typology of interest groups can be found in Ornstein and Elder, pp. 35–53.

13. For a discussion of lobbying techniques, see Carol S. Greenwalk, *Group Power: Lobbying and Public Policy* (New York: Praeger Publishers, 1977), pp. 68–84. Also see Ornstein and Elder, pp. 53–58.

14. For an examination of this bargaining process, see Martin and Susan Tolchin, *To the Victor: Political Patronage From the Clubhouse to the White House* (New York: Random House, 1971).

15. Ornstein and Elder, pp. 58–65.

16. Carol S. Greenwald, pp. 75–76.

six

Administrative Agencies

Quarterbacks of the Decision-Making Systems

Some individuals in the system are more powerful than others, although it is wrong to exaggerate these inequalities. Members of Congress are extremely active and important, and so are the White House staff and the Washington lobbyists. The administrative agencies, however, have some powerful advantages over the other institutions in the systems. They do for decision-making in government what good quarterbacks do for a football team. There are ten other players on the field, another team, coachs, owners, and fans, but the quarterback is the key person. He needs to know the capabilities of his team and the opposition. In much the same way, the leadership of an administrative agency orchestrates the decision-making system. The agencies are the nerve centers of the decision-making systems. They organize the system, guide it, and are usually more responsible than others in the system for success or failure.

Successful agency leadership depends on continued good relations and support throughout the decision-making system, and to some extent with the media and the public. Support of the other members of the system has to be cultivated and maintained. One of the most important tasks of the agency is to know what changes can be made and how quickly, and to know how to bring about the necessary forward momentum to keep a program moving. To accomplish these tasks, administrative agencies have at their disposal the tools of expertise, longevity, institutional memory, and rule-making authority delegated by Congress.

Expertise is housed primarily, although not exclusively, in the bureaucracy. The bureaucracy attracts people with interest and commitment to the programs over which they preside. There generally is strong linkage between the agency leadership and the interest groups participating in the decision-making system. These relationships tend to concentrate information about the program and the environment in which it operates in the agency. Consequently, the agency almost always enjoys technical superiority over the other actors in the decision-making system.

Bureaucratic agencies enhance their expertise by compartmentalizing into small, manageable areas of specialty. Individual bureaucrats have the luxury of concentrating their attention in specific areas of expertise. Congressmen must run for reelection and respond to their constituencies in a variety of ways, while many lobbyists spread themselves across a broad range of programs. Agencies, lacking most of these outside distractions, are better organized to specialize than are Congress or the interest groups. Furthermore, the agencies are much larger. They have the staff to focus on specific policy problems.[1]

The agencies of the bureaucracy are the record keepers and the historians of the decision-making systems. These are classical functions of bureaucracies. Memory and access to data are important sources of power. Usually the people in agencies have been with government for many years, or if they were outside for part of their careers, they often were associated with programs they now manage. Stability of relationship to an issue gives an individual a substantial advantage in decision-making and is one of the factors in successful management at the program level. Stability, however, also makes it difficult to integrate or coordinate similar or competing government programs.[2]

Those dealing with government look to the bureaucracy for information about existing programs and plans for future programs. The ability to be selective about the use of data and the timing of its release enhances the position of agencies in decision-making. Some agencies regularly supply friendly legislators with important information on critical issues at the right time. Press releases can be timed to aid certain legislators while hindering others. Wise bureaucrats take advantage of their positions to know what all the actors in the decision-making system are doing and what they need to support their positions.[3]

As bureaucrats possess a certain amount of expertise and often control the quantity and the quality of information pertinent to current issues, it is not surprising that their advice and participation often help to shape the decisions of elected officials. This occurs in several areas, including drafting of legislation, preparation of budget requests, and preparation of testimony for others or themselves. The most important agency powers, however, are those delegated by Congress. It is with these powers that agencies interpret, shape, and even create the law. Increasingly, the attention of business executives is drawn to the action of the administrative agencies, because some of the most important decisions affecting business are made by bureaucrats in their rule-making activities.

Rule-Making in Administrative Agencies

The dynamics of policy-making in a modern state have expanded the role of bureaucracies in decision-making. Although theory as well as the Constitution clearly hold that laws should be written or policy made by Congress with presidential concurrence, the system has not worked quite that way for years. Almost from the beginning, Congress found it necessary to delegate law-making or policy-making powers to administrative agencies,[4] which have the time and expertise to develop standards in policy areas. Agencies are given substantial power to write rules and regulations, to interpret, clarify, and implement the legislative intent of Congress. Thus, most of the rules and regulations to which the business community must respond are the output of the executive branch operating under delegations of authority from Congress.

One can better understand this process if one thinks of government policy-making taking place in three consecutive stages. The first stage is legislative; Congress passes a bill and the president signs it into law. The remaining two stages are administrative. An administrative agency clarifies the law and makes it ready for application. In the third stage, the agency administers the law and while doing so elaborates, evaluates, and changes it. Rule-making is a continuous process.

The last two stages are especially important. Usually Congress writes its laws in broad terms. Congressional legislation is generally vague and sometimes fraught with ambiguities spawned by political compromise. The administrative agencies must make the law operational by eliminating these ambiguities and developing well-defined procedures for implementation. Sometimes the law takes different or occasionally new directions as a result of agency rule-making activities. It is for this reason that business executives need to carefully observe this stage of the policy-making process. The stages of policy-making are portrayed graphically in figure 6.1.

The legislation creating the Federal Communications Commission is a good illustration of the processes of congressional delegation to an agency. The legislation, passed in 1932, is brief. Congress only set up the agency, authorized the number of commissioners to be appointed, and described generally the commission's field of activity or jurisdiction. The operational part of the legislation was a simple statement that the Federal Communications Commission should regulate wireless communications in the United States in the "public interest, convenience and necessity." It is under that broad delegation of power that the agency decided myriad questions about the regulation of the radio, television, and telecommunications industries. Under that broad grant, thousands of rules and regulations have been written on technical subjects as well as on social and political issues.

Every agency of the federal government has such powers delegated to it by Congress. The Department of Agriculture has great latitude over the agricultural sector of the economy through its powers to write rules and regulations in all of its program areas. The Internal Revenue Service has broad discretionary powers to write rules and regulations that affect all of us.

As the authority delegated to agencies is such a powerful tool, and as the Constitution makes it clear that legislative authority should reside in the legislature, considerable effort has been taken to oversee the administrative policy-making process. These efforts are designed to assure that the fundamental rights of citizens are not violated. In 1946, Congress passed the Administrative Procedure Act, which contains certain requirements for administrative agencies in their rule-making procedures. For example, agencies must announce in the *Federal Register* any proposed changes in existing rules and regulations or proposals for new ones. Agencies must give interested parties the right to submit testimony or even to appear at a hearing in the agency when the rule change or new rule is being considered. This is one of the assurances that public views will be heard while agencies are drafting rules and regulations. (For more information on the *Federal Register*, see Appendix C.)

Figure 6.1

Know your federal regulations

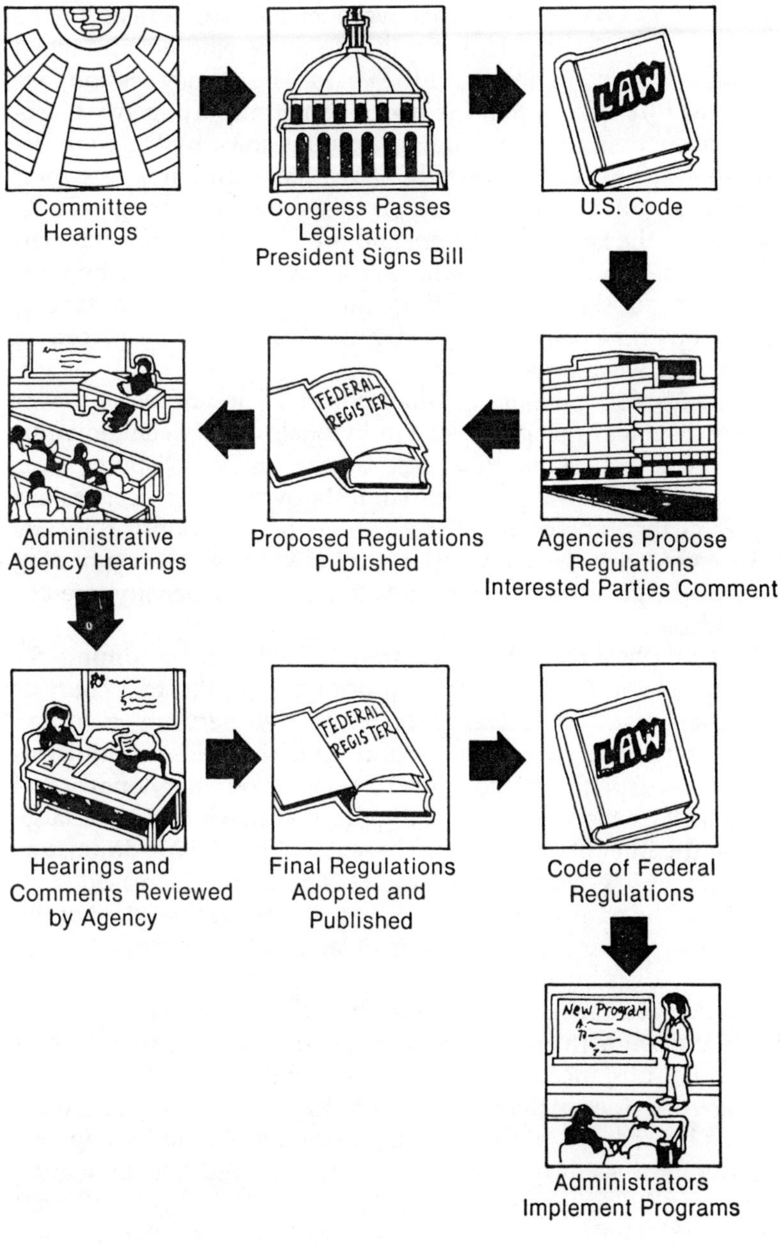

Hearings in the Agencies

When an administrative agency is engaged in its rule-making activities, its hearings are similar to those before a congressional committee. Hearing rooms in administrative agencies are similar to the hearing rooms on Capitol Hill, familiar to those who have watched important televised hearings over the years. The agency sessions are presided over by agency staff members, sometimes by agency directors, or, in the case of the regulatory commissions, by the commissioners themselves. Witnesses submit written testimony, state their positions orally, and answer questions posed by the hearing officers. Transcripts of the hearings are kept and used by the agency in reaching a decision. Anyone desiring to testify may do so simply by notifying the clerk of the agency. If there are many who want to testify, oral testimony time could be limited, but seldom are limits placed on the amount of written testimony.

Agencies also have judicial-like powers. They have the power to resolve disputes arising between individuals or between individuals and the government on a case-by-case basis. Disputes over licenses awarded in the past and contests over future licenses are examples of this type of activity. Hearings on violations of agency rules and regulations by corporations or individuals, where a finding in favor of the government could result in a fine or penalty, are another example.

These quasi-judicial hearings are presided over by administrative law judges and operate under procedures similar to a court of law. These judges are an elite corps of civil servants recruited through competitive examinations, and validity of these administrative processes depends to a considerable degree on their honesty and integrity, just as the validity of the judicial systems rests to a large degree on the integrity of judges. There are about 1,100 administrative law judges in government today. This figure has increased from 780 in 1974. The number assigned to agencies shows the extent of the judicial type of discretionary powers delegated to agencies and how that power is distributed through government (table 6.1).

The rules and regulations of administrative agencies may be appealed to the courts in most cases. The courts, however, are reluctant to review the substance of decisions based on the agency's expertise. The review activities of the courts are generally confined to questions of agency procedures, authority, or jurisdiction. Should an agency violate due process of the law in its hearing procedures, the courts may overturn its decision. In doing so, the courts will generally not decide on the merits of the case, but simply remand the decision

Table 6.1

Administrative law judges by agency

Agency	*No. of administrative law judges*
Agriculture Department	5
Civil Aeronautics Bureau	19
Civil Service Commission	1
Coast Guard	16
Commodity Futures Trading Commission	4
Consumer Products Safety Commission	1
Drug Enforcement Administration	1
Environmental Protection Agency	7
Federal Coal Mine Safety & Health Commission	12
Federal Communications Commission	14
Federal Energy Regulatory Commission	19
Federal Maritime Commission	7
Federal Trade Commission	13
Housing and Urban Development	1
Interior Department	21
Alcohol, Tobacco, Firearms Bureau	1
International Commerce Commission	62
International Trade Commission	2
Labor Department	49
Maritime Administration	3
National Labor Relations Board	100
National Transportation Safety Board	6
Nuclear Regulatory Commission	1
Occupational Safety & Health Review Commission	48
Postal Rate Commission	1
Postal Service	2
Securities and Exchange Commission	9
National Oceanic & Atmospheric Commission	1
Social Security Administration	675
TOTAL	1,101

Source: Office of Administrative Law Judges, U.S. Civil Service Commission, 1978.

back to the agency for another hearing with the instructions that this time the hearing be conducted properly.

After a rule has been adopted by the agency, it is published in the *Code of Federal Regulations*. The *Code* is fully indexed and conveniently organized by agency or major program. The *Code,* therefore, contains all the rules and regulations that any given agency has passed. Also, all of the amendments to the rules and regulations are included in the *Code*. (See Appendix D for a description of the *Code of Federal Regulations*.)

A key document in understanding the roll of the agency and one of enormous importance to business is the *Federal Register.* The *Register* brought some order to the administrative chaos that existed prior to its first publication in 1936. Before that time, there was no single document that contained all the official actions of agencies, including proposed rules, adopted rules, hearing notices, and application forms. Consequently, there was no way for the government to communicate with the public about administrators' actions except through mimeographed announcements, the press, and selected mailing lists. The *Federal Register* was created by Congress to end the fundamental unfairness inherent in a system where crucial government information was disseminated in a haphazard way.

The *Register* is published daily and subscribed to by several thousand people. Several thousand copies are also distributed free of charge. All proposed changes in agency rules, regulations, and forms are announced in the *Federal Register.* A period of time is given for those who wish to comment on these rules and regulations. The final determination of the agency is also printed in the *Register* before it is entered into the *Code of Federal Regulations.*

It is the delegated powers from Congress which make administrative agencies central to the policy-making process. Congress can, and often does, overrule agencies. Furthermore, the decision-making system operates in such a way as to assure members of Congress that bureaucrats take their views into consideration at all times. Sometimes congressmen even testify at agency rule-making hearings. Nevertheless, agencies have a considerable advantage in the policy-making process because of their permanence, their expertise, and their access to records. The legal authority to write rules and regulations further enhances their power in the process.

In 1978, President Carter was embroiled in a conflict with the House over a procedure known as a legislative veto. The House attempted to pass an authorization bill that included a veto clause that irked the president. The legislative veto shortcuts the legislative process by allowing either the House or a specific committee to veto rules or regulations written by an administrative agency.[5] Supporters of the legislative veto have argued that it is a device for monitoring and controlling bureaucratic behavior. They see it as an essential tool for a legislative body attempting to stay abreast of government programs. Opponents see it as a device for Congress to meddle in the affairs of the executive branch. They argue that Congress has delegated power by statute and cannot call it back by the action of one house or one committee of the legislature. Furthermore, it could slow the policy-making processes of government enough to affect adversely all those concerned. The Senate rejected this legislative veto approach late in 1978, but supporters of the idea will surely be heard from again.

The legislative veto proposal is only one manifestation of the constant tension between the agencies and congressional committees over the question of delegated powers. This tension and the vigilance it generates is healthy and offers more insurance that the voices of elected officials are heard clearly in the halls of agency policymaking. In a technologically complex society where expertise is required in decision-making, some balance must be sought between experts and elected officials. The competitive interaction in our policy-making systems helps to achieve a reasonable balance.

In recent years, lobbyists, or interest-group representatives, have come to realize the importance of agency activity. Traditionally, lobbyists devoted most of their energies to Capitol Hill. In fact, the term "lobbyist" emerged because the interest-group representatives often met with members of Congress in the lobbies immediately adjoining the House and Senate chambers. Modern lobbyists can still be found on the Hill, but increasingly they spend more time working in the agencies. This diversification of interest-group activity further underscores the importance of administrative agencies in policymaking.

The Executive Office of the President

Although the president seldom is directly involved in the hundreds of decision-making systems of government, members of his staff are often active participants. The top staff people are busy serving the president on the most immediate and most crucial matters of international affairs and major domestic problems. The atmosphere is intense, unpredictable, and occasionally chaotic. There are less visible, less high pressure parts of the Executive Office, however, where the presidency links up with decision-making systems.

The three components of the Executive Office of the President that attempt to influence the domestic decision-making system on behalf of the president are the White House Office, the Domestic Policy Staff (formerly the Domestic Council), and the Office of Management and Budget (figure 6.2). The other components of the Executive Office of the President have highly specialized tasks and are involved in decision-making systems related to those tasks.

The White House Office was established by the Reorganization Act of 1939. The staff is composed of personal advisors to the presi-

Figure 6.2

Executive office of the president

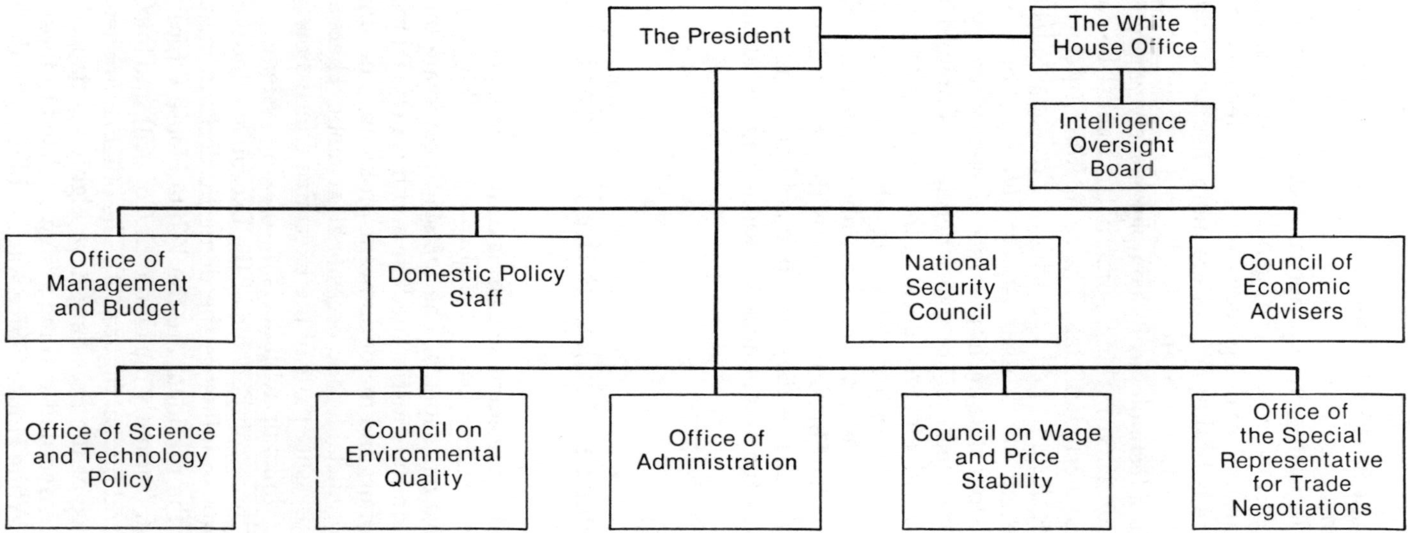

dent and numbers between sixty and seventy people. Upon assuming office, each president seeks to shape the Executive Office in a manner consistent with his needs, goals, and working style. The White House Office is one place where the president has great flexibility. He usually seeks to blend loyalty and expertise in the people chosen to become his close, personal advisors.

Within the White House Office, the president appoints a chief counsel, a press secretary, and a public relations officer. He also appoints special assistants to the president in areas such as consumer affairs, minority affairs, ethnic affairs, and women's issues. Each of the special assistants is likely to have a deputy assistant and a few staff people to provide support services. The White House Office staff is responsible for facilitating and maintaining communication with Congress, heads of executive departments and agencies, the media, the public, and special-interest groups. They are the president's personal staff and his eyes and ears outside the White House.[6]

In July 1970, President Nixon implemented one of the recommendations of the Advisory Council on Executive Management (Ash Commission) and created the Domestic Council. The president felt that the institutional arrangements for dealing with domestic policy under his three immediate predecessors lacked continuity, clear lines of responsibility, techniques for planning and reviewing actions, and mechanisms for follow-through. What the president wanted was a systematic way of handling domestic policy similar to the way the National Security Council handles foreign policy. He needed an agency, with some legitimacy, short of the president to resolve disputes as well as an analysis branch to help clarify and rationalize demands.[7]

President Nixon assigned the following responsibilities to the Domestic Council:

1. formulate and coordinate domestic policy recommendations to the president;
2. assess national needs and coordinate the establishment of national priorities;
3. provide a rapid response to presidential needs for policy advise on critical domestic issues;
4. provide continuous review of ongoing domestic programs from a policy standpoint;
5. operate through a series of ad hoc project committees which deal with either broad program areas or specific problems; and
6. utilize staff support from departmental or agency experts, or its own staff.

The associate and assistant directors of the council acted as project managers. Each would deal with a few key issues. The planning staff provided the general support and coordination. The issues dealt with by the Domestic Council usually reflect presidential priorities. The deployment of staff serves as a guide to the issues to which the president is willing to commit resources—time, money, people, influence, and public leadership.

Under Presidents Nixon and Ford, the Domestic Council focused on planning and follow-through activities. It acted as a conduit and processor of proposals coming to the White House. The staff helped to articulate options by developing arguments for and against each policy issue. These options included the recommendations of both departmental and Executive Office staff as well as the comments of the Domestic Council.

Many of the ideas of the Domestic Council materialized in the president's State of the Union message or in special messages to Congress on the budget or specific legislation. The messages to Congress were usually accompanied by supporting data explaining the president's position.

The follow-through activities of the Domestic Council included monitoring proposals to insure they were implemented successfully, working with Congress on legislative language, and making decisions on legislative tactics, including final compromises. The Domestic Council representatives also provided a political perspective in the annual budget review. The Domestic Council was also charged with analyzing and communicating program results. This was done through the media, speeches, press conferences, and White House briefings. The Domestic Council prepared the necessary materials and also analyzed public opinion polls and political information to determine the reaction to the president's domestic policies and to uncover, if possible, new issues and problems requiring attention.

The Carter administration found the domestic policy process in place too chaotic and too inefficient for its working style. In mid-1977, an Executive Office reorganization plan was recommended to strengthen the role of the president's chief domestic policy advisors. The new process was aimed at increasing the president's control over the development of major domestic programs.[8]

Not until early 1978 did the new reorganization plan become operational. The reorganization that ended the Domestic Council and replaced it with a domestic policy staff has helped to clarify some of the lines of responsibility within the Executive Branch. However, White House influence on the programmatic decision-making systems of government has not changed markedly following the reorganization.

The Office of Management and Budget

Another unit in the Executive Office of the President with substantial power to affect policy is the Office of Management and Budget.[9] OMB was created by President Nixon in 1970 to give the old Bureau of the Budget more responsibility in the management field. The director and deputy director were initially appointed by the president without Senate confirmation. Now these appointees must be confirmed by the Senate. The politically sensitive nature of these two positions has made them targets of controversy almost from the beginning.

OMB has a staff of around six hundred professionals. Their major areas of responsibility are to assist the president in the preparation of the budget and in the formulation of his fiscal program. They are also charged with control and administration of the budget. These responsibilities necessitate a continuous dialogue with the agencies and departments of government, first on budget questions, then on legislative issues, and finally on administrative matters.

OMB participates fully and regularly in the policy process. If a bureau head wants to initiate a new program or make substantial changes in an existing one—changes that require congressional action—the proposal must be approved by OMB. The proposal must have the written blessing of OMB before it can move forward to Capitol Hill. Added to its regular budget functions, this legislative clearance function makes OMB one of the most powerful—perhaps the most powerful—organization in Washington. Presidents rely heavily on OMB as they attempt to influence policy, control costs, or exercise leverage on programs controlled by the decision-making systems of government.

OMB is also charged with aiding the president in improving the efficiency of government services, expanding coordinating mechanisms among agencies, promoting the development of improved plans of administrative management, advising the president on legislation ready for his signature, planning and implementing information systems to produce program performance data, planning and conducting program evaluations, and developing programs to recruit, train, motivate, and evaluate career personnel.

As the president seeks to influence the outcome of issues in the hundreds of decision-making systems, he has at his disposal a personal staff of specialists, a domestic policy staff, and, probably his strongest weapon, OMB. All of these resources together are impressive, but on any given issue they will not assure the president victory.[10]

Interest groups, Congress, and agency bureaucrats each have resources at their disposal. Depending upon the degree of coordination, timing, resource commitment, and perseverence, these actors can stall and often defeat a presidential program, or they can accelerate the process and move an issue to a swift and positive conclusion. The decision-making systems work primarily because there is a degree of balance in them. No one component alone dominates the others unless there is a major national crisis. Short of that, each of the actors seeks to achieve the best possible compromise consistent with stated goals and objectives.

It is to the operation of the decision-making systems which we now turn. Knowing what the components of the system are facilitates an understanding of how to participate effectively in the processes of support, challenge, and change necessary to move decision-making in desired directions.

Notes

1. See Francis E. Rourke, *Bureaucracy, Politics and Public Policy,* 2nd ed. (Boston: Little, Brown and Co., 1976), pp. 13–18.

2. For a discussion of cooperation between program managers and congressmen, see James A. Thurber, "The Actors in Administering Public Policy: Legislative Administrative Relations," *Policy Studies Journal* 5, no. 1 (Autumn 1976): 56–65.

3. See Randall B. Ripley and Grace L. Franklin, *Congress, the Bureaucracy and Public Policy,* (Homewood, Ill.: Dorsey Press, 1976), pp. 64–67.

4. See A. Lee Fritschler, *Smoking and Politics,* for more details on the policy-making powers of administrative agencies.

5. Edward Walsh, "President Trying to Blunt Hill Weapon Against Bureaucrats," *Washington Post,* 1 July 1978.

6. See Grant McConnell, *The Modern Presidency,* 2nd ed. (New York: St. Martins Press, 1976), pp. 68–72; and Thomas A. Timberg, *The Federal Executive: The President and the Bureaucracy* (New York: Irvington Publishers, 1978), pp. 13–15.

7. An analysis to the Domestic Council can be found in Raymond J. Waldmann, "The Domestic Council: Innovation in Presidential Government," *Public Administration Review* 36, no. 3 (May–June 1976): 260–68. Also see Dom Bonafede, "White House Staffing: The Nixon-Ford Era" in *The Presidency Reappraised,* 2nd ed., edited by Thomas E. Cronin and Rexford G. Tugwell (New York: Praeger Publishers, 1977), pp. 160–61, 169–70.

8. David Broder, "Shaping the Administration's Policy: New Process for Domestic Issues," *Washington Post,* 12 February 1978.

9. For a discussion of OMB, see Timberg, *The Federal Executive,* pp. 106–8;

also McConnell, *The Modern Presidency,* pp. 72–73; and Dorothy Buckton James, "The Future of the Institutionalized Presidency," in *The Future of the American Presidency,* ed. Charles W. Dunn (Morristown, N.J.: General Learning Press, 1975), pp. 105–6.

10. Richard E. Neustadt, *Presidential Power: The Politics of Leadership,* 2nd ed., (New York: John Wiley and Sons, 1976).

seven

The Decision-Making System in Operation

The decision-making systems of government are constantly in motion; colliding, overlapping, and competing. To track and influence them, one has to watch closely and acquire the skills to maneuver them in desired directions. Dealing with government—influencing decision-making processes to achieve desired outcomes—has become a specialized task. It is time-consuming, intricate, and requires special training or experience. But like many modern specialties, learning the basics is not difficult. Applying them successfully takes common sense, practice, and time.

Effective participation in government decision-making has become a full-time job. Special-interest groups, corporations, and even universities have turned their representational activities over to knowledgeable people whose major responsibility is dealing with government. This chapter illustrates how interested observers can become active participants in decision-making systems. It examines these systems at the local, state, and national levels, for policy made in Washington often relies for its success on the administrative talents and managerial capabilities of state, county, and city officials.

First Step: How to Locate Decision-Making Systems

Having learned what a decision-making system looks like, the first step is to locate the system responsible for the policy or program in question. The process of location and identification is relatively easy. To identify the specific system one is interested in, use the *U.S. Code* and the *Congressional Quarterly Almanac.*[1] The *U.S. Code* is a compendium of all legislation passed by Congress and signed by the president. It contains information about which agency is responsible for managing the program. The *Almanac* contains information on other aspects of the decision-making system. It leads the reader to the subcommittee that heard the legislative proposals, and lists interest groups, executives, public officials, and others involved in the development of the legislation. The *Almanac* is a good chronicle of government decision-making systems.

To become more informed, read the congressional hearings and committee reports. All of these materials will identify the programs, the actors, and the major controversies associated with a given decision-making system. At this point, a useful document is the *U.S. Government Manual.*[2] The *Manual* is published annually and is the most comprehensive guide available of the agencies, bureaus, and offices of government, the Executive Office of the President, and the two houses of Congress. Included in the *Manual* are descriptions of the government agencies, some background on their creation, an organization chart, and a listing of the top management officers and their titles. The index to the *Manual* lists government agencies according to the substantive area in which they operate. For example, one of the headings in the index, "Aviation," has nine agencies listed under it. In the section of the *Manual* that describes agencies is a list of the programs for which each agency is responsible. This will quickly narrow the possible number of agencies that can be administratively responsible for a specific program.

Once the key agency is located, interested parties can become directly involved in the decision-making systems. A productive first call or visit might be to an agency's public information office. The telephone number and the name of the director of public information are listed in the *Manual.* This person will be able to give additional up-to-date information on the program being administered, including special features of the legislation, targeted groups, evaluation criteria, budget allocation, intergovernmental considerations, and important regulations.

Instead of going first to the administrative agency, another entry point into the decision-making system is Congress. After locating the appropriate statute, one can identify from the *Congressional Directory*[3] the committee or subcommittee of the Congress that wrote the legislation and is responsible for oversight. Also listed in the *Congressional Directory* are the membership of the appropriate committee and some biographical information about its members. This is a very useful guide; it contains the telephone numbers and office numbers of members of Congress by committee and by congressional district. The *Directory* is published every session of Congress by the Government Printing Office. A privately published document, the *Congressional Staff Directory*[4] provides biographical information on the members of Congress, office staffs, committee, and subcommittee staffs. Another useful publication in dealing with Capitol Hill is the *Almanac of American Politics*,[5] which gives a summary of the members' voting records and their ratings by various constituency organizations like the Americans for Democratic Action and the Americans for Constitutional Action. In addition, biographical information on the members, recent election results in the district, and characteristics of the district are also presented.

Once an appropriate direction has been chosen, the next step is to make an appointment with a staff member on the Hill or a mid-level bureaucrat in the agency. This person will be able to provide the most current information available and, more important, can provide the names and institutional affiliations of all the major actors in the decision-making system. Staff members are able to name the important interest groups concerned and in what way they are concerned. Key White House people can also be identified. At that point, some time must be spent gathering information about the decision-making system's past activities, future plans, and what seem to be the current issues motivating it. This task is not as difficult as it might seem.

Tracking Decision-Making Systems

One of the best sources for following a decision-making system is the specialized press that has a vested interest in, and therefore monitors, the specific system. Associated with nearly every decision system in Washington is a group of reporters who are writing for either a trade publication or an independent publication that services a group of specialized subscribers interested in one particular functional issue, aging or mass transit, for instance. *Printer's Ink* is a major publication in advertising, while *Aviation News* covers the airline industry.

There are hundreds of these publications in Washington. They are available by subscription or in libraries across the country to satisfy the research needs and interests of specialized client groups. Talking with a reporter on the staff of one of these publications can produce good information on either the substance or the process of the programs and issues his publication covers. In some cases the publication with the best information may be a relatively small newsletter service operated out of a private home. The owner-reporter may be a one-person business, where the owner collects information by monitoring a decision-making system, turns it over to a typing service which prepares camera-ready copy for the printer, who in turn delivers the finished newsletter to a mailing service. Though these operations are relatively small, they fill an important specialized information gap that the larger media outlets cannot cover.

Two of the most important publications for those following decision-making systems are *The Congressional Quarterly* and *The National Journal.* Of course, they cover only the major and most controversial decision systems. They also, however, report the actions and deliberations in Congress. Actors involved in the systems find the publications essential.

At this point, one should have enough information to prepare a system diagram for a specific program by writing names, addresses,

Figure 7.1

A government decision-making system

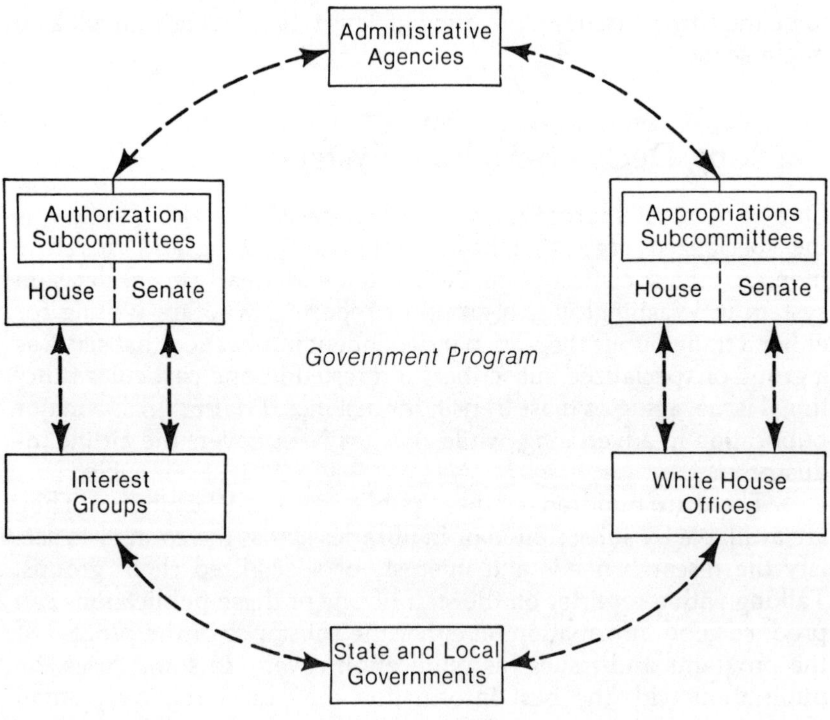

and telephone numbers of key actors beside the appropriate boxes. This tailored diagram can be used as a map of the system in question (figure 7.1). Now the time has come to follow the system carefully and to meet regularly with the individuals in it. Learn what is on their minds; how they see the future of the program in question; how they would like to see it changed; and how they plan to move ahead in the coming months. In the course of these discussions, one can refine one's judgment on the influence of various individuals and begin to build the kinds of analytical and forecasting capabilities that those in close contact with human systems develop over time.

There are consulting or lobbying firms that track decision-making systems for clients. Larger organizations do it for themselves, but for smaller corporations not interested in setting up a Washington office, these firms can be helpful. On behalf of their clients, they prepare reports on specific issues based on input from the generalized media, the specialized media, government reports, the *Congressional Record*, the *Federal Register*, and other sources. If a client wants to become actively involved, these organizations will set up appointments, arrange for appearances at agency or congressional hearings, and even help write testimony for the hearings. Also, the major representational groups, like the U.S. Chamber of Commerce, National Association of Manufacturers, and the AFL-CIO, track and participate in these decision-making systems for their members.

Decision-Making Systems in Action

After locating the system and learning about its background and agenda, it is necessary to learn how to become an effective participant. Some additional information on the environment in which systems operate is helpful. The U.S. Constitution does not establish or encourage the development of a coordinated management system. In fact, the Constitution sets up a system of divided or shared powers which makes it very difficult, at times, for government officials effectively to manage programs. A source of ongoing debate in political science and public administration circles over the years has been between those who want to invest more power in chief executive officers—presidents, governors, and mayors—enabling them to manage government programs more effectively, and those who prefer the decentralized power system the Constitution encourages.

The decision-making systems that have emerged over the years are one means government has devised to compensate for the requirement of separated powers set forth in the Constitution. These systems informally bridge the separation of powers to insure that the processes of government are not stalled. It is through these systems that the separated institutions of government come together to compromise differences, make public policy, and manage programs. These decision-making systems make government in general more stable and predictable.

The systems operate in a constitutionally created state of near anarchy. To a great extent, they are held together by the fear of what would happen to the political process if the systems disintegrated. The actors know that should disintegration occur, the stability and predictability so necessary to government management would disappear. Cooperation and compromise would be all but impossible; the participants would lose control of the program; and the outputs of the political system would become quite unpredictable.

There is a high premium placed on keeping the decision-making structure together. One can imagine each participant in the decision-making system going through a mental calculation whenever a new proposal surfaces: "How much do I agree or disagree with this proposal? Do I disagree with it so strongly that I am willing to risk obstructing or possibly even destroying the decision-making system? Or can I bend and seek a compromise with others to keep the decision-making structure and function?" One alternative is to devise obstacles so great that it becomes virtually impossible to process the issue through the system. Once all parties agree that the issue has been successfully stalled, it is tabled, and the system either moves on to other issues or becomes temporarily dormant. The customary answer is to keep the system together, to move slowly or incrementally. The alternative might be confusion, even chaos, the loss of predictability and control over government programs.

Initiating Change in the Systems

The nature of the environment in which the decision-making systems work provides a clue as to how to interact with these systems. There are essentially two choices, two modes of operation, each quite different from the other. One approach is to work with the system, support it, and try to bring about incremental change within it. There are several ways of supporting a decision-making system that is making policy one favors: work for the reelection of the elected members of the system, provide information to strengthen the system, and persuade others to support the system by building broader-based coalitions.

There are many access points through which individuals and groups can make their views known and through which change can be sought. It is possible to testify in hearings held by administrative agencies or by congressional committees and subcommittees. Calls can be made on federal agencies in the executive branch, the White House staff, congressional and committee staff, and members of Congress to try to persuade them to adopt a new position or modify the one they currently hold.

When persuasion and working within the decision-making system fail, the other approach is to find or create an alternate or competing decision-making structure. This deprives the original system of the chance to process the issue and is likely to produce a radically different outcome. The first approach is more prudent and the one most often selected. The second is chosen only at considerable risk; the chances of losing the fight are great.

In 1967, President Lyndon B. Johnson was faced with such a choice. His advisors had developed a proposal for granting the District of Columbia a modicum of home rule by changing the commission form of government to a mayor-council form, with the top officials appointed by the president.

Past efforts to reorganize the District of Columbia government had been thwarted by recalcitrant members of the House District Committee, parliamentary maneuvers, the Washington Board of Trade, and grass-roots lobbying efforts. Any effort to effect change would require a different strategy than the legislative route through the District Committees of the House and the Senate.

Johnson's advisors understood the nature of decision-making systems and the odds against successfully navigating a D.C. governmental reform bill through the established decision-making system. The only legitimate choice open was to try and process the issue through another system. They recommended that the president introduce a reorganization plan for D.C. government to Congress. A reorganization plan would be sent to the House Committee on Government Operations, where it would probably receive a much more favorable hearing than a bill sent to the House District Committee.

By finding an alternative decision-making system the president and his advisors achieved their goal of reorganizing the ninety-three-year-old governmental system in the District of Columbia.[6]

Strategy I: Redefining the Issue

When decision-making systems fail to respond to advocates of incremental change, then more extreme strategies are required. One of these involves redefining the issue. An interesting characteristic of public decisions is that they can be defined in at least two, but usually many more, ways. For instance, the debate over requiring health warnings on cigarette packages and in cigarette advertising could be, and was for many years, defined as a commercial issue. There are commercial aspects of every phase of cigarette production. It involves those who make their living producing tobacco leaf, those who manufacture cigarettes, those who advertise cigarettes, and those who sell cigarettes.

It is also, however, a health issue. Since there is little doubt among medical researchers and practitioners that smoking is harmful to health, there have been frequent attempts to require health warnings on cigarette packages. For many years these proposals were sent to a decision-making system accustomed to dealing with commercial and economic issues. The output from that system was quite predictable: nothing happened. This was quite natural coming from a system more attuned to corporate health than to personal health. Very often the type of decision that emerges from government depends upon the characteristics of the system processing the decision. Consequently, a major strategy for those desiring change in decision-making is to redefine the issue in such a way that it is placed in a different decision-making system with different actors who are more likely to respond to different information sources and points of view.

The food stamp program was conceived to distribute surplus food to the poor and the needy. The program was delegated to the Department of Agriculture to administer. In the 1960s, Americans became much more aware of the scope and intensity of poverty across the country. Many liberal interest groups saw the food stamp program as an obvious vehicle for relieving hunger and ameliorating poverty. These groups felt that the Agriculture Department was too conservative in its approach to surplus food distribution. Representative Jamie L. Whitten (D-Miss.), past chairman of the House Appropriations Subcommittee on Agriculture, who has often been called the "permanent secretary of agriculture," strongly supported the Agriculture Department's point of view.

The battle was joined. The liberals saw food stamps as a social welfare issue which should be administered by HEW. The conservatives viewed it as a surplus food program to be handled by the Agriculture Department. For more than a decade the issue has been the subject of intense debate, hyperbole, compromise, and vote trading with minor adjustments being made to satisfy periodic pressures. The liberal groups have not been successful in redefining the food stamp program so that it can become part of a welfare decision-making system.[7] They have achieved a modest victory, however. Beginning in 1979, recipients no longer had to pay for their food stamps.

Strategy II: Reorganization

Another strategy is to build new coalitions with other interested parties and to work either to move a program from one decision-making system to another or to create an entirely new system. Government reorganization is often designed for this purpose. Moving a program from one bureau to another or from one subcommittee to another has the effect of changing actors, changing coalitions, and probably changing outcomes. A federal effort to relieve traffic congestion in large cities, for example, would substantially change in emphasis if it were moved from a highway-oriented decision-making system to a mass-transit-oriented one. It is not difficult to see how officials from the Urban Mass Transportation Administration, the U.S. Conference of Mayors, and the American Public Transit Association, with the support of protransit members of Congress, might propose solutions different from those offered by the Federal Highway Administration, state highway departments, the American Automobile Association, and their congressional allies.

An interesting example occured in 1978, when the Carter administration proposed the creation of a separate Department of Education. A number of individuals and groups supported the bill, reasoning it would give education a more prominent place in the decision-making arena by giving it independent status, hence greater visibility and more political clout. Others supported the bill because they felt it would put the spotlight on numerous educational programs that were not receiving the rigorous evaluations they deserved.

The reorganization proposal was opposed by a number of special-interest groups, as well as by the Departments of Defense and Agriculture, whose educational programs were scheduled to be transferred to the new Department of Education. Sensing that their decision-making systems might be reorganized out of existence, they fought to preserve their turf, existing power relationships, and institutionalized channels of access. Others opposed the new department for fear of creating another large bureaucracy. The proposal was not enacted in the rush to adjourn the Ninety-fifth Congress, despite great pressure from the Carter administration and the National Education Association. However, the pros and cons have now been ar-

"Get those wheelchairs in a circle—the president's comin' back!"

ticulated, and the political struggle is certain to be continued in the Ninety-sixth Congress.[8]

The importance of reorganization or redirection as a change strategy cannot be overemphasized. Greater efficiency or adherence to some allegedly scientific principles of administration are the most common arguments for shifting an activity from one bureau to another or for creating a new governmental unit. In reality, government organization reflects national priorities and problems. The recent creation of the Department of Energy, for example, was a confirmation that energy policy is now sufficiently important to warrant its own cabinet-level agency instead of being fragmented and treated piecemeal by agencies concerned primarily with other matters. Issues elevated to cabinet status within the past fifteen years include housing and urban development and transportation, while environmental protection, occupational safety, and equal employment opportunity issues are among those receiving their own lower-level but separate agencies.

Strategy III: Escalate the Controversy

A third strategy is to escalate the controversy to a higher level of decision-making. The president, secretaries of cabinet departments, and the leadership of Congress are not directly involved in decision-making systems. Their role in trying to bring about change is similar in operational terms to those outsiders who desire to influence the systems. They use the strategies of persuasion, redefinition, reorganization, and coalition building that others use. There is one major difference, however: these individuals, because of their high-level positions in government, are much more powerful that the ordinary participant. Because of their extraordinary power, actors interested in bringing about a major change attempt to get the president, department heads, or congressional leaders involved on their behalf to change the focus and the balance of power and hence the outcomes of specific issues.

Perhaps the two most illustrative examples of this strategy were the War on Poverty and Medicare. In both cases, the decision-making systems began to process these issues as they would any major piece of domestic legislation. One important difference between these two and hundreds of other proposals was that billions of dollars were involved, and this money was in essence being redistributed from people paying higher taxes to those people in need who paid relatively low taxes.[9] When the stakes of politics are high and a sizable redistribution of tax dollars is involved, it is difficult for the lower-level decision-making systems to generate the necessary compromise and consensus to produce a bill.

When deadlock occurs in such issues of national importance, it usually means that the decision-making must be elevated to a higher level. Congressional leadership, the cabinet, and probably the president become involved. At this level, any compromise reached is likely to be very broad in scope.

The Economic Opportunity Act of 1964 was an example of decision-making systems resolving many small conflicts but being unable to bridge the wide ideological chasm between conservative and liberal congressmen. As Ripley and Franklin point out,

> Individual members of the House and Senate, particularly those in strategic committee positions, were important in helping make decisions, as were individuals scattered throughout the administration and relevant executive branch agencies. However, these individuals could not make binding decisions by themselves. A much broader set of decision-makers got involved including all Senators and Representatives (through floor action), the President and his top advisors, and a large variety of interest groups.[10]

An analysis of the passage of Medicare is not markedly different from the War on Poverty. Once again a piece of legislation on the public agenda involved billions of dollars. There were very strong conflicting views about the scope of a federally supported health insurance program. Favoring action were the AFL-CIO, the National Council of Senior Citizens, and a host of public-welfare organizations. Opposing any federal entry into a national insurance program were the American Medical Association, the insurance industry, and business organizations in general.[11]

Two factors helped to resolve the conflict over a federally funded health insurance program. First, this issue had been debated in Congress and the White House intermittently since 1935. Very few new ideas and arguments were being raised for or against the issue. Second, in 1964, the American people elected an overwhelmingly Democratic majority in both houses of Congress to work with a president sympathetic to Medicare. Not only was there a Democratic majority in Congress, but it was a majority with a liberal outlook and a determination to enact social legislation.

Recognizing that the tide was going against them, opponents sought the best possible compromise. To do this they had to remove the issue from the specialized health system and elevate it to the highest levels of governmental decision-making. The strategy proved successful in the Medicare bill because it contained more amendments they supported than it would have otherwise.

Decision-making systems process the issues on the government's agenda. All of the actors involved in these issues know how the systems work. Opponents and proponents mobilize their resources to achieve their objectives. However, options are still open to the actors to redefine the issue, reorganize the decision-making system or elevate the controversy to the highest levels of government.

Notes

1. *Congressional Quarterly Almanac* (Washington, D.C.: Congressional Quarterly, Inc., published annually).

2. Office of the Federal Register, National Archives and Records Service, General Services Administration, *United States Government Manual 1977/78* (Washington, D.C.: U.S. Government Printing Office, 1978).

3. United States Congress, *Official Congressional Directory* (Washington, D.C.: U.S. Government Printing Office, 1978).

4. *Congressional Staff Directory,* ed. Charles B. Brownson (Mount Vernon, Va.: The Congressional Staff Directory, 1978).

5. Michael Barone, Grant Ujifusa, and Douglas Matthews, *The Almanac of American Politics: 1978* (New York: E. P. Dutton, 1977).

6. For a discussion of this strategy, see Royce Hanson and Bernard H. Ross, "Washington," in *The Government of Federal Capitals,* ed. Donald C. Rowat (Toronto, Canada: University of Toronto Press, 1973), pp. 93–99.

7. For an excellent discussion of this issue, see Nick Kotz, *Let Them Eat Promises: The Politics of Hunger in America* (New York: Anchor Books, 1971); also Phillip M. Gregg, "What Difference Will Food Stamp Reform Make?" *The Bureaucrat* 7 (Winter 1978): 22–33.

8. For a discussion of the arguments surrounding the proposal for a new Department of Education, see Joel Havemann, "Carter's Reorganization Plans—Scrambling for Turf," *National Journal,* 20 May 1978, pp. 788–92.

9. For a discussion of redistributive domestic policy, see Randall B. Ripley and Grace A. Franklin, *Congress, the Bureaucracy and Public Policy* (Homewood, Ill.: Dorsey Press, 1976), p. 122.

10. See Ripley and Franklin, p. 123. For a discussion of the War on Poverty legislation, see Sar A. Levitan, *The Great Society's Poor Law* (Baltimore: Johns Hopkin Press, 1968); and Daniel P. Moynihan, *Maximum Feasible Misunderstanding: Community Action in the War on Poverty* (Glencoe, Ill.: The Free Press, 1969), chapter 5.

11. For a discussion of the Medicare struggle, see Ted Marmor, *The Politics of Medicare,* rev. ed. (Chicago: Aldine, 1973); also Eric Redman, *The Dance of Legislation* (New York: Simon and Schuster, 1973).

eight

Business Executives and the Intergovernmental System

One of the most difficult concepts to understand about the American political system concerns the dichotomy between policy-making and policy implementation. In our system, broad policy goals and objectives are legislated by Congress. Administrative agencies then develop rules and regulations to guide the states, counties, and cities charged with the responsibility of implementing the programs.

There are few domestic programs administered solely by the federal government: the postal system, Tennessee Valley Authority, major regulatory programs, and Social Security, among others. Most other domestic programs are funded in part by the federal government but implemented and managed at the state and local level. Air and water pollution control projects, airport and road construction, welfare and education programs, and mass transit are only a few examples of government programs that operate through the intricate intergovernmental systems established by the U.S. Constitution as well as by experience and necessity. To understand how power is distributed and exercised in the political system, one has to know how the intergovernmental system functions.

The importance of state, county, and city government was underscored earlier by including them in the decision-making system diagram used in this book. Their impact upon the system is dramatic, because in many respects these subnational units of government are the operational components of the system.

Currently, the federal government is appropriating approximately $80 billion to be channeled to the state and local governments through the grants-in-aid system. A large share of these funds are expended in contracts with business firms. The grants-in-aid system is the third most significant expenditure in the federal budget, behind Social Security and defense. If a reasonable overhead were to be added to this $80 billion intergovernmental transfer, it would probably make grants-in-aid the largest single expenditure in the federal budget. In other words, the federal government is in the business of financing programs administered by state and local governments, and such funds have become an increasingly important source of revenue for state and local governments. Businessmen dealing with state and local government should realize that a large portion of state and local funds come to these governments from Washington through the grants-in-aid system. Understanding how decisions are made in this intergovernmental system is of great importance to business executives.

Number of Governmental Units

The size and scope of the federal government and its many activities are overwhelming. The size and scope of the subnational system are equally impressive and even more complex. More impressive is the large number of governmental units involved in administering programs and policies at the local level (table 8.1). While the total has decreased by over 11,000 units in the past fifteen years, there still remain over 80,000 units of government in the country. Municipalities, townships, and counties have remained relatively constant in this period. The major changes have taken place in the number of school and special districts, with the former decreasing because of consolidations and the latter increasing because of the public recognition of the need for specialized service-delivery mechanisms.

The number of governmental units in the country automatically creates some problems. Most of these units exercise some executive, legislative, and administrative powers, making them autonomous units of government. Consequently, it is difficult for federal agencies to exercise oversight of the programs funded by Washington but administered by these jurisdictions.

Management of the intergovernmental system has become one of the most challenging problems facing public-sector officials today. With so many political jurisdictions, it is difficult for the federal government to try and legislate to encompass the variety of national needs even within a specific functional area. The large number of jurisdictions also means uneven quality in the administration of federal programs and many problems in trying to coordinate programs in a metropolitan area. The picture that emerges is one of a large, complex system that is highly fragmented. It is often difficult to

Table 8.1

Scope of the subnational system: number of governments in the U.S.

Type of government	*1962*	*1967*	*1972*	*1977*
Total	91,237	81,299	79,269	80,171
U.S. Government	1	1	1	1
State Governments	50	50	50	50
Local Governments	91,186	81,248	78,218	80,120
Counties	3,043	3,049	3,044	3,042
Municipalities	18,000	18,048	18,517	18,856
Townships	17,142	17,105	18,991	16,822
School Districts	34,678	21,782	15,781	15,260
Special Districts	18,323	21,264	23,885	26,140

Source: U.S. Bureau of the Census

know what neighboring jurisdictions or jurisdictions of a similar size are doing well or poorly. The result is a system in which service and tax boundaries overlap. There is duplication of services, and, consequently, some resources are poorly allocated and wasted. Major problems arise when metropolitan areas attempt a region wide program that requires fiscal or at least administrative concurrence from all area jurisdictions. In metropolitan areas with hundreds of political units, this can be a monumental and often an impossible task.

The state and local systems that implement federal policies and programs are highly decentralized. It becomes a serious management problem for the federal bureaucracy to monitor the quality of federal programs as well as state and local compliance with rules, regulations, and guidelines. Federal agencies often rely on interim reports and self-evaluation as the only means of assessing compliance and quality control. There are far too many political units and far too few federal evaluators and auditors to do a professional job. Selective investigations by congressional committees or studies conducted by the Office of Management and Budget and the General Accounting Office occasionally uncover serious incidents of mismanagement, noncompliance, or fraud.

On the other hand, this decentralized administrative system can be viewed as a check against unwise or autocratic federal policy-making. Since federal programs are filtered through a subnational administrative system, they are subject to state, county, and city modifications—within limits—which tailor the program more appropriately to the needs of the specific jurisdiction. This final check reduces the likelihood of federal programs causing serious problems for any region, state, or class of cities.

Picket-Fence Federalism

Federal, state, and local government programs are linked together in a fashion sometimes referred to as picket-fence federalism (PFF).[1] In the mid and late 1960s, there was a rapid expansion in the number of grant programs authorized and funded by the federal government. These programs required state, county, and local administrators to implement them. PFF depicts the relationship of national to subnational decision-making and administrative units (See figure 8.1).[2]

As federal programs are normally funded and administered along functional lines, the slats in the picket fence represent the major program areas as they span the three levels of government. Functional specialists and program managers on all levels are linked by federal legislation, program funding, and operational guidelines. Program by program, federal bureaucrats work directly with state and local bureaucrats. Elected officials at the state and local level find themselves excluded from policy decisions, for the authority and fund for programs is generated by the federal government and transmitted through bureaucrats. State and local elected officials do have the strength to counterbalance the increased powers federally funded programs invest in state and local bureaucrats. When state and local agencies fail to provide the quantity and the quality of service citizens demand, problems arise. Citizens find themselves at a disadvantage in trying to apply pressure on local elected officials to influence the administration of policies and programs, for the program guidelines and funding are from federal, not state or local, sources.

The bureaucratic agencies that accrued power through grant-in-aid programs are supported by a number of well-organized and influential special-interest groups who know how to gain access to key administrators. The imbalance that crept into the system was not easily or quickly recognized.

Recently, local elected officials began to exercise greater oversight functions on federally financed grant programs. In addition, the federal government has also changed some of its funding approaches. More money is now allocated to state and local governments with fewer restrictions, giving elected officials greater discretion in how it is spent. Still, the system is heavily dependent upon bureaucrats for administrative and policy decisions.

The conflict between state and local elected officials and three levels of bureaucrats is now being fought in part in the courts. *Shapp v. Casey*[3] arose in 1976 when the Pennsylvania state legislature passed two bills, one requiring that all federal funds coming into the state be deposited in the general fund and be subjected to the state

Figure 8.1

Picket-fence federalism: a schematic representation

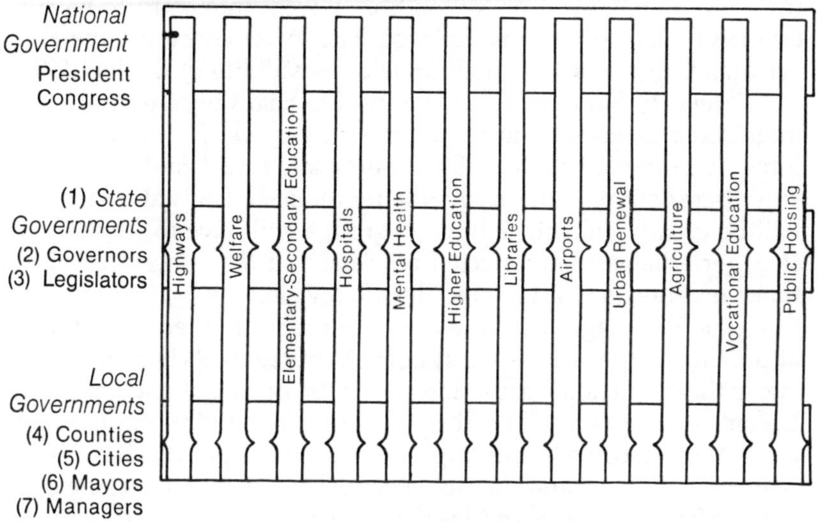

The Big Seven

(1) Council of State Governments
(2) National Governors' Conference
(3) National Legislative Conference
(4) National Association of County Officials
(5) National League of Cities
(6) U.S. Conference of Mayors
(7) International City Management Association

Source: Deil S. Wright, "Intergovernmental Relations: An Analytical Overview," The Annals of the American Academy of Political and Social Science, *November 1974, p. 15.*

appropriations process. The second bill mandated that all federal funds be appropriated to state agencies through specific line items in the state budget. The first bill was passed over the governor's veto. The governor, as head of the executive bureaucracy, was unwilling to see power move from the bureaucracy to the legislature. The state treasurer, acting under existing law, refused to release federal funds for a program. Governor Milton Shapp went into court to have the two laws declared unconstitutional. The lower court and the Pennsylvania Supreme Court both upheld the validity of the legislation.

The U.S. Supreme Court's refusal to hear the case means there might be a major shift in where and how power is exercised in the intergovernmental system. State bureaucrats will find their power and discretionary authority markedly reduced. Legislative authority will be greatly enhanced. Interest groups will have to forge new or stronger alliances with elected officials, and the concept of picket-fence federalism will undergo drastic revisions.

The PFF diagram also reveals a number of other characteristics about the intergovernmental system. As bureaucrats become specialists in their functional areas and rise in the management hierarchy, it becomes more difficult for them to move into a different functional area. A low-income housing specialist, for example, reaches a certain management level and can no longer easily decide to become a program officer in the Urban Mass Transportation Administration. As a result, the opportunities for career advancement and higher salaries eventually are confined to one functional specialty. Therefore, bureaucrats in the health, welfare, or education field usually find the greatest opportunities for new jobs by moving around the decision-making system on their own level of government, as lobbyist, staff member, or agency bureaucrat, or by moving to a different level—federal, state, or local—within their functional area. High-level U.S. Office of Education officials often wind up as state education administrators or local school system superintendents, and local or state transportation policy-makers often find jobs in the Urban Mass Transportation Administration.

It is easy to qualify for jobs at any level within functional specialties, for individuals spend a large part of their professional careers working on programs funded by the same committees and using the same guidelines promulgated by the same agencies. Most functional specialists read the same professional and trade journals and attend the same national conferences. While this tends to increase expertise and encourage greater specialization, it decreases job mobility and limits the influx of new people with new ideas into the specific program area. The top bureaucrats in each functional area on all levels of government know one another. They talk with each other about programs and after a while can begin to anticipate each other's response to certain questions. This tends to reinforce a policy of gradual and limited change.

Within functional areas of specialization on state and local levels, decision-making systems exist similar to those operating on the federal level. The relative influence of actors within these systems varies, depending upon factors such as: length of governor's or mayor's term; full-time/part-time status of legislature or council; reelectability of the executive; staffing of legislative bodies; and powers allocated by constitution or charter to the executive or the legislative body. It is important to understand that political issues are processed in essentially the same manner on all levels of government. The components of the systems are there, and each seeks to achieve the most favorable consideration of its point of view. If a reasonable compromise can be agreed to, the issue will be successfully resolved. If not, the issue will be tabled or withdrawn, and the actors in the system will turn to other issues or participate in other decision-making systems.

Grants-in-Aid, Lifeblood of the Intergovernmental System

The politics and administration of the intergovernmental system is shaped by the dollars channeled through grants-in-aid to state and local government. A grant-in-aid is money given to those governments for specific purposes. Expenditure of the money is usually subject to conditions specified in the statute of the administrative regulations (table 8.2).

There are two classifications of grants, formula and project. Formula grants are distributed to state and local governments according to a formula written into the law by Congress. Depending upon the subject of the grant, the formula could be based upon population, tax effort, per capita income, number of senior citizens, or number of poor people. These grants are noncompetitive. State and local governments do not compete for a percentage of the budgeted dollars; the money is theirs by law.

Project grants are directed towards specific problems. These grants are not spread uniformly to state and local governments, but are awarded on a competitive basis. Eligible governments submit grant proposals seeking funding for their projects. Business executives are occasionally called upon by state and local officials to assist

Table 8.2

Federal grants-in-aid as percentage of state-local receipts from own sources, 1960–1980 (dollar amounts in billions)

	Federal grants		*State-local receipts from own sources*[b]		*Federal grants as a percent of state-local receipts from own sources*
Fiscal year[a]	*Amount*	*Percent increase*	*Amount*	*Percent increase*	
1960	$7.0	5.3	$41.6	10.1	16.8
1961	7.1	1.3	44.9	7.9	15.8
1962	7.9	11.0	48.7	8.5	16.2
1963	8.6	9.4	52.2	7.2	16.5
1964	10.1	17.5	56.5	8.2	17.9
1965	10.9	7.5	61.6	9.0	17.7
1966	13.0	18.9	67.0	8.8	19.3
1967	15.2	17.6	73.9	10.3	20.6
1968	18.6	22.0	82.9	12.2	22.4
1969	20.3	8.9	93.9	13.3	21.6
1970	24.0	18.6	105.0	11.8	22.9
1971	28.1	17.0	116.6	11.0	24.1
1972	34.4	22.3	131.6	12.9	26.1
1973	41.8	21.7	146.9	11.6	28.5
1974	43.4	3.6	158.9	8.2	27.2
1975	49.8	14.9	171.4	7.9	29.0
1976	59.1	18.6	190.2	11.0	31.0
1977	68.4	15.8	221.0	16.2	31.0
1978	77.9	13.8	245.4	10.9	31.7
1979 est.	82.1	5.4	270.0	10.0	30.4
1980 est.	82.9	1.0	N.A.	N.A.	N.A.

[a]Data for 1960 through 1976 are for fiscal years ending June 30; for 1977 through 1980, for fiscal years ending September 30.
[b]As defined in the national income accounts.
N.A.—Not available

Source: ACIR staff computations.

in the preparation of grant proposals. Awards are determined mostly on the merit of the proposal, with the political considerations—occasionally even partisan ones—taken into account.

There are two types of project grants—categorical grants and block grants. Categorical grants are for narrowly defined purposes such as those found in the health and the education fields. Block grants are for broad program areas which leave more discretion for state and local officials on how the money is to be spent. Two examples of block grants are the community development block grant program, administered by HUD, and the Comprehensive Employment and Training Act, administered by the Labor Department.[4]

The total number of grant-in-aid programs in the system is difficult to determine. It is estimated at about five hundred, much below the figure often expressed by exasperated observers of the grant-in-aid process. In 1978, the U.S. Advisory Commission on Intergovernmental Relations counted 492 "federal categorical grant-in-aid programs available to state and local governments."[5] Project grants are more numerous than formula grants, and within project grants, categorical outnumber block grants.

The impact of the grant-in-aid system is most vividly demonstrated by examining the dollars involved and the percentage they represent of total federal outlays. A review of selected years, 1960, 1970, 1975, and 1979, indicates clearly how important federal domestic programs are to the governments in the system (table 8.3). In

Table 8.3

Historical trend of federal grant-in-aid outlays (dollar amounts in millions)

	Composition of grants-in-aid			*Federal grants as a percent of federal outlays*		
	Grants	*Grants for payments of individuals*	*Other grants*	*Total*	*Domestic*[a]	*State and local expenditures*[b]
1950	$2,253	$1,421	$832	5.3	8.8	10.4
1955	3,207	1,770	1,437	4.7	12.1	10.1
1960	7,020	2,735	4,285	7.6	15.9	14.7
1965	10,904	3,954	6,950	9.2	16.6	15.3
1970	24,018	8,867	15,151	12.2	21.1	19.4
1971	28,109	10,789	17,320	13.3	21.4	19.9
1972	34,372	13,421	20,951	14.8	22.8	22.0
1973	41,832	13,104	28,728	17.0	24.8	24.3
1974	43,308	14,030	29,278	16.1	23.3	22.7
1975	49,723	16,105	33,618	15.3	21.3	23.2
1976	59,037	19,511	39,526	16.1	21.7	24.7
TQ	15,909	5,122	10,787	16.8	22.6	25.5
1977 estimate	70,424	23,513	46,911	17.1	23.1	26.7
1978 estimate	71,581	25,459	46,122	16.3	22.3	25.0

[a]Excludes outlays for the national defense and international affairs functions
[b]As defined in the national income accounts

Source: Special Analyses: Budget of the U.S. Government, Fiscal Year 1979, p. 184.

1960, grants totaled $7 billion, representing 7.6 percent of total federal outlays and 14.7 percent of state and local expenditures. By 1970, grants were $24 billion, 12.2 percent of federal outlays and 19.4 percent of state and local expenditures. In 1975, the figures were $49.7 billion, 15.3 and 23.4 percent. The 1979 estimates are $85 billion, 17 and 26.2 percent.

Grants-in-aid are an integral part of the intergovernmental system. Government decision-making systems cannot be understood unless the importance of the intergovernmental system in implementing federal programs and policies is recognized (figures 8.2 and 8.3).

Figure 8.2

Federal grants to state and local governments

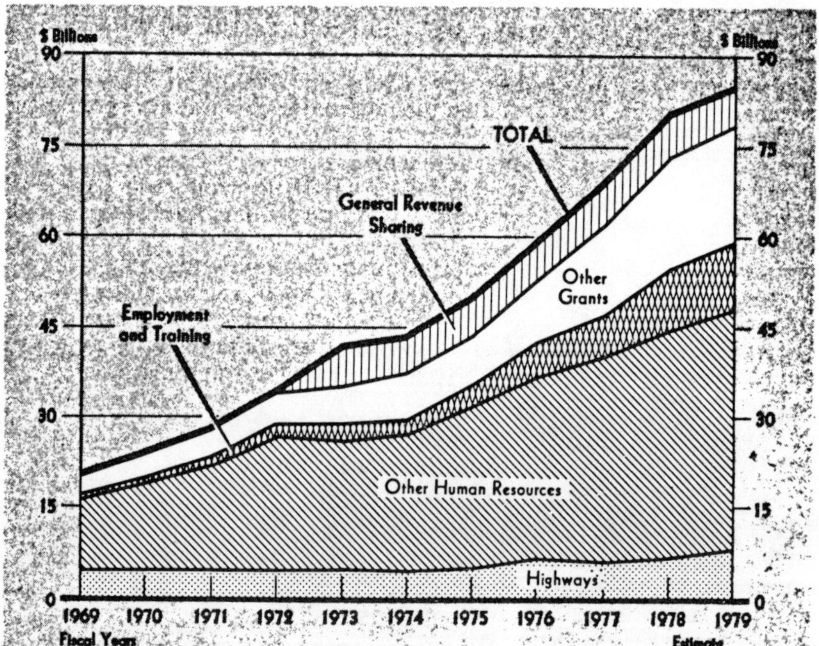

NOTE: Federal aid to state and local governments is defined as the provision of resources by the federal government to support a state or local program of governmental service to the public. The three primary forms of aid are grants-in-aid (including shared revenues), loans, and tax expenditures. Unless specifically indicated to the contrary, reference to "federal aid" or "grants" in this analysis is confined to grants-in-aid, including shared revenues.

Source: Special Analysis: Budget of the U.S. Government, *Fiscal year 1979, p. 175.*

Figure 8.3

Distribution of federal sector expenditures by category

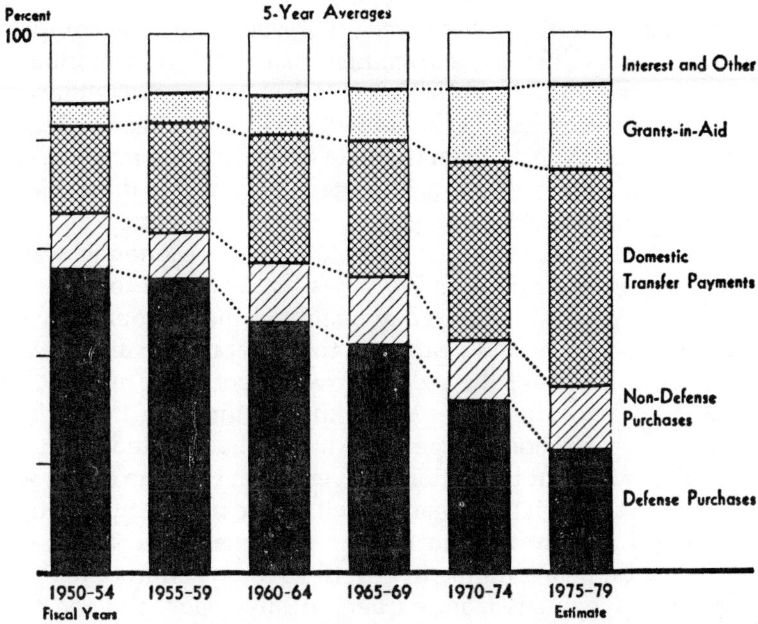

Source: Special Analysis B, Budget of the U.S. Government, *Fiscal Year 1979, p. 50.*

A Balance Sheet of Power in the Intergovernmental System

A balance sheet of the political resources in the intergovernmental system shows that the assets of politics are shared by all three levels of government. State, local, and national governments each control certain political resources. Although the forces for sharing and cooperation are great, the forces for conflict and stalemate are at least equally as great. These are the forces that make it so difficult to create a decision-making structure designed to deal with nationwide problems.

One of the fundamental reasons for the continual conflict in intergovernmental relations is that power—legal, political, and economic—is seldom in the hands of one government at any one time. Power seesaws back and forth in the federal system depending on the issue involved and the time at which the issue is being considered. Power is not static in any political system, but in a federal system it is more dynamic than in others.[6]

Consider the political power assets of state and local governments in relation to those of the federal government. The comparative list of assets (table 8.4) shows, first, that in terms of number or variety, the state and local governments have more assets than the federal. This reflects the fact that the whole legal-political system in the United States evolved from the state base. Even the most cursory examination of state laws yields important insights into the nature of intergovernmental relations. It was in the states that almost all of the rules and regulations of the United States social-economic system were written. In addition, it is the states that continue to make the decisions that affect the day-to-day quality of most peoples' lives.

Questions of war and peace and the general state of the economy are in the hands of the federal government. Still, many forget that it was not until the great wars of this century that the national government began to loom large in the national polity. Indeed, it was not until the 1930s that the national government began to take a serious interest in the social problems besetting the nation. By that time, the states had already worked out the processes of economic and social regulation that continue to govern us today. Education, the licensing of professionals from barbers to physicians, and the rules and regulations that affect issues from the environment of neighborhoods to the administration of business or universities are nearly exclusively in the hands of state and local officials.

The list of assets is suggestive of the distribution of political power in U.S. intergovernmental relations. Political parties are organized at the state and local levels. This is where most officials are elected, where all party officials have their roots, and where all nominations for all elective posts in this country originate. The only two national offices in the United States are the presidency and the vice-presidency. Almost everyone who tries for political office starts by going directly to the state and local party officials to obtain the nomination.

Students of intergovernmental relations recognize that most national officials are actually local officials on location in Washington, but this rather obvious fact is frequently overlooked by those who argue that the increasing fiscal dependence of state and local governments on the national treasury has meant a loss of local power and a corresponding increase in national power. The party organization of the United States did not move toward centralization as the national government took on more of those functions previously within the domain of state and local governments.

Table 8.4

A comparison of state-local and federal political assets in intergovernmental decision-making

State-local governments	*Federal government*
1. Political Party Control—election of national officials	1. Money—treasury increases tied to GNP through income tax structure
2. Weak national enforcement mechanisms	2. Authority to Write And Enforce Guidelines—delay, threats of delay, cutoffs, etc.
3. Project Administration—proximity, expertise, contract letting, etc.	3. The Federal Courts
4. Federal Bureaucratic Momentum—money must be spent, professionalism, fear of injuring wrong people, one-year budget cycle, etc.	4. Policy-making Initiative
5. Interest Group Support	
6. Public Support—grass-rootism, etc.	

The full impact of politics and the manner in which it is organized in the United States occurs when Congress enters a dispute between the national and the state and local administrations in grant-in-aid matters. The national bureaucracy's power of the purse succumbs quickly to the demands of local officials. Local officials mobilize the political support of their congressional delegation. Any "unreasonable" demand on the part of federal officials is received unsympathetically by Congress.

Congressional power is the root support for the second item on the state-local side of the balance sheet, the absence of powerful, even adequate federal enforcement mechanisms. Congress does not appropriate sufficient money to allow federal agencies to employ large inspection staffs to police and enforce the guidelines under which state and local governments spend federal money. This is to some extent a deliberate policy. Few members of Congress are anxious to support a corps of federal inspectors who would monitor or evaluate the actions of the local officials who run the political mechanisms that sent them to Congress in the first place and keep returning them there each election year.

The U.S. Office of Economic Opportunity is a dramatic example of a federal agency attempting to require important changes in the way local governments make decisions. The provision requiring "maximum feasible participation" of those affected by the decision-making process simply could not be enforced against the wishes of state and local officials. Eventually this federal agency was dismantled.[7]

Congressional support is not the only political asset that state and local officials have in their favor. Pressure groups, depending on the issue, can be counted on to support the position of state and local officials when that position comes into conflict with the national bureaucracy. Organizations of state and local governments—such as the Council of State Governments, National Association of Counties, National League of Cities, U.S. Conference of Mayors, National Governors' Association—and organizations of government officials—such as the International Association of Chiefs of Police and many others—more often than not find themselves in agreement with state and local governments instead of the national government.

Those groups representing building contractors and building supply manufacturers know that local governments let the contracts on public-works projects even though the biggest share of the money comes from Washington. Furthermore, those who champion the position of state and local officials have the benefit of years of thoughtful philosophy and less thoughtful political rhetoric to back them up. The American mythology greatly favors strong state and local prerogatives over a powerful domestically active federal government.

Political Assets of the Federal Government

The political assets of the national government have been until recently almost exclusively related to money. A paradox of the United States federal system is that while political power remains at the base of the system, public economic power has risen to the top. The passage of the Sixteenth Amendment in 1913 set the stage for the shift. The income tax produced a constantly growing source of revenue for the national treasury, a source of revenue tied to the expanding economy. It is also relatively easy to collect.

In the 1940s and 1950s, the difference in dollar resources became dramatic. State and local revenues, tied largely to property values and retail sales taxes, tended to increase more slowly than inflation. They failed to rise sufficiently to meet the needs of state and local governments. Fiscal imbalance between state and local governments and the federal government grew. At the same time the needs of an increasingly urban society outstripped the fiscal capacity of state and local governments. The disparity among governments in resources—financial and political—shapes the operation of the intergovernmental system. The national government has the power to withhold funds when grant guidelines are not met, but Congress comes down on the side of state-local governments in most disputes.

Furthermore, federal agencies are not strong advocates for fund cutoffs. Bureaucrats have professional interests in the programs they administer; in other words, national bureaucrats would rather see some program in operation than none at all. Consequently, "federal bureaucratic momentum" is listed on the balance sheet as a local government power. Combine this with the one-year funding cycle agencies operate under, and it is apparent that there is great motivation for federal agencies to spend. Agencies try to avoid ending the year with a surplus if they want Congress to appropriate the same or an increased amount in the next budget cycle. Agencies must rationalize schemes to allow them to move ahead with a program *even* when there are incidents of noncompliance with the rules by state and local governments; they believe it is better to have a program with some violations than no program at all.

President Roosevelt's advisor Harry Hopkins discovered how few effective tools he had to compel the states to meet matching requirements of the emergency relief program he ran in the early New Deal days. He admitted this to a conference on relief programs in 1934:[8]

> Whether we have been right or wrong in going after the states I don't know. I tell you it isn't any fun, but what can you do? Here's the state of Kentucky. It would not put up money and you say, "You put up some money or we won't give you any." They do not put it up. Who gets licked? The unemployed. They always get licked. . . . Believe me, that is a tough order to give. It is going to be a long time before I give another one. There will have to be somebody else to cut off this food from the unemployed.

Termination of programs, even if the federal bureaucracy is able to do so, seldom affects the officials in state or local governments who are unwilling to cooperate. Instead, it hurts those for whom the programs are devised.

The U.S. has not succeeded in creating a national policy-making machinery through political and management efforts. The $80 billion the federal government now spends on state and local programs has not changed the well-defined power relationships that existed at the time the Constitution was written. Power still resides at the base of the political system with state and local governments.

Increased demands to deal with national programs on a national basis have led the national government to increase its grant-in-aid spending and to attempt to increase its control or influence over state and local decision-making. It has not succeeded, as the impressive array of powers listed on the state-local side of the balance sheet indicates. However, the federal courts are now beginning to change the balance.

It is ironic that in this decade, nearly two hundred years after the Constitution was written, the balance in powers between state and local governments on the one hand, and the national government on the other, is beginning to change. The irony is deepened by the certainty that federal power will be strengthened by the courts. They are beginning to require that the conditions of federal programs, the rules and regulations written by federal agencies, be enforced. It is also true that in recent years our political system has begun to avoid processing very controversial issues. The political stakes are often high and the rewards of victory pale by comparison with the penalties for defeat. Issues of this nature often are brought to the courts for resolution.

Recent issues include: school busing to achieve racial integration, residency requirements for welfare recipients, and abortion. Many local governments have been mandated by the courts to undertake busing programs to achieve an acceptable degree of racial integration in the schools. The costs of these court-ordered edicts must be borne by local residents.

When a Connecticut court struck down as unconstitutional residency requirements for welfare recipients, it had an impact on almost every major city in the country. Welfare recipients could now move and collect their welfare checks more rapidly from the local government paying the highest amount in the area.[9]

Even though the U.S. Supreme Court has ruled on the abortion issue, efforts have been underway to urge Congress to pass legislation outlawing federal funding for abortion. For two successive years, the House and the Senate have been unable to agree on the language of such a measure.[10] One indirect result has been that appropriations bills for the Departments of Labor and HEW have been stalled, delaying paychecks for thousands of employees.

When the decision-making systems decline to act on controversial issues and the courts are required to resolve them, the whole system suffers. Action by court decree occasionally resolves the political impasse, but it also may require huge additional expenditures as well as further complicating the intergovernmental management system.

Proposals for Change and Improvement: The New Federalism

With so much money involved, there have been periodic recommendations on how to restructure the intergovernmental system to make it more equitable and more accessible. Most of these suggestions stem from a fear that the federal government is too involved in the lives of citizens at the state and local level and that too much money is being allocated at the discretion of federal bureaucrats.

One response to these fears was called New Federalism, and it was orchestrated by the domestic policy advisors to President Nixon. New Federalism was based on the assumption that for forty years money and political power had been flowing from states and localities to Washington. The Nixon program sought to arrest this flow and reverse it so that money and political power would flow back to states and local governments.[11]

Part of the problem in implementing New Federalism was the failure of the Nixon administration to analyze several key assumptions about the intergovernmental system. It is doubtful that the federal government really has all of the power with which it is credited. It is possible that real power resides not with national policy-makers, but with state and local governments who have the responsibility for administering the programs and hence great discretionary power. After all, with all those units of local government, it is virtually impossible for the federal agencies adequately to monitor the implementation of these programs. Congress also has great difficulty in trying to oversee the federal agencies. This means that astute state and local officials who understand oversight limitations realize they have a good deal of administrative authority and freedom in program implementation.

Another questionable assumption of the Nixon administration was that federal agencies and Congress would want to give up all the power they had been amassing since the 1930s. An axiom of politics is that people rarely give up power voluntarily; it is usually taken from them. Even if the federal government had wanted to give up some of its power, it is not certain that state and local systems were capable of receiving and exercising this power.

Finally, there was some evidence that a number of local officials did not want additional broad grants of power. With this new power there was certain to be increased responsibility and accountability. It would become increasingly difficult to blame the federal government for everything that went wrong if more and more decision-making authority resided with the local government. Local officials accustomed to receiving federal funds with accompanying guidelines might not want to tackle the special-interest groups and entrenched bureaucrats if federal money were suddenly to become less encumbered.

Revenue Sharing

New Federalism had several components, but the two with the greatest impact upon the intergovernmental system have been revenue sharing and regionalization. The general revenue sharing program passed in 1972 called for expenditures of $30.2 billion over five years. The money was divided one-third for state and two-thirds for local governments. One important feature of the program was the relatively few restrictions placed upon how federal money could be spent. State and local discretion in expenditures is a hallmark of the program.[12]

At the same time Congress was passing the general revenue sharing bill, it was working on the consolidation of categorical grants into larger block grants. This program, named special revenue sharing, resulted in block grants in the employment, education, transportation, and community development fields. The block grant approach is far less restrictive than the categorical grant system and gives local officials greater discretion in how to spend their money.

In 1976, Congress passed a new revenue sharing bill extending the program until 1980 and slightly increasing each year's payments to states and local governments. Since revenue sharing funds are usually deposited in state and local governments' general revenue accounts, it is difficult to trace program expenditures. However, after an initial flurry of expenditures for capital expense projects, local governments began to spend revenue sharing funds on the same programs on which they normally spend their own tax dollars.[13]

It appears that Congress is moving toward a three-part federal aid mix: categorical grants to stimulate and support state and local programs of specific national interest; block grants to provide greater flexibility in broader functional areas of national interest; and revenue sharing aimed at reducing some of the fiscal disparities in the intergovernmental system and at the same time helping state and local governments to meet their own needs (table 8.5 and figure 8.4).

Regionalization

In 1969, the Nixon administration established ten Federal Regional Councils (FRC) in ten large cities to combine federal agencies and coordinate programs at the subnational level[14] (figure 8.5). The goals of the regionalization program were to:

1. devolve administrative responsibility and decision-making authority back to states, counties, and local governments;
2. invest FRCs with power to make decisions, thereby eliminating the need for local governments to go to Washington for all decisions;
3. reduce confusion, and cut lead time, paperwork, and response time;
4. encourage and increase regional flexibility and diversity; and
5. assist state and local governments to become responsive to their constituents.[15]

Table 8.5

Federal aid by category, selected fiscal years, 1966–1975 (in millions)

Category	*1966*	*1968*	*1972*	*1974*	*1975 (estimate)*
Revenue sharing	–	–	–	$6,106	6,176
General support aid[1]	$238	$294	$490	624	1,361[2]
Block grants[3]	–	57	415	3,352	5,232
Specific purpose grants[4]	12,722	18,248	35,035	36,058	39,880
Total federal grants	$12,960	$18,599	$35,940	$46,040	$52,649

[1]Includes federal aid to state, local, and territorial governments that is available for general fiscal support or is available for distribution among programs involving two or more budgetary functions when the distribution among those functions is at the discretion of the recipient jurisdiction. The types of aid included are payments in lieu of taxes, broad-purpose shared revenues, and the federal payment to the District of Columbia.
[2]Includes proposed energy tax equalization payment.
[3]Includes total of block grants although a portion may be granted for specific projects under the discretionary allocation provided for by statute. Also, where outlays data are not available obligations have been used and adjusted where additional information is provided. Social services amounts included beginning with 1974 when formula allocation of funds was provided.
[4]Includes target grants like Model Cities and the Appalachian Regional Commission program.

Sources: Special Analyses Budget of the United States and Budget Appendix, *various years.*

Figure 8.4

Breadth of functional focus of various types of grants

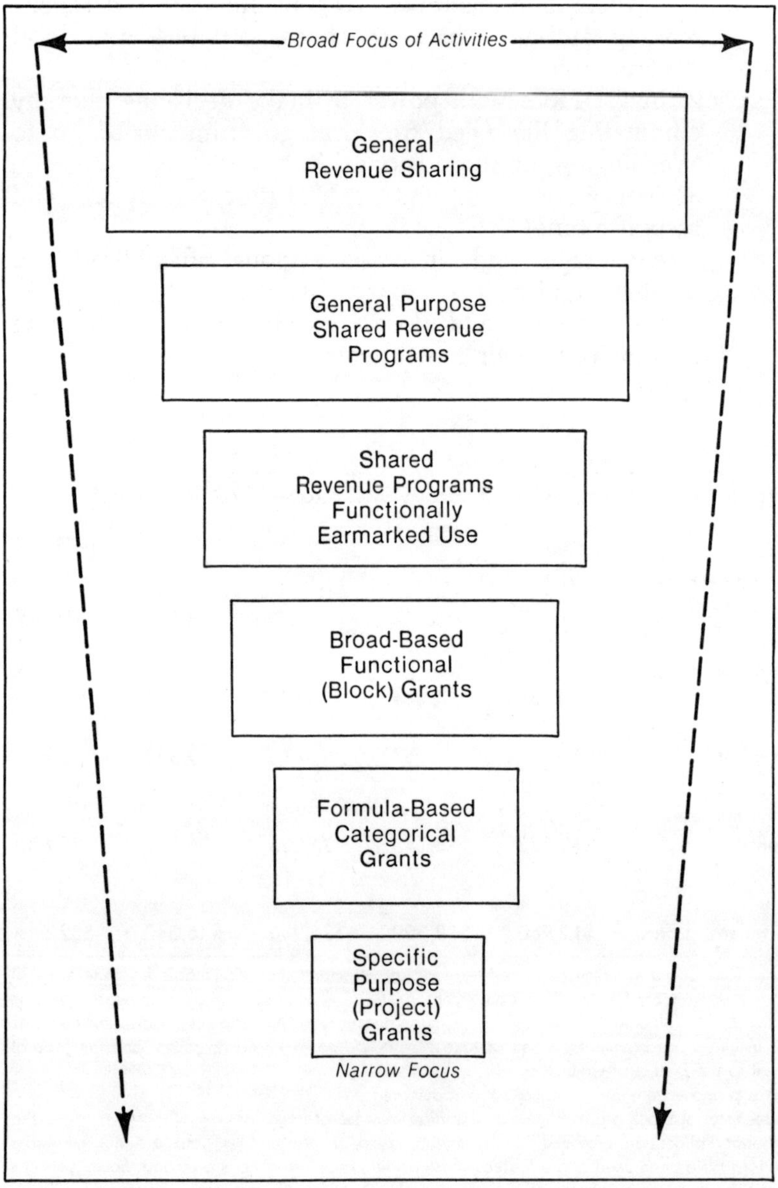

Source: Categorical Grants: Their Role and Design *(Washington, D.C.: Advisory Commission on Intergovernmental Relations), 1978, p. 108.*

The FRCs were also charged with providing planning and management assistance to state and local governments. This included introducing new management, budget, and evaluation techniques and assistance in gathering, processing, and disseminating information that focuses on the specific needs of local governments in the region.

The FRCs have met with varying degrees of success. Some have been staffed with professionals of proven ability; others have not. Coordination among agencies has been difficult in some areas, while other FRCs have been successful at this. Communication with local governments and community groups has been uneven in performance; continuity of agency representatives and rotating the leadership of the FRC have also caused problems.

The concept behind the FRCs is sound. Getting all the federal departments to support the concept and to transmit that support throughout the agency is difficult. The future of the FRCs depends upon many factors, but one of the most important is how well they service the large states and the big cities in their region. If they are able to provide fast and satisfactory information as well as some administrative discretion, they may be able to convince governors and mayors to use the regional centers and reduce their dependence upon Washington.

This seems doubtful for two reasons. During the 1960s, when American cities were plagued by riots, the mayors, unable to obtain the aid they considered necessary from states, began to seek help from Washington. It did not take long for the big-city mayors to become national figures. They forged strong alliances with bureaucrats in key federal agencies who could fund urban programs, as well as with key representatives, senators, and congressional staff. It would be extremely difficult to alter seriously these communication networks and political alliances.

The other reason centers around the Carter administration's ambivalence towards the FRCs. No move has been made to dismantle the regional centers, but there is little indication that they are to be strengthened.

It is important to remember that in the United States, decision-making systems are organized around programs and encompass all three levels of government. In this complex maze of institutions—national, state, and local—the decision-making systems operate. They provide stability and predictability in government policy-making. They also make it possible for government programs to be managed. Knowledge of these systems and how they operate is crucial for anyone seeking to participate in public policy-making in meaningful ways

Figure 8.5

Source: Responsive Federalism, Report to the President on the Federal Assistance Review *(Office of Management and Budget, 1973)*, *p. 6.*

Notes

1. Terry Sanford first discussed this idea in *Storm Over the States* (New York: McGraw-Hill, 1967), pp. 80–81. Also see Deil S. Wright, *Understanding Intergovernmental Relations* (North Scituate, Mass.: Duxbury Press, 1978), pp. 61–63.

2. For a discussion of this concept, see Wright, *Understanding Intergovernmental Relations.*

3. For a discussion of *Shapp v. Casey,* see *Intergovernmental Perspective* 4 (Fall 1978): 5–6, and *Intergovernmental Perspective* 5 (Winter 1979): 28. With the change of governors in Pennsylvania, the case was renamed *Thornburg* v. *Casey*

4. For a discussion and analysis of the grant-in-aid system, see *Categorical Grants: Their Role and Design* (Washington, D.C.: Advisory Commission on Intergovernmental Relations, 1977), pp. 1–9 and chapter 4.

5. *A Catalog of Federal Grant-in-Aid Programs to State and Local Governments: Grants Funded FY 1978* (Washington, D.C.: Advisory Commission on Intergovernmental Relations, 1979), pp. 1–4.

6. Richard H. Leach, *American Federalism* (New York: W. W. Norton, 1970), p. 59.

7. Daniel P. Moynihan, *Maximum Feasible Misunderstanding: Community Action and The War on Poverty* (Glencoe, Ill.: Free Press, 1969).

8. James T. Patterson, *The New Deal and the States: Federalism in Transition* (Princeton, N.J.: Princeton University Press, 1969), p. 72.

9. See *Shapiro v. Thompson,* 394 U.S. 618 Sup. Ct. 1322; 22 L. Ed. 2nd 600 (1969).

10. *Roe v. Wade,* 410 U.S. 113 Sup. Ct. (1973).

11. "The Administration of New Federalism: Objectives and Issues," *Public Administration Review* (special issue), ed. Leigh Grosenick, September 1973. Also see Richard P. Nathan, *The Plot That Failed: Nixon and the Administrative Presidency* (New York: John Wiley and Sons, 1975), pp. 12–34.

12. See Richard P. Nathan, Allen D. Manvel, and Susannah E. Calkins, *Monitoring Revenue Sharing* (Washington, D.C.: The Brookings Institution, 1975). Also see Paul R. Dommel, *The Politics of Revenue Sharing* (Bloomington: Indiana University Press, 1974); and Richard P. Nathan and Charles F. Adams, Jr., *Revenue Sharing: The Second Round* (Washington, D.C.: The Brookings Institution, 1977).

13. David A. Caputo and Richard L. Cole, *Urban Politics and Decentralization* (Lexington, Mass.: Lexington Books, 1974). Also David A. Caputo and Richard L. Cole, "General Revenue Sharing Expenditure Decisions in Cities Over 50,000," *Public Administration Review* 35, no. 2 (March–April 1975): 136–42.

14. Executive Order 11647.

15. *Responsive Federalism: Report to the President on the Federal Assistance Review* (Washington D.C.: Office of Management and Budget, 1973), pp. 3–9.

nine

Strengths and Weaknesses

A Critique of Government Decision-Making Systems

The decision-making systems examined in this book have evolved over the last two hundred years and have played a large role in the country's development. The systems both incorporate and reflect the special mixture of ideology and pragmatism that characterize American life. They provide the avenues for participation and popular control which democracy demands. They compete with each other and provide for a shared system of powers in the way they function. These features help to guarantee that no individual or small group of individuals control government. Thus, these decision-making systems preserve the goals of those who wrote the Constitution: dispersed and fragmented power is controlled power. At the same time, the decision-making systems provide government with the ability to decide, to manage, and to function in a complex, modern era.

Although the decision-making systems do a remarkably good job of reconciling the conflicting goals of dispersed power and management efficiency, they do have shortcomings. They work reasonably well when focused on specific, well-defined issues, such as programs in health, agriculture, education, and road building, for example. These programs are processed rather efficiently because they have the virtue of being specific in definition and scope, their purposes are widely understood and they have their own groups, clientele, or supporters.

When issues get bigger and more complex, the decision-making systems do not perform as well. When an issue or a program becomes very visible, involves too many competing and conflicting interests, and when the stakes in the program are exceedingly large, the government decision processes fail to coordinate, plan, and manage. They become too large, unwieldy, and conflict ridden.

Energy policy is an example of a policy so large that it affects almost everything that government does. It has both domestic and international ramifications as well as important economic consequences touching both national health and personal well-being. It is simply too big for one, or even two or three related decision-making systems to handle. When large issues like energy policy arise, the small, well-defined decision systems give way to large, less systematic decision processes involving large numbers of people and the higher echelons of government. The president and cabinet secretaries become involved directly in policy-making instead of bureau chiefs and others at lower levels. There is debate on the floor of the House and the Senate at earlier stages in the policy-making processes instead of pro forma floor action taken after committees and subcommittees have done their work. And a large number of interest groups become actively involved. The results are often time-consuming, chaotic, and unpredictable.

Decision-making systems also fail to perform well when there is a need to coordinate programs operating within more than three or four established systems. To control inflation, for example, the government needs to bring enormous numbers of separate programs into synchronization. Trade-offs must be made between programs. The structure and processes for accomplishing these objectives are weak and ill defined. Presidential and congressional leadership are required to bring numerous disparate programs together, to create new ones, and to encourage state and local governments to establish supportive programs. Government is not well equipped to deal with huge and complex problems like energy and inflation.

Given the problems of governing a complex, multi-interest, and diverse society, the decision-making systems that have evolved over the years are impressive only when called upon to manage small, well-defined programs. Fortunately, most government activity falls into these categories.

A closer look at government management processes throws some light on the operations of government decision-making systems and the prospects for reforming them. The issues involved in managing decision processes explain, or at least help to clarify, some of the problems government has in dealing with the larger issues of public policy facing the country today.

Pluralism, Bargaining, and Incrementalism: A Triad of Decision-Making Characteristics

The approach to public policy-making described in this book has been called the pluralist-bargaining-incremental, or PBI, system.[1] It is pluralist because it provides access for a wide variety of economic, social, and ethnic groups, each of which works within the political system to advance its own interests. As these interests frequently conflict, the various groups must bargain among themselves, through their legislative and bureaucratic allies, in order to gain as many of their objectives as possible or to protect themselves against encroachments by other groups. The different groups are by no means evenly matched, but very seldom is one so dominant as to gain more than small, incremental changes in an established policy at one time.

The PBI system has its share of defenders; arguing against it is difficult in a democratic society. One of the most articulate defenders has been Charles Lindblom, who has called PBI, approvingly, "the science of muddling through."[2] This approach, he says, is preferable to the more rational, comprehensive planning strategy frequently suggested as an alternative method of setting policy. For one thing, muddling through guarantees a certain amount of stability in a given policy area, for change is slow and difficult. The incremental approach guards against any sudden, radical changes in the way in which government addresses a problem and is thus more democratic in providing all interested groups with the opportunity to participate in policy-making. Government decisions evolve out of compromises reached by groups and individuals instead of being made by a few technically trained planners who are not accountable to the public. Perhaps the most important part of Lindblom's argument is his contention that rational comprehensive planning simply will not work in government.

> It is impossible to take everything important into consideration unless "important" is so narrowly defined that analysis is in fact quite limited. Limits on human intellectual capacities and on available information set definite limits to man's capacity to be comprehensive.[3]

Lindblom's article on the science of muddling through was written in 1959. Since that time, dissatisfaction with the PBI approach has grown steadily, and a variety of attempts have been made to inject greater rationality into the policy-making process in the name of efficiency, modernity, and better management.

PBI is biased in favor of the status quo. The stability it offers is more aptly described as stagnation, for agencies and programs established in response to yesterday's problems often prove incapable of changing to meet today's crises. Public agencies must operate in a turbulent social, political, and technological environment. To justify the tax dollars spent on them, they should be able to forecast and adapt to at least some of this turbulence.

Proponents of PBI underestimate the extent to which bargaining power and effectiveness is concentrated on one side in many, if not most, issues. The discussion in the earlier chapters of this book has pointed out that many government policies are initiated in direct response to requests from specific interest groups. These groups are prepared to invest substantial resources in promoting acceptance of their pet policies, which may be higher price supports, a protective tariff, increased funding for a social welfare program, or stiffer regulations to protect against "unfair" competition. Opposition to these policies is likely to be scattered and relatively indifferent, unless the opponents happen to have an intense interest in the specific issues. This is unlikely, for there are not enough hours in the day to mount an effective campaign against every organized interest seeking special favors from government. Special-interest groups often claim that adoption of their proposed policies will serve the broader public interest. This may or may not be true. The main point, however, is that the decision on whether or not to adopt the policy usually hinges not on a well-balanced assessment of its merits, but rather on the lobbying effectiveness of, and selective information provided by, its proponents.

The PBI approach wastes scarce resources, because it often produces contradictory policy results. That is, one policy-making subsystem succeeds in establishing, obstensibly in the public interest, a program that might diminish the effectiveness of another program, also initiated in the public interest. For example, the money spent on cancer research and on antismoking campaigns is, to some extent, negated by the money spent for tobacco price supports and marketing assistance. To carry this example a step further, the elimination or reduction of price supports would undercut economic development efforts and exacerbate unemployment in the tobacco-growing and tobacco-processing areas of the country. Thus, the issue contains both health and economic concerns. Legitimate interests are involved on both sides, but thus far the PBI approach has yet to come up with any long-range solutions, such as programs through which tobacco farmers and tobacco industry workers can make the transition to producing other products without suffering undue economic hardship. Instead, the economic interests continue to get their price supports, and the health interests continue to get their research and education programs. This is mostly attributable to the difficulty involved in coordinating policies processed by different decision-making systems.

Incremental Change or No Change at All?

Some question the ability of reformers to bring about fundamental or major changes in decision-making, given the nature of the systems. Programs do tend to take on a life of their own, and it is difficult, although not impossible, to eliminate them. Herbert Kaufman, in an effort to determine whether government organizations are immortal, studied the major subdivisions of ten executive departments in the federal government. (Only the Defense Department was excluded.) He found that of the 175 subdivisions in existence in 1923, 148, almost 85 percent, were still around in 1973. Furthermore, in most of the twenty-seven deaths, the activities were not terminated; they were reassigned or taken up by other units for the most part.[4] Thus, once government becomes involved in a policy area, as a regulator, a provider of services, or a subsidizer, the chances are very good that it will stay involved.

Part of this organizational longevity is attributable to the bureaucrat's much publicized desire for job security and propensity for empire building. But government employees acting alone cannot keep an unpopular or unproductive program afloat, much less expand it. They need allies, both on Capitol Hill and among organized private interests. And, of course, opinion differs widely on which programs are unpopular or unproductive. A dairy farmer might decide that too much money is spent on aid to families with dependent children and not enough on milk price supports, while a welfare recipient might reach the opposite conclusion. As a general rule, however, the proponents of a given governmental activity feel more strongly about it than do its opponents. This is because the typical government program provides substantial benefits to a relatively small group while imposing only small incremental burdens, in the form of higher taxes or higher prices, on the vast majority. These increments add up. Sometimes they produce political backlashes which usually endanger the most politically vulnerable, though not necessarily the least deserving or most costly, special-interest programs. For the most part though, there is a bias in the U.S. governmental system toward continuing, not terminating, government programs. If blame for this situation must be placed on someone, the words of the late Walt Kelly, creator of "Pogo," seem appropriate: "We have met the enemy and he is us."

One thing that our decision-making system does well is to provide the basis for competition. Decision centers compete with each other for control of programs and budgets. These elements of competition are not insignificant factors in providing incentives and management improvement. They are especially helpful where there is no possibility, as in government, to compete over sales and profits.

Big Issues and Government's Response to Them

In the routine kinds of programs that confront government daily, the decision-making centers characterized by pluralism, bargaining, and incrementalism serve the country rather well and process a majority of issues in a fair and efficient manner. There is, however, a large area of government decision-making where these centers do not work well, if at all. Major issues of war, the economy, and delicate diplomatic maneuvers must be orchestrated by the president and his closest associates. The president can accomplish what the formal decision-making system cannot because he can involve the actors quickly and blend their ideas and opinions in a much shorter time than if the issue had to be processed by the larger decision system.

Also, new issues, particularly when they burst on the scene unexpectedly, are not handled well by these specialized decision-making systems. It is in these types of issues that the president and his cabinet can be most effective. The president can decide where an issue should be placed in some instances and can play a major role in shaping the decision-making system that will handle that issue.

The issues government handles with great difficulty are typically very big, and their solutions, if they exist, are far beyond the capabilities of conventional decision-making systems. Big issues lack identifiable political or social boundaries. They do not lend themselves to piecemeal solutions, like so many other social and political issues. There is a major difference between modern problems like energy and the troubled cities of the Northeast, and historical problems like the Great Depression of the 1920s and 1930s.

The federal government's response to the Depression was very conventional in terms of operational style. Several new programs were created in that period to work towards solutions to various discrete aspects of the Depression. The Social Security program was created, along with guaranteed bank loan programs, the Works Progress Administration, the Civilian Conservation Corps, the Securities and Exchange Commission, and other programs designed to bring the nation out of the great economic collapse. There was very little need to coordinate these programs. They operated almost independently of each other, within the conventional government decision-making systems.

There are fundamental differences between government's response to the Depression and its response to modern difficulties like energy shortages and inflation. Franklin D. Roosevelt did little to change the decision-making processes of government or the way they operate. He created more of them, and consequently, there was more government at the end of the Great Depression than there was before it. But it was more of the same. Energy policy development in the 1970s is a remarkably different story.

The current effort to develop a national energy policy shows the inability of decision-making systems to process an issue that is large and difficult to break up into smaller, discrete, manageable pieces. The importance of cheap energy to our economy and our life-style is overwhelming. Energy supply affects the way we live, what we eat, how we dress, our transportation system, international affairs, and a host of other important items. No decision-making system in government is large enough to encompass all or even a major portion of the issues directly tied to energy. Consequently, the government seems to be floundering without being able to come up with a coherent energy policy. Some programs, such as highway building and natural gas price regulation, seem to promote consumption, while other programs, such as tax write-offs for home insulation and a host of publicity campaigns, appear to favor conservation.

Senator William Proxmire (D-Wis.) appearing on "Face the Nation" in July 1978, was asked why the Congress had failed to pass the president's energy program. Proxmire's reply is illustrative of what happens when too many issues are grouped together into a "national policy" and the political system is asked to process the policy as a whole:

> Three parts of that program can be passed right away. I wrote to the president, together with other senators, urging that he separate that program into its parts. We can pass energy conservation, coal conversion; and we can pass the utility rate reform. What we can't pass is the deregulation of natural gas and the crude oil equalization tax. And if the president insists on that, we won't pass an energy bill at all this year. If he separates it out we'll pass something.[5]

Three Big Issues: Energy, Cities, and Regulation

The politics of the creation of the Department of Energy illustrates the problem clearly. In the spring of 1977, the bill was debated on the Hill and attacked in a very conventional manner. The congressional criticism of the Carter proposal was that the Department of Energy would be too powerful; it would give more power to the proposed secretary of energy than is traditional or desirable in the American scheme of things.

Senator John Glenn (D-Ohio), a member of the committee that wrote the bill, complained, on the other hand, that Congress was not creating an energy czar. In fact, he argued that the proposed Department of Energy would be weak because it would not contain power to deal with some of the major aspects of energy policy. The Department of Transportation, not the Energy Department, would continue to police standards for automobile fuel efficiency under the bill. Forty percent of the nation's crude oil is consumed by automobiles. This omission from the purview of the Department of Energy immediately removed a major portion of energy policy from the new agency's control. Offshore oil leases would still be under control of the Department of the Interior, and there was considerable debate over who should set the wellhead price of natural gas. Should it be the Federal Power Commission or the newly created Department of Energy. A compromise was reached on that point, with a kind of independent commission created within the new department to handle the task.

Congressional response to the creation of the Department of Energy was typical. Historically, we have preferred to divide power and deal with issues at a low level. Energy is probably one of those issues that cannot be handled well that way, yet the creation of an agency that could deal with the whole energy situation seems unthinkable in contemporary political terms.

Another big issue, similar to energy in its implications for government decision-making systems, is the problem of the northeastern and north central cities. These cities have the common characteristic of being small geographically and surrounded by large suburban jurisdictions with governments of their own. Over the years various federal and state policies have inadvertently encouraged both the middle class and industry to leave the central cities and establish themselves in the suburbs. This, of course, is a serious problem for cities—the tax base deteriorates while public-service expenses are likely to increase.

The GI Bill of Rights passed after World War II as a measure to reward veterans and reassimilate them into American life is but one example of legislation with unintended but serious negative consequences for northeastern cities. The no-down-payment home mortgage provision of the GI Bill put the federal government in the business of encouraging the middle class to leave the cities. One could read the debate on the GI Bill in Congress and the hearings and not find the word "cities" mentioned. Why not? The GI Bill was con-

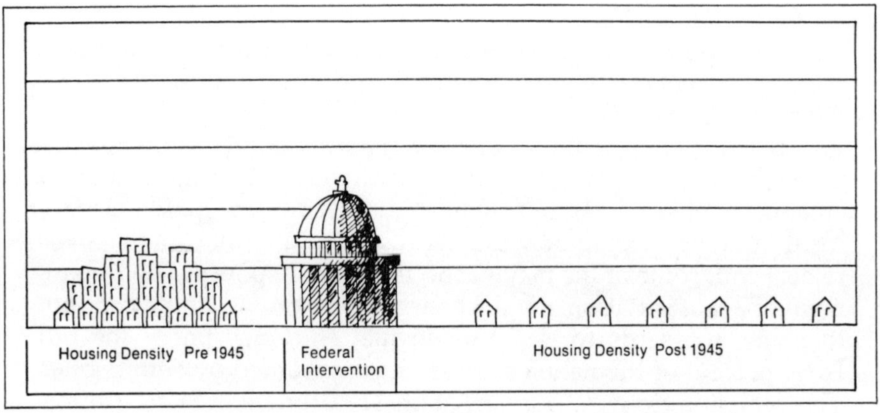

Source; Illustration by David Battle Design. Reprinted from Nation's Cities, *November 1977.*

sidered by a veteran's decision-making system which did its job well but had no interest or expertise in the problems of central cities. Highway programs and urban mass transit programs make it easier for the middle class to move in and out of cities, and for industry to locate itself in suburban areas. These issues were discussed and decided traditionally by highway decision-making systems and mass transit decision-making systems, again with little concern for their impact on the central city. Even today there is no place in the national government where the cities can be looked at as a whole.

Government regulation of business is also this kind of problem. Individual agency regulations, although unpopular, are not overly troublesome to industry as a whole. There are complaints about specific programs and the way they are run, but these complaints usually involve questions of incremental change, fine tuning, and amendment. What is developing as one of the most serious problems with business regulation is the competition and contradictions between regulations and the inability of the government to see the cumulative results of regulations as they impact on a specific corporation. There is an analogy in medicine. Every drug sold in the United States is tested by the government and is probably safe. Consumers know reasonably well what happens when they take a specific drug. But what happens when an individual takes a combination of different drugs in the same day? No one really knows what the result might be. Similarly, no one in government has the capability of assessing the impact of the variety of government regulations on a particular industry or corporation. These and other areas of large, complex, and interconnected problems are a growing concern for government and business.

The nature of the decision-making systems and their inability to process large and visible issues helps to explain why it is impossible in our system of government to develop a truly national policy in areas such as urban development, energy, transportation, or health.

Notes

1. Louis C. Gawthrop, *Administrative Politics and Social Change* (New York: St. Martin's Press, 1971), p. 17.

2. Charles E. Lindblom, "The Science of Muddling Through," *Public Administration Review* (Spring 1959): 79–99.

3. Ibid, p. 89.

4. Herbert Kaufman, *Are Government Organizations Immortal?* (Washington, D.C.: The Brookings Institution, 1976), p. 34.

5. Transcript, *Face the Nation,* CBS-TV, 9 July 1978, pp. 15–16. Used with permission.

ten

Two Approaches to Reform

Management Improvement and Presidential Government

There are two approaches to making government more responsive to the big issues. The first approach can be labeled *management improvement.* It attempts to reform the existing decision-making systems by improving the way programs are managed and by instituting new techniques designed to bring the diverse and competing systems together to work in closer harmony. Many of these management improvements are borrowed from business; others are original. While all are designed to improve management, most do not alter the basic structure of decision systems, although some would redistribute power among the actors.

The other approach, *presidential government,* strengthens the decision-making authority of the president by investing the office with additional powers or strengthening the powers already there. This approach tends to reduce the importance and the impact of the specialized decision-making systems, permitting the president (or governor or mayor) to exercise greater decision-making authority. There are important implications to strengthening the role of the chief executive in decision-making. The public dislikes this idea, even though demands for presidential action, especially during times of crisis, increase. Most presidents are reluctant to take on more power, particularly in the areas of domestic policy. Presidents know the political consequences of too much power. They also know that chances for success in most policy areas are limited and problematic. There are few political incentives to visible, active involvement—the chances for failure are too great. Yet if the decision-making systems of government cannot be improved to resolve some of the big issues, presidential activity and power will, of necessity, increase.

The list of proposed management improvement reforms of the decision systems is long. It includes government versions of planning-programming-budgeting systems (PPBS), management by objectives (MBO), and zero-based budgeting (ZBB). Recently, many legislators have become aware of the need to control the government spending that results from PBI's "something for everybody" philosophy. Sunset legislation and the Budget Reform Act of 1974 are two products of this new awareness. Program evaluation and various impact analysis statements are two other techniques employed to improve the management capabilities of the decision-makers.

Planning Programming Budgeting Systems

PPBS grew out of the developmental work done in systems analysis and operations research during the 1950s. Much of this work was done at the Rand Corporation, the Air Force "think tank" in Santa Monica, California. Another organization heavily involved with these techniques was the Ford Motor Company, whose president, Robert McNamara, became John Kennedy's secretary of defense in 1961. The department at that time was, according to Otis L. Graham, Jr.,

> a good example of a bureaucracy out of control of its top management, including the President. . . . Instead of being an integrating policy instrument, the DOD budget was a bookkeeping device for dividing funds between the three services. . . . After the funds were allocated, there was no performance measurement, so that next year's budget was not likely to be altered by some demonstrable failure.[1]

McNamara found this situation intolerable and with the help of several top aides, including Charles Hitch and others from the Rand Corporation, set out to centralize programming and budgeting authority in the secretary's office. PPBS was the vehicle used for this purpose.

PPBS was quite simple in concept, if not in execution. It involved the following basic steps:

1. identify precise, measurable objectives;
2. identify alternative approaches to accomplishing each objective;
3. select the most efficient or cost-effective alternative;
4. monitor each program to make sure objectives are being reached, more or less on schedule, and to receive feedback concerning program operations;
5. use the feedback to improve program performance; and
6. integrate each of these steps with the budgetary process so that planning decisions can actually be implemented.

In 1965, Lyndon Johnson was sufficiently impressed by the performance of PPBS in the Defense Department to order its implementation in the twenty-one largest civilian departments and agencies. There were problems, however, both in the way in which the technique was disseminated to the nondefense agencies and in PPBS itself. Allen Schick has suggested,

> PPB died of multiple causes, any of which was sufficient. PPB died because of the manner in which it was introduced, across the board and without much preparation . . . because new men of power were arrogantly insensitive to budgetary traditions, institutional loyalties, and personal relationships . . . because of inadequate support and leadership with meager resources invested in its behalf . . . because good analysts and data were in short supply and it takes a great deal of time to make up the deficit.[2]

In some cases, PPBS was forced upon agencies that were making their own attempts to develop rational planning and management systems. For example, the State Department's Comprehensive Country Programming System required the identification of goals, objectives, and performance measures even more explicit than those demanded by PPBS. According to Mosher and Harr, this was one reason that senior Foreign Service officers, reluctant to surrender their traditional autonomy to State's top management, favored DOD's technique over that developed in their own agency.[3] After a four-year struggle, PPBS was selected in 1967 as the State Department's planning and programming system.

The heavy-handed way in which PPBS was imposed on federal agencies caused some officials to subvert, consciously or unconsciously, the system's effectiveness. The most serious problem was the failure in many agencies to integrate program planning with budgeting, an omission that obviously weakened, if not destroyed, the relationship between planning and implementation. But other problems intrinsic to PPBS made its complete acceptance by federal agencies highly unlikely, even under the best of circumstances. For example, goals and objectives in the public sector, unlike those of private organizations, are based on legislative mandates. Thus, they often reflect political compromises among groups with sharply differing aims. As Harry Havens of the U.S. General Accounting Office puts it, "A premium is placed on 'fuzzing up' issues which, if made too clear, would stimulate conflict and thus destroy the consensus."[4] Thus PPBS, with its need for precise, measurable objectives, would appear ill suited for a governmental system in which such clarity is dysfunctional.

Allen Schick marks June 21, 1971, as the date of PPBS's death within the federal government. That was the date of an Office of Management and Budget memorandum informing federal agencies that they were no longer required to include in their budget submissions the multiyear program and financing plans, program memoranda, and other documents associated with PPBS.[5] But as many observers, including Schick, have pointed out, only the forms and procedures of PPBS, not its essential concern for rationality, have died. The problems of incrementalism remain. The PPBS experience has left us at least with several skilled policy analysts, improved data-gathering mechanisms, and a greater commitment to rationality.

Management by Objectives in Government

Peter Drucker popularized the term "management by objectives" in 1954, in his book *Practice of Management.*[6] The method's antecedents are diverse, and its history can be traced back at least as far as Frederick Taylor, whose concept of "scientific management" included strong emphasis on identifying unambiguous, quantifiable objectives. Although MBO, both before and after Drucker's book, has been most closely associated with private-sector organizations, governmental involvement with it has been far from negligible. In the 1930s, several federal agencies, including the Forest Service and the Social Security Administration, experimented with goal-setting for individual employees. In the mid-1950s, the California State Training Office promoted a form of MBO called program management that emphasized holding managers accountable for results obtained instead of simply for resources used.[7]

"The way I look at it—it's organizing ability that counts!"

In the early 1970s, public-sector MBO acquired new popularity and was expected to take on new roles. The business oriented Nixon administration promoted it as a way of controlling the federal bureaucracy, which it perceived as populated primarily by hostile New Deal Democrats. At the same time it was seen as a successor to PPBS and thus as a procedure for allocating resources.

Goals and objectives proposed by mid-level managers were to be passed up the line to top administrators within the agencies and then to Office of Management and Budget officials, who would decide on the funding level for each agency's programs. There are some key differences between MBO and PPBS, however. For one thing, MBO is less rigid; agencies are not required to meet uniform reporting requirements or to adhere to inflexible schedules. MBO is a general management style rather than a specific budgeting technique. Because it lacks this emphasis on uniformity, attempts to use it for resource allocation were inappropriate. For example, the information (program objectives) coming to the Office of Management and Budget from the Labor Department was not necessarily comparable to that emanating from Interior or Agriculture.

The flow of information under MBO is supposed to be from the bottom up, whereas with PPBS the flow was from the top down. MBO emphasizes participatory management, the process whereby individual workers communicate to top management, through the objectives-setting process, their understanding of operating constraints and possibilities. PPBS, on the other hand, relies upon the judgments of technically trained experts, skilled in statistical analysis, who report directly to top-level officials. MBO can thus help organizations avoid those difficult situations created when operating officials must implement programs forced on them by "outsiders" who may or may not understand the practical problems involved.[8]

Sherwood and Page point out that MBO is based on four assumptions:

> 1. Objectives can be stated precisely.
> 2. Organizations are essentially "closed" and participants in the decision (objective-setting) process are easily identified.
> 3. Sufficient information is available to administrators to enable objectivity in analysis, decision-making, and evaluation of outcomes.
> 4. Organizational members at all levels will internalize prescribed objectives and cooperate in securing their achievement.[9]

As in the case of PPBS, the most serious obstacle to a successful MBO program is the difficulty in agreeing on objectives precise enough to be useful. Bargaining among individuals and groups with diverse interests is as likely to produce ambiguous objectives in the bureaucracy's middle layers as it does in Congress. Aplin and Schoderbek believe that the problem is especially acute in those agencies providing social services. They quote one administrator as saying, "You simply cannot measure our contribution to society."[10]

There are other problems associated with implementing MBO in the public sector. One is that until recently most civil service pay systems did not allow employers to reward workers for exceptional service. There were provisions for slight merit increases, but these tended to be given automatically to all but the most incompetent employees instead of being reserved for the most effective. For the most part, the government worker's pay is determined by formal qualifications and length of service, not by quality of work. A related problem is that workers who fail to meet their objectives cannot be penalized as easily in government as in the private sector. Civil service systems are typically designed to protect workers from capricious and politically motivated harassment from their supervisors. Unfortunately, management finds itself hampered in its efforts to provide effective supervision even when competence, and not political loyalty, is at issue.[11] The civil service reforms of 1978 will give managers more flexibility in rewarding exceptional performance.

Although MBO is no longer viewed as the latest miracle drug for curing government's management ills, its spirit, like that of PPBS, still lives. As it is more an attitude toward management than a formal program, it is not likely to be terminated by an OMB directive. Its greatest contribution may be as a means of introducing participatory management to government, thus facilitating communication within bureaucratic organizations and perhaps motivating public employees to provide more effective service.

Zero-Base Budgeting

Zero-base budgeting came to the federal government from private industry through state government. The term was coined by Peter Pyhrr, who developed the approach while at Texas Instruments in the late 1960s.

> The basic concept of attempting to reevaluate all programs and expenditures every year—hence the term zero-base—is not new. However, to my knowledge the only formalized attempt at zero-

> base budgeting was an unsuccessful attempt by the Department of Agriculture in the early 1960s, which did not resemble the methodology used successfully in both industry and government.[12]

According to David Beam, ZBB "has much in common with the performance budgeting strategy urged by reformers since the Taft Commission of 1912 and recommended in the 1949 report of the First Hoover Commission."[13] John Rehfuss says that ZBB, in contrast to PPBS,

> is a throwback to an older budgetary emphasis on management. . . . The primary personnel skill is administration, not economics. The information flow is upward, not downward. Planning responsibility is dispersed to line managers and is not centralized. Finally, the role of the budget agency is efficiency, even economy, not policy determination.[14]

Pyhrr wrote an article on ZBB for the November/December 1970 issue of the *Harvard Business Review* which was read by the newly elected governor of Georgia, Jimmy Carter. Carter brought Pyhrr to Atlanta, and Georgia became the first state to implement a ZBB system. Several others followed suit, including New Jersey, Texas, Montana, and Illinois. The ZBB approach received its greatest impetus after Carter was elected president in 1976 and began fulfilling his campaign promise to institute it throughout the federal government.

According to Pyhrr, in government ZBB involves four basic steps. The first is defining the decision units, those meaningful elements within the organization for which budget decisions will be made. These may correspond to the budget units defined by traditional budget procedures or they may be program elements, activities, or functions within the traditional units. The second step is to analyze each decision unit in a "decision package." This package describes each decision unit in such a way that management can evaluate it in relation to competing decision units and decide whether or not to approve it. A decision unit may have several decision packages, each describing an alternative method of accomplishing the unit's objectives as well as a separate funding level. Thus, decision unit A may have four alternative methods, each described at three funding levels, making a total of twelve decision packages. The third step is to evaluate and rank all decision packages and develop the appropriations request. The final step is to prepare detailed operating budgets reflecting those decision packages approved in the budget appropriation.[15]

Conceptually, ZBB resembled MBO in its participatory management orientation. Front-line operating officials are supposed to make the key decisions concerning acceptable alternative methods and funding levels. Unacceptable alternatives never get sent up the organization ladder. But when ZBB was implemented in Georgia, thousands of decision packages were generated, far too many for top-level officials to review intelligently. Since the problem could only be worse at the federal level, the Office of Management and Budget allowed agencies to submit "consolidated" decision packages, which inevitably muddied or obliterated the perspectives and priorities of operating officials. Allen Schick believes this decision by OMB was in effect an abandonment of ZBB's managerial purposes. However, this is no great loss, he feels, since experience with ZBB in the states has shown that the managerial emphasis has caused some expenditure shifts within budgets but has not promoted basic examinations of programs or objectives.[16]

As with its predecessors, PPBS and MBO, ZBB burst on the federal scene accompanied by extensive hoopla and hyperbole. Perhaps this is an inevitable part of the political process. However, even its creator admits, "We can't realistically expect major funding reallocations among major agencies [from the procedure]." Pyhrr does believe, however, that we can expect the elimination of low-priority programs, resulting in increased availability of money for high-impact programs and a general increase in governmental effectiveness.[17] Schick is more skeptical, but nevertheless finds some grounds for optimism.

> ZBB by itself cannot override the much stronger incentives to seek larger budgets and expanded functions. What ZBB can do is much more realistic and modest, but nonetheless important. It can stimulate the redirection of resources within budgets and programs, encouraging agency officials to shift from less to more productive activities.[18]

Preparation of the 1980 budget took ZBB a step further. The Office of Management and Budget introduced the concept of interagency zero-based budgeting. In this new procedure, agencies are required to work together to develop their budgets, particularly their priority schemes under ZBB procedures. Agency officers were required to sit in the same room and justify programs together.

The interagency ZBB process is a significant new procedure for decision-making systems. It attempts to bring two or more systems together at the agency level. This new procedure could give the president more leverage over competing decision systems by forcing agreement on program cutbacks or consolidation before the budget is sent to Congress.[19]

Sunset Laws

Although zero-base budgeting is designed primarily for executive agencies in government, while sunset laws were conceived as legislative tools, there are similarities between the two approaches. Each is a reform measure currently generating widespread interest. Each has a readily identifiable source as well as roots extending further back into the earlier years of this century. Sunset's equivalents to Peter Pyhrr and Texas Instruments are Common Cause and the state of Colorado. The basic idea, however, goes back at least as far as Justice William O. Douglas's tenure as chairman of the Securities and Exchange Commission during the 1930s. Douglas told Franklin Roosevelt that regulatory agencies should self-destruct (he probably did not use that term) after ten years.[20] More recently, Theodore Lowi has proposed a Tenure of Statutes Act, providing for automatic termination of programs after a specified period of time.[21]

Both ZBB and sunset have been implemented in several states—fifteen in sunset's case, with another dozen or so considering the idea. The most important similarity between the two, however, is that each requires that current governmental programs actively justify their continuation. According to Bruce Adams and Betsy Sherman of Common Cause, "Sunset is designed to force legislatures to carry out their oversight responsibilities. In the absence of affirmative action by the legislature, the status quo is changed rather than continued."[22] Thus sunset, like ZBB, is a reaction to the frequently heard complaint that government programs, once established, are difficult to terminate.

Stripped to its fundamentals, the sunset concept contains only two components: a requirement that all programs or agencies included in the legislation be terminated after a specified period of time unless the legislature decides otherwise, and an evaluation process for making such decisions. But sunset's proponents recommend several additional features to enhance its effectiveness. For example, Common Cause's founding chairman, John Gardner, has suggested that:

> 1. the sunset mechanism be phased in gradually, beginning with those programs to which it seems most applicable;
> 2. programs and agencies in the same policy area be reviewed simultaneously to encourage coordination and efficiency;
> 3. membership on legislative oversight committees be ro-

tated regularly to encourage objectivity in program review; and

4. public participation, through open hearings and free access to information, is essential.[23]

Evaluation is the crucial component of sunset and, some believe, its greatest weakness. Obviously government activities should not be terminated capriciously, and no useful purpose is served by terminating the more beneficial programs. Also, since the wisest course in some cases may be to modify rather than eliminate a program, legislators will need good evaluation data when deciding on the precise changes to be made. But for many of the reasons already mentioned, evaluation is far from an exact science.[24] There is, for example, the question of objectives. There is a premium in government placed on keeping them ambiguous in order to preserve ad hoc coalitions of diverse interests. An evaluation would require the specification of precise, measurable objectives. Depending on how those objectives are defined, and the relative weights assigned to each, the final report could be positive, negative, or almost anything in between.

Implementation of a sunset law would also require some consideration of the trade-off between, as Robert Behn put it, workload and neutrality. If it is to enjoy widespread support, sunset legislation must be perceived as an across-the-board attack on government waste. It must not be seen as a device to be used solely against the military-industrial complex or the welfare establishment. An even-handed attempt to review all government programs would place an unreasonable strain on limited evaluation resources. And the criteria for choosing those activities most appropriate for coverage under sunset are far from universally agreed upon. Behn, commenting on the hearings for a sunset bill proposed by Senator Edmund Muskie, noted, "Although everyone applauded the neutrality of the sunset concept and praised the virtues of terminating useless programs, no one suggested a single program that might just possibly be a candidate for termination."[25]

Another problem with sunset laws is the question of who should be in charge of evaluating a given program or agency. Most sunset proposals place this responsibility with the legislative committee having jurisdiction over the policy area in which the program or agency operates. These committees usually consist of people with vested interests in the status quo. They are not likely to evaluate their own programs critically or to look at them from varying points of view. Gardner's suggestion that committee membership be rotated on a regular basis is aimed at this problem. However, such a reform would be extremely difficult to accomplish. Few legislators, if any, would be willing to abandon their favorite programs or those favored by their constituents to the tender mercies of critical newcomers. In fact, if Congress could be made to accept the idea of rotating committee assignments, legislative oversight might improve so much that no formal sunset provisions would be needed at all.

In spite of these problems, the sunset concept can make a contribution toward greater governmental effectiveness and efficiency. The problem lies, as it did with ZBB and the earlier executive-oriented reforms, in separating the genuine benefits from the overly optimistic expectations of some of its supporters. Once again, the comments of Allen Schick are useful:

> Rather than being perceived as a termination process, sunset can more profitably be regarded as a reauthorization process, as an opportunity for Congress to make periodic adjustments and corrections in the course of federal programs. When a program is scheduled for expiration, Congress would have a full range of alternatives. In a few cases—only a few—Congress might allow the program to lapse by not renewing its authorization. In a greater number of programs, Congress probably would extend the authorization without making significant changes in its charter. In many programs—perhaps the largest number—Congress would deploy sunset as an opportunity to examine how the program has operated, and delve beyond the mere authorization into substantive law to make such adjustments as it deems appropriate. If sunset is enacted, this third category will contain the bulk of its benefits.[26]

Congressional Budget Reform

Congress has played an important role in reforming decision-making processes by developing methods to bring competing decision centers closer together. Criticism over the way Congress prepares the federal budget has long been widespread. A basic concern has been the generally uncoordinated nature of the process, with no congressional unit responsible for taking the larger view of national priorities or for relating budgetary decisions to broader economic policy. Another complaint has been with substantive legislation containing entitlement programs, which put almost three-fourths of federal spending outside congressional control. Another recurring problem is the disruption of executive branch operations caused by congressional inability to pass appropriations bills before the new fiscal year begins.

Perhaps the greatest impetus for reform, however, came from within as members of Congress sought to reverse a long-term tendency toward presidential usurpation of their traditional powers. This conflict acquired new intensity in the early 1970s, when President Nixon impounded congressionally appropriated funds as part of his efforts to control federal spending. When Nixon challenged Congress to limit spending in fiscal 1973 to $250 billion, many members agreed on the sum but felt strongly that they, not the president, should be the ones to decide how the money was allocated. A Joint Study Committee on Budget Control was created and instructed to find ways of increasing congressional control over the budgetary process. The result of the committee's work, and of subsequent hearings and debate, was the Congressional Budget and Impoundment Control Act of 1974.

According to James Finley, the act brought about the following major changes in congressional institutions, procedures, and timetables for handling budgetary matters:

> 1. New Budget Committees were established in the House and Senate.
> 2. A Congressional Budget Office (CBO) was created.
> 3. Congress instructed itself to make coordinated overall decisions on revenue and spending relationships before making individual revenue or appropriations decisions.
> 4. A revised budget timetable was established.
> 5. The role of the General Accounting Office (GAO) in providing budget related information was strengthened.
> 6. More information was required from the executive branch.
> 7. Anti-impoundment laws were strengthened.[27]

The newly created budget committees play a crucial role in the process. After receiving budget requests from the executive branch and various analytical reports from other congressional units by mid-April, "they must, within a rigid time schedule, establish a congressional position or target as to overall size and functional mix that will be observed in subsequent consideration and passage of appropriations and other legislation."[28] These targets are communicated to the various appropriations committees through a concurrent resolution. Next, the appropriations committees report their spending bills, which are reviewed by the budget committees. The budget committees then issue a second concurrent resolution which is, in effect, a final budget ceiling that informs the appropriations committees of the amounts by which changes in their spending bills must be made. These changes are made by late September, approximately one week before the new fiscal year begins on October 1.

Some skeptics have been pleasantly surprised by Congress's ability to adhere to the rigid timetable it set for itself. If this continues, executive branch agencies will enjoy greater predictability and stability for their own planning and operations than in the past. But this was a relatively minor objective of the act. Has congressional budget reform been a success in any more meaningful ways? The answer depends, of course, on the criteria for success. Ironically, the Congressional Budget and Impoundment Control Act resembles in an important way most other major legislation to emerge from the pluralist-bargaining-incremental system it sought to control. That is, different people supported the act for different, and possibly conflicting, reasons. John Ellwood and James A. Thurber suggest that a broad coalition of support assured a solid majority in favor of budget reform:

> 1. Both conservatives who wanted to cut spending and liberal Democrats who wanted to increase spending and change priorities saw the reform as a means to achieve their ends.
> 2. Both members of the appropriations and revenue committees, who wanted to limit back-door and uncontrollable spending, and liberal Democrats, who tended to be on the very legislative committees that would be most hurt through such control, supported the reform.
> 3. The reform was supported by members who saw the elimination of back-door and uncontrollable spending as a first step toward allowing greater short-term congressional control over the budget, and by members who felt that the only way to achieve congressional budget control was some form of forward planning and/or advanced budgeting.[29]

Some liberals are of two minds concerning the act's ultimate implications for public policy. According to Neil Kotler, a legislative assistant to Representative John Conyers, (D-Michigan),

> If the process works as intended by its reformer-advocates, it could consolidate and enhance control over the legislative process in this area, whereas formerly the diffusion of power largely benefitted wealthy, organized and powerful interests. Therefore,

> it is not surprising that the new budget institutions in Congress have stirred resentment and resistance from old line committees. . . . The new budget system may, of course, become merely a more efficient tool for consolidating and implementing the dominant interests.[30]

Thus, the success of the act should not be judged in terms of specific policy outcomes—more for butter and less for guns or vice versa. The act's greatest value may lie in the assistance it provides the political process in setting those priorities. According to LeLoup, "Staff members in both Budget committees and the Congressional Budget Office report noticing a change in the awareness and understanding of legislators."[31]

In this respect, congressional budget reform is similar to the other reform measures discussed above. None of them will alter the fact that ours is a diverse society, inhabited by people with a wide variety of frequently conflicting interests. However, each reform holds the promise of forcing our political and government institutions to consider alternative policies and their consequences intelligently and, most important, to make their final decisions more explicit and thus more easily susceptible to public scrutiny.

Program Evaluation

In the 1960s the Great Society social programs pumped billions of dollars into governments on all levels. Congress, in the 1970s, felt the need to tighten its control over expenditures. Numerous cases of misappropriation of funds, embezzlement, and poor judgment in planning and development prompted Congress to require more formalized evaluations of some of these programs.

Some evaluations were carried out by the agency or organization running the program. In other cases, third-party, outside evaluators were required. Additionally, Congress put more pressure on the federal agencies to evaluate the programs they were administering so that Congress could be more aware of the social benefits resulting from the programs it was funding. On many occasions Congress asked its investigative unit, the General Accounting Office (GAO), to conduct extensive evaluations of federal programs.[32]

The movement for evaluation of public programs becomes even stronger as government learns to build evaluative mechanisms into its program requirements. Congress has learned that sophisticated program evaluation techniques are valuable tools in an effort to better manage and to moderate some of the excessive programs generated by interest-group, White House, and bureaucratic pressures.

Other reforms have been instituted to try and make the domestic program system more manageable. Two of the most far-reaching are directives issued by OMB in response to legislative mandates. They are known as OMB Circulars A-85 and A-95.

Notes

1. Otis L. Graham, Jr., *Toward a Planned Society: From Roosevelt to Nixon* (New York: Oxford University Press, 1976), p. 171.

2. Allen Schick, "A Death in the Bureaucracy: The Demise of Federal PPB," *Public Administration Review* 33, no. 2(March-April 1973): 148–49.

3. Frederick and John Harr, *Programming Systems and Foreign Affairs Leadership* (New York: Oxford University Press, 1970), p. 239.

4. Harry Havens, "MBO and Program Evaluation, or Whatever Happened to PPBS?" *Public Administration Review* 36, no. 1 (January-February 1976): 41.

5. Schick, "A Death in the Bureaucracy," p. 146.

6. Peter Drucker, *Practice of Management* (New York: Harper and Row, 1954).

7. Frank P. Sherwood and William J. Page, Jr., "MBO and Public Management," *Public Administration Review* 36, no. 1 (January-February 1976): 6.

8. Bruce H. DeWoolfson, Jr., "Public Sector MBO and PPB: Cross Fertilization in Management Systems," *Public Administration Review* 35, no. 4, (July-August 1975): 393.

9. Sherwood and Page, "MBO and Public Management," p. 8.

10. John C. Aplin, Jr. and Peter P. Schoderbek, "MBO Requisites for Success in the Public Sector," *Human Resources Management* 15, no. 2 (Summer 1976): 34.

11. Ibid, pp. 34–35.

12. Peter A. Pyhrr, *Zero-Base Budgeting: A Practical Management Tool for Evaluating Expenses* (New York: John Wiley and Sons, 1973), p. xi.

13. David Q. Beam, "Public Administration is Alive and Well—and Living in the White House," *Public Administration Review* 38, no. 1 (January-February 1978): 73.

14. John Rehfuss, "Zero-Base Budgeting: The Experience to Date," *Public Personnel Management* 6, no. 3 (May-June 1977): 187.

15. Peter A. Pyhrr, "The Zero-Base Approach to Government Budgeting," *Public Administration Review* 37, no. 1 (January-February 1977): 2–7.

16. Allen Schick, "The Road from ZBB," *Public Administration Review* 38, no. 2 (March-April 1978): 179. Also see Thomas P. Lauth, "Zero-Base Budgeting in Georgia State Government: Myth and Reality," *Public Administration Review* 38, no. 5 (September-October 1978): 420–30.

17. Pyhrr, "The Zero-Base Approach to Government Budgeting," p. 8.

18. Allen Schick, "Zero-Base Budgeting and Sunset: Redundancy or Symbiosis," *The Bureaucrat* 6, no. 1 (Spring 1977): 19.

19. Philip Shabecoff, "Federal Agencies, for Budget Efficiency, Were Required to Rank Programs Against Other Departments," *The New York Times,* 5 January 1979.

20. William O. Douglas, *Go East, Young Man: The Early Years* (New York: Random House, 1974).

21. Theodore J. Lowi, *The End of Liberalism: Ideology, Policy and the Crisis of Public Authority* (New York: W. W. Norton, Inc., 1969), pp. 309–10.

22. Bruce Adams and Betsy Sherman, "Sunset Implementation: A Positive Partnership to Make Government Work," *Public Administration Review* 38, no. 1 (January-February 1978): 78.

23. Ibid, pp. 78–79.

24. See Alice M. Rivlin, *Systematic Thinking for Social Action* (Washington, D.C.: The Brookings Institution, 1971).

25. Robert D. Behn, "The False Dawn of the Sunset Laws," *The Public Interest* 49 (Fall 1977): 116.

26. Schick, "Zero-Base Budgeting and Sunset: Redundancy or Symbiosis," p. 25.

27. James J. Finley, "The 1974 Congressional Initiative in Budget Making," *Public Administration Review* 35, no. 3 (May-June 1975): 272.

28. Ibid.

29. John Ellwood and James A. Thurber, "The New Congressional Process: The Hows and Whys of House-Senate Differences," in Dodd and Oppenheimer, eds., *Congress Reconsidered* (New York: Praeger, 1976), pp. 168–69.

30. Neil G. Kotler, "The Politics of the New Congressional Budget Process: or, Can Reformers Use It to Undo the System of Privilege?" in Marcus G. Raskin, ed., *The Federal Budget and Social Reconstruction: The People and the State* (New Brunswick, N.J.: Transaction Books, 1978), pp. 5–24.

31. Lance T. LeLoup, *Budgetary Politics: Dollars, Deficits, Decisions* (Brunswick, Ohio: King's Court Communications, Inc., 1977), p. 235.

32. Two useful works in understanding program evaluation are Michael Quinn Patton, *Utilization-Focused Evaluation* (Beverly Hills, Calif.: Sage Publications, 1978); and Carol H. Weiss, *Evaluation Research: Methods of Assessing Program Effectiveness* (Englewood Cliffs, N.J.: Prentice-Hall, 1972). A different approach developed by a former government executive is Laurence H. Silberman, "If Not the Best, At Least Not the Worst," *Commonsense* 1, no. 1 (Summer 1978): 18–26.

eleven

Reforms in the Intergovernmental System

All the reforms discussed so far in this chapter are directed at improving the operation of decision-making systems in the national government. As the reader knows, in domestic programs the national government management processes are only the tip of the iceberg. Attempts to improve management practices in the intergovernmental system have been frequent in the last twenty years. Circular A-85, for example, is designed to permit state and local executives, through their Washington-based national organizations, sometimes referred to as public-interest groups (PIGs), to review and comment on major issuances of federal rules, regulations, guidelines, and organizational changes that could have an impact on state and local governments.

The circular was issued in response to the Intergovernmental Cooperation Act of 1968, which provided for a variety of viewpoints to be heard on federally developed or assisted programs. The circular defines guidelines for agencies to use in seeking state and local governmental review and comment. The Advisory Commission on Intergovernmental Relations (ACIR) is the administering agency that transmits the proposed rules and regulations to the public-interest groups. ACIR submits an annual report to the director of OMB on how the process is functioning.

The record of response by the public-interest groups varies tremendously. In some cases, irrelevant material is submitted to them for review, while in other instances the time is too short for serious review and comment by their staffs. This has dampened some of the initial enthusiasm for the program. Furthermore, agencies have often been unresponsive to changes suggested by the public-interest groups.[1]

OMB Circular A-95 established a project notification and review system to strengthen the management capabilities of local executives and to coordinate specific federal programs on the metropolitan level. Designated agencies composed of locally elected officials were assigned the review and comment function on grant applications at the metropolitan level. Regional and state bodies were also designated as acceptable review agencies. The review agencies, sometimes called clearing houses, were often involved in the early stages of the grant application process. This permitted preliminary ideas to be discussed and moderated before final decisions were made.

Initially, A-95 coverage included about fifty federally funded programs. Most of the programs covered were bricks and mortar, but some planning assistance programs in health, law enforcement, and community action were included. In 1971, A-95 regulations were expanded to include an additional fifty programs.[2]

Both Circulars A-85 and A-95 are devices initiated by the federal government to reform the decision-making process. Each circular attempts to restore some authority to elected officials, thereby reducing the powers of the bureaucracy. An additional check has been added to an already complex and lengthy system to minimize possible errors generated by undue pressures from interest groups and bureaucrats.

Presidential Initiatives in Decision-Making Systems Reform

Presidents employ various techniques and strategies to improve the management of decision systems. These include reorganization and impact analysis statements. Most presidential initiatives are designed to increase cooperation among decision-making systems and to enhance the president's influence within them.

When public-sector executives, particularly the president, announce plans to reorganize departments of government, they imply that the present system is unsatisfactory and unmanageable; a new arrangement of agencies, bureaus, offices, and key personnel is required to meet the working style of the executive. Thus, proposed reorganization is a strategy for disrupting existing power relationships and lines of communication so that executives can bring new groups of people together to form decision-making systems more in tune with their thinking.

Except where executives are granted extraordinary power to reorganize government, reorganization plans often meet stiff resistance. Most of the actors in the system view reorganization as a threat to their positions and fight to weaken if not defeat such proposals. In the past fifteen years many states have given their governors sweeping reorganization power to assist them in modernizing their executive branches. Governors have been quick to learn the political ramifications of their efforts to reorganize.[3]

In 1971, President Nixon sent a reorganization proposal to Congress which would have created four supercabinet departments composed of six major existing departments and several other agencies. They were to be called Department of Community Development, Department of Economic Affairs, Department of Human Resources, and Department of Natural Resources. The rationale for the reorganization appeared sound. The president sought to:

1. eliminate fragmentation and duplication;
2. combine programs with similar orientations;
3. sharpen the focus of each department;
4. give each department more responsibility; and
5. make each department head more accountable to Congress, the president, and the people.

However, many sound reorganization proposals have failed because the political realities of the situation were accorded more weight than the rationale for reorganizing. In this case, the proposed reorganization would have drastically altered the existing power relationships. Congress, the bureaucracy, and interest groups all sensed what a severe jolt this would be to existing decision-making systems and moved quickly to see that the president's plan did not receive serious consideration.[4]

By centralizing more decision-making authority in four key cabinet secretaries, President Nixon hoped to tighten up government and make it more responsive to his wishes. The actors in the affected systems saw this as a serious threat which, if left unchallenged, would have forced Congress to restructure the committee system to better oversee the new departmental alignment, require interest groups to revamp their strategies and tactics to conform to the new access points, and force the bureaucrats to reacquaint themselves with a host of new actors.

President Carter has been given a broader set of reorganization powers than either of his two predecessors. He too is finding that reorganization politics is a difficult and potentially dangerous game. While the White House staff and the Executive Office have been relatively easy to reorganize, President Carter has found that reorganizing the executive agencies has far-flung ramifications that reverberate throughout the political system. Although President Carter invested more time and resources in reorganization planning than other recent presidents, the results have been disappointing. Civil service reform, including the elimination of the Civil Service Commission, was the president's outstanding achievement in the area of reorganization.

Impact Analysis Statements

Impact analysis statements are perhaps the most dramatic step taken by presidents to coordinate the activities of the traditional decision-making systems. Instead of evaluating programs after they have been implemented to determine how they impact on one another, impact statements must be written before programs can be implemented. This enables the administering agency, an elected executive, and, increasingly, the courts to determine the advantages and disadvantages of a given program before it is implemented. Impact statements also force the personnel of decision-making systems to look at other systems. The statements are aimed at reducing overlapping and contradiction. Requiring an environmental impact statement in a highway construction program, for example, assures that highway builders look at how the proposed construction affects agriculture, air and water pollution, housing, and other matters outside of the traditional highway decision-making system.

Impact statements are most commonly found in the areas of environment and occupational safety and health. Noise, air, water pollution, as well as dangerous and unsafe working conditions are the major issues in current impact statements. Impact statements serve as another technique for bringing decision systems together, at least temporarily, to develop coherent, cross-system decisions. By requiring an impact analysis, government establishes a check to filter out the possible negative consequences of decisions processed by two or more systems.[5]

In March 1978, President Carter announced his National Urban Policy. One executive order that was part of the policy required an urban impact analysis to be performed for every proposed major domestic program. The president wanted to minimize the negative impact federal programs might have on large urban centers and maximize any advantages.

The impact analysis outlined by Carter is another tactic designed to fine tune the political system and make it function better. Impact analysis provides the president another weapon with which to manage the complex, competing decision-making systems. If a proposed new program is determined to have a negative impact on urban areas, the president has a legitimate reason to modify or veto the program. It is worth speculating on how the no-down-payment home mortgage provision of the G.I. Bill might have been different had the urban impact requirement been on the books in the 1940s. Would the opportunity for veterans have been conditioned by provisions to encourage more building in the central cities and less far-reaching suburban development? Would highway construction have been planned differently to minimize damage to central-city neighborhoods? These questions are imponderable. Difficulty of foresight in these complex policy areas and strong political pressures might have negated any of the positive effects of the impact statement requirement. Yet, forced to go through the impact statement analysis, government officials would have had the opportunity to anticipate and ward off at least the worst unintended consequences of these programs.

Public Demands for Decision-Making System Reform

Occasionally decision-making systems receive a shock from the public which alters the routine functions and brings about important reforms. Such was the case in June 1978, when the Voters of California passed Proposition 13, which restricted taxation in four ways: property taxes were limited to 1 percent of the market value of real property; the assessed value of real property for tax purposes was set at the 1975–76 level; state taxes could only be increased by two-thirds vote of both houses of the state legislature; and local taxes—other than property taxes—could only be increased by two-thirds of those voting in an election.[6] The tax-cutting idea spread to other jurisdictions.

The Proposition 13 movement was a reaction, at least in part, to the incremental nature of the American political system: additions and deletions, whether programmatic or financial, are accomplished in a slow, careful manner consistent with the give-and-take nature of our political system. Proposition 13 and other such major changes force the system to take stock. Incrementalism and the competing decision-making systems now had to be looked at as a whole. Trade-offs were forced, because spending decisions had to be made under a firm expenditure ceiling

In situations like Proposition 13 and similar measures, the rules governing decision-making systems are altered. Political leaders find their ability to respond to pressure is strengthened. Knowing there are limits on the dollars available, they can more easily say no to interested parties with less fear of reprisal at the ballot box.

Felix Rohatyn, chairman of the Municipal Assistance Corporation in New York City, summed up this point in a speech:

> Most of the meaningful decisions required from government today are unpleasant; they involve vocal, powerful, competing interests. They involve living up to over-commitments made by previous office-holders unwilling to face facts in their own time and place.
>
> The politician, every day, has to reconcile the hard realities of the moment with the impossible promises he and his predecessors made in the past on taxes, on services, on labor costs, on jobs. Everywhere he wants peace, he wants to be loved, he wants to make everyone happy, he wants to be reelected.[7]

Agencies of government heretofore concerned primarily with how much more to ask for in each succeeding fiscal year, now find they are being asked to cut costs, programs, and personnel in an effort to deal with a declining resources situation.[8]

In crisis situations, such as those brought about by Proposition 13, decision-making systems are temporarily altered, thereby increasing the power of the chief executive. In those circumstances where executives fail to act, legislative bodies are generally called upon to assume an increased role in decision-making systems.

American government tends not to move on tough decisions until the crisis stage or something close to it has been reached. The reasons should be clear when one understands the nature of the decision-making process. A crisis is sometimes required to bring about coordination and cooperation between decision-making systems. Sometimes crisis points are created artificially by writing deadlines into law. In 1978, New York City moved right up to its deadline of June 30, on an extension of the federal loan guarantee program for city financing. The deadline date was known two full years in advance, yet the decision was taken at the last minute. Why? The issue was so large and so controversial it was impossible to force an end to the "after you, Alphonse" routine in which various decision-makers were involved. The decision on New York City financing included labor unions, city officials, state officials, banking groups, and the federal government. Each of these groups was waiting to see what the other would do. The force that brought them together was the June 30 deadline, which, if not met, would probably have resulted in a declaration of bankruptcy for the city. The decision was made at the eleventh hour. At times, when problems are big, tough, and involve many people, an "artificial" device like a deadline is necessary to move the various competing decision-making centers to reach agreement.

The number of attempts at management improvement in government have over the years been extensive and impressive. Some of the techniques are original; others have been borrowed from business and adapted to the peculiar demands of public management. They all attempt to make decision-making systems operate effectively, and, to tie them closely together by encouraging a more unified, coherent set of government policies. The Congressional Budget Office and sunset laws attempt to give Congress the means to coordinate and evaluate the bigger picture. These reforms help members of Congress make choices between programs on a reasonably informed basis. Civil Service reform, reorganization, and other reforms supported by presidents assist the president to become more effectively involved in policy-making by giving him better tools to both evaluate and influence the activities of decision-making systems.

Still, no amount of management improvement will reconcile all of the conflict, duplication, and inefficiency caused by competing decision-making systems. Management improvements will not help, because the problems in the systems are not caused solely by management deficiencies. They are instead political problems. Management improvement will not resolve the differences between proponents of nuclear power and environmentalists. Those who see the use of nuclear reactors to generate electrical power as the only sensible way to energy self-sufficiency cannot be easily reconciled with environmentalists who foresee the worst possible disasters resulting from increased nuclear use. The decision-making systems responsible for public health will not find management solutions to their conflicts with the systems fighting for the continuation of tobacco price supports and programs designed to promote the sale of tobacco products abroad. These conflicts are the stuff of politics. Government managers learn the art of dealing reasonably with these issues while learning the skills of good management.

But what about the big issues beyond the grasp of decision-making systems? What happens, for example, if management reform and program management techniques fail to bring decision-making systems together to manage in a reasonably effective way the complexities in the intergovernmental system, a possible energy crisis, inflation, and the older cities of the Northeast? What if Congress, through its newly created mechanism, the Congressional Budget Office, fails to bring decision-making systems into some semblance of synchronization with each other? And what does the future hold for the management of intergovernmental programs? Will management reform make a difference in this field?

The most likely answer to these questions is that the operations of decision-making systems will improve at least marginally. Whether or not they will be able to resolve the bigger, more complex issues of our times is an open question. If they fail, the demands for the president to move in or at least exert more influence will grow. Thus, the country would move more rapidly in the direction of a stronger presidency.

Presidential Government: A Solution to the Big Problems?

As used here, the term *presidential government* means increasing the power of the president to make decisions that were left, in the past, to the decision-making systems described in this book. Presidents have always participated in these systems, but usually on a sporadic basis and often as an outsider. In times of emergency, especially in instances of armed, international conflict, presidents manage without regard to decision-making systems. Increasing the managerial powers of the president makes him less of an outsider to these systems and more of an insider. In fact, in some areas in recent years—inflation and economic stabilization, for example—the president is empowered to act on his own.

At the extreme, presidential government is unilateral action by the president in times of national emergency, acting under constitutional authority as commander-in-chief. Although these powers are related to the war powers granted by the Constitution, they have been used by presidents at times in other situations. The area of executive agreements and executive privilege is legally clouded and politically controversial. Over the past several years, presidents have used these prerogatives to gain more discretion and power. "The general drift of authority and responsibility to the President over the past two centuries is unmistakable," according to a recent scholarly study of the presidency.[9]

Recently, Congress delegated enormous power to the president in the area of energy and inflation. The Economic Stabilization Act of 1970 was used by President Nixon to issue wage and price controls the next year. Also, Nixon allocated oil reserves during the Arab oil embargo under power delegated to him by Congress. These are extraordinary powers for presidents in peace time, indicating that when established decision-making systems fail, more power gravitates to the president to solve problems.

The use of extraordinary powers by the president is limited by the courts. The courts serve as a check on presidential powers even in times of national emergencies. In 1952, the Supreme Court ruled that President Truman's seizure of the steel mills during the Korean War was unwarranted and beyond his constitutionally granted authority.[10] Control of the steel mills was immediately returned to the private sector.

Political pressures and political tradition are two strong forces working to keep presidential power in check. Presidents know that taking power even in times of emergencies involves taking risks. If the situation is worsened by presidential actions, the consequences could be defeat at the polls for himself and his allies.

Still, one can imagine situations in the areas of energy, inflation, and the cities where the traditional decision-making systems—even with the benefit of improved management—do not respond well and the president feels obliged or is encouraged to take a stronger hand. President Carter's inflation control program is an example of the difficult choice confronting presidents faced with tough, big issues. The first step in his program was voluntary guidelines combined with a variety of efforts to use the traditional decision-making systems to help stabilize the economy. Alfred Kahn, the president's inflation fighter, threatened to use the government's procurement powers to encourage government suppliers to keep prices down. Budget mechanisms were used to keep budget requests of the competing decision-making systems down to a reasonable level. Deregulation of certain industries, trucking, for example, was examined to see if prices in those industries could be brought down by changing or even eliminating federal regulations. Kahn was placed in the White House to help the president orchestrate an anti-inflation program that depended mostly on persuading the existing decision-making centers to act in ways that would help reduce inflation. If these attempts fail, the president might be encouraged to shift to wage and price controls. In this case, the commensurate shift in power away from the decision-making systems to the presidency would be enormous.

At this time, the list of activities of the government to improve decision-making systems is much longer than the list of actions taken to enhance presidential power. How long this situation will last depends in part on how well the decision-making systems respond to the problems facing government. However, should the number of large, complex issues grow, it is likely that increased power will accrue to the presidency.

Notes

1. For a discussion of Circular A-85, see *Improving Federal Grants Management* (Washington, D.C.: Advisory Commission on Intergovernmental Relations, 1977), pp. 135–37.

2. The development and implementation of A-95 is discussed in *Regional Decisionmaking: New Strategies for Substate Districts,* vol. 1 (Washington, D.C.: Advisory Commission on Intergovernmental Relations, 1973), pp. 143–65.

3. See *State of the States in 1974: Responsive Government for the Seventies* (Washington, D.C.: National Governors Conference, 1974), pp. 19–24.

4. See Richard P. Nathan, *The Plot That Failed: Nixon and the Administrative Presidency* (New York: John Wiley and Sons, Inc., 1975), pp. 60–62, 68–69, 134–135. Also see Douglas M. Fox, "The President's Proposals for Executive Reorganization: A Critique," *Public Administration Review* 33, no. 5 (September-October 1973): 401–6.

5. Eugene Bardach and Lucian Pugliaresi, "The Environmental Impact Statement vs. the Real World," *The Public Interest* 49 (Fall 1977): 22–38.

6. For an analysis of Proposition 13, see John Quirt, "Aftershocks from the Great California Taxquake," *Fortune,* 25 September 1978, pp. 74–84; and John Shannon and Carol S. Weissert, "After Jarvis: Tough Questions for Fiscal Policymakers," *Intergovernmental Perspective* 4, no. 3 (Summer 1978): 8–12.

7. Felix G. Rohatyn, "Statesmanship from the Private Sector," *The New York Times,* 12 July 1978.

8. For a discussion of different institutional responses to the problem of reduced resources, see Charles H. Levine, ed., "Symposium: Organizational Decline and Cutback Management," *Public Administration Review* 38, no. 4 (July August 1978): 315–57.

9. Louis Fisher, *The Constitution Between Friends: Congress, the President and the Law* (New York: St. Martin's Press, 1978), p. 247.

10. *Youngstown Co. v. Sawyer* 343 US 579 (1952).

twelve

Business and Government in the Future

Some Speculation

Some problems are handled well by government, others are not. If a program fits neatly into one or a few closely related decision-making systems, the chances are good that government will process that program with relative efficiency. If a program does not fit into a decision-making system, the result is likely to be chaotic management, unpredictability, and a program to which outsiders have difficulty relating.

Business executives should look at government relations on a program-by-program basis. Most government programs conform to the pattern of decision-making described in this book. Most of the older regulatory programs, for example, are handled by these types of systems. Food and drug programs, housing programs, a wide variety of health programs, soil conservation, and hundreds of others could be added to the list. In these cases, business executives might not like the government program or the way it is being run, but at least they can develop strategies to deal with those in government responsibile for the program.

On the other hand, when business executives are faced with large, controversial problems—like energy—which spill over into several dozen decision-making systems, the result is quite different. Trucking deregulation, for example, will be handled within the identifiable confines of one decision-making system. On the other hand, programs focusing on the probable causes of cancer in humans are split among several systems and agencies, including (but not only) the Consumer Product Safety Commission, Environmental Protection Agency, Food and Drug Administration, and the Occupational Safety and Health Administration.

With no one system dominant, one cannot predict how a program will develop, who is in charge, or what the policy outcome might be. In these cases, it is nearly impossible for executives to develop effective strategies. The best one can do is to attempt to break the larger issues up into smaller, manageable portions that fit more neatly into operating decision-making systems. This is a difficult task. In some cases, division into smaller pieces cannot be accomplished. Then executives can work with government officials to improve management and help to define and redefine programs in such a way that existing or new decision-making systems can handle them. Good relationships with these officials will facilitate that process.

Relationships between business and government have run the gamut from legal action, name-calling, and recalcitrance to cooperation, information-sharing, and joint endeavors. The prospects for improved business-government relationships will greatly influence the political and economic climate of the 1980s. A sound, intelligent relationship, based on fact and reason, is critical to a nation committed to solving numerous social, economic, and managerial problems.

Both business and government have experienced changes over the past ten years that have made it more difficult for the two sectors to keep informed of each others' activities and consequently to make intelligent decisions in major areas of public policy. Change, as Saul Alinsky once said, means movement; movement means friction; friction means heat; and heat means controversy.[1] The motion, its causes, the friction, its causes, and the way government deals with these phenomena have been major considerations of this book. Now we turn to some speculation on the future.

Changing Business-Government Relations

Change sometimes generates myths that blur reality. Stereotypes develop and are passed around a company, an industry, or a government agency until they become accepted as facts. In the beginning of the book we tried to isolate a number of myths and present facts and figures to place business-government relations in perspective. Two areas where there seemed to be a great deal of misunderstanding were bureaucracy and government regulations. We have analyzed the bureaucracy by reviewing its size, growth, place of employment, pay scales, retirement system, and agency size. Business executives who negotiate and communicate with government organizations should have an accurate picture of the bureaucracy with which they are dealing.

Similarly, the facts surrounding the initiation of much government regulation are clouded by myth and self-interested press releases and speeches from both government and business. The recent changes in government regulation are important to business organizations today. We have shown that a sizable amount of recent government regulation is general rather than specific. In the past, most government regulations were issued by agencies authorized to issue rules and regulations for specific industries, such as ICC, FTC, and FCC. Today, more regulations apply to all business organizations regardless of their industry. These regulations are being issued and enforced by agencies such as OSHA, EPA, and EEOC. The type of regulation, the method of promulgation, implementation, and enforcement are changes that require adjustments in businesses if they are to reduce tensions and improve their relationships with government.

Most observers predict that government regulation will increase over the next several years. In some industries, however, pressures towards deregulation seem strong. Deregulation, which aims to reduce inflation by increasing competition, is likely to become more prevalent in the 1980s. The airline deregulation of 1978 will probably be followed in the coming months by deregulation of the trucking industry. Fighting inflation through increasing competition by decreasing regulation has wide appeal across the political spectrum.

On the other hand, deregulation in social and environmental areas will not come easily, even when the argument includes promises to reduce inflation by lowering industrial production and management costs. The bulk of regulations in this area are very controversial, for they are manifestations of popular contemporary social and political movements. The process of determining whether or not a regulation is worth the price is both difficult and highly subjective; according to some, regulations geared to save lives or improve the quality of life are worth almost any price. Data can be brought together to support the arguments of the regulators as well as the deregulators.

The Regulatory Council, set up by President Carter on October 31, 1978, has high on its agenda the mandate to develop a data base to measure the impact of regulations on the economy. This will take a considerable length of time. Even if the goal is achieved, it is not likely to end the debate over the costs and benefits of regulatory policy.

The pressures for *increasing* federal regulatory activities are substantial. They can be organized under the following headings:

1. consumer pressures on government;
2. activities of certain industries to encourage government to regulate on their behalf;
3. the development of new technologies; and
4. changing ideologies and bureaucratic momentum.

The pressures favoring the *decreasing* federal government regulation of business include:

1. political pressures brought by business on government;
2. decisions of government agencies to both simplify and reduce certain regulatory standards;
3. better management of federal regulatory programs across agencies;
4. successful court decisions in suits brought by business against government regulatory policy; and
5. the desire to control inflation.

The Forces Behind Increasing Regulation

It is difficult to assess precisely the extent of consumer and public support of business at any given time. It is important to know how the public feels about business, however. Public attitudes will determine, in part, the level of government regulation of business in the future. There seems to be a decline in the public's faith in leadership, whether of corporations, government, or academic institutions. The extent of the decline is uncertain, but there is no doubt that the public holds business leadership in less esteem than it did ten years ago. According to pollster Louis Harris, in 1979, only 18 percent of those questioned had great confidence in business leadership. In 1966, that confidence level was measured by Harris at 55 percent (table 12.1). There seems to be little hope of reversing this trend in the short run, but many corporate leaders are beginning to do something about it, through an intensified use of public-relations techniques.[2] Business executives are not the only ones suffering from a loss of public confidence; the national government and the press itself were big losers.

Table 12.1

Great deal of confidence in institutions: 1966–1979

The Harris Survey asked: "As far as people in charge of running (READ LIST) are concerned, would you say you have a great deal of confidence, only some confidence or hardly any confidence at all in them?" (The figures are for "great deal of confidence.")

	1979 (percent)	*1977 (percent)*	*1976 (percent)*	*1966 (percent)*
Medicine	30	55	42	73
Higher education	33	41	31	61
Organized religion	20	34	24	41
U.S. Supreme Court	28	31	22	50
The military	29	31	23	62
Television news	37	30	28	41[a]
White House	15	26	18	XX
Major companies	18	23	16	55
Executive branch of government	17	23	11	41
Local government	XX	21	19	28[a]
State government	XX	19	16	24[a]
The press	28	19	20	29
Law firms	16	16	12	24[a]
Congress	18	15	9	42
Organized labor	10	15	10	22
Advertising agencies	XX	11	7	21

[a]Indicates 1973 data

Source: Harris, Louis, "The ABC News-Harris Survey," vol. 1, no. 27. New York: Chicago Tribune-New York News Syndicate, 5 March 1979. Reprinted with permission.

Those who seem to score the highest over time are organized religion and state and local governments.

The press will undoubtedly continue to cover the mistakes of industry more thoroughly than its innovative products or positive contributions. Auto recalls, unsafe auto gasoline tanks and tires, dangerous levels of chemicals in rivers, and similar stories will continue to make good copy for the press, as it should. Even as business works to improve its image, catastrophes, some small, some spectacular, will cancel out these efforts. Image enhancement is an uphill struggle. It is doubtful that it will make a significant improvement in public attitude toward business in the next few years. If this prediction is accurate, there will be little public pressure to deregulate based on an improvement of public attitudes toward business.

As government regulations stay on the books for periods of time, some industries develop new products that profit from those regulations. The air and water pollution equipment industries are an example. There is every reason to believe that several major corporations will continue to press for retention and even extension of government regulations in the areas where their products become more marketable by virtue of those regulations. These fortunate corporations are in the position of doing well by doing good. The natural forces of industrial expansion and protection would seem to work in favor of keeping those regulations on the books.

Furthermore, some corporations, large and small, almost certainly will continue to pressure government for regulations that enhance their market positions. There are no signs of change here, and one should not expect them. Corporations will continue to pursue their economic self-interests—even when those efforts include using favorable regulations. The trucking industry and the major trucking unions support current trucking regulations. They can be expected to make that point forcefully in debates over deregulating this industry.

Special-interest actions before regulatory agencies like the FTC will continue; also, there is reason to believe that corporations facing bankruptcy will continue to go to government for low-interest loans or other bail-out measures rather than face dissolution. In short, it is questionable how much support there is in industry for deregulation. It is easy enough to ask for an end to the regulations that hamper, but is industry willing to support a weakening of those regulations that give them a special advantage?

REMEMBER THE GOOD OLD DAYS WHEN WE ONLY HAD TO SMOKE A FEW CIGARETTES AND EAT SACCHARIN?

Increased regulatory activity parallels the development of sophisticated technology. As technology improves and expands, the extent of government regulatory activity seems to increase. Discoveries of harmful chemicals in food products or in the environment will certainly lead government to either ban or limit distribution of those products. The invention of devices to improve the efficiency of internal-combustion engines will strengthen the government's hand in forcing automobile manufacturers to adhere to higher mile-per-gallon standards. The list of possibilities here is endless. It is not possible to predict what technological developments will bring in the next few years. It is likely, however, that we will experience continued advances, and the level of government regulatory activity will increase accordingly.

Excesses in certain industries, both real and alleged, could lead to public demands for more, not less regulation. In the insurance industry it has recently come to light that several companies are selling unnecessary numbers of questionable policies to the poor and semiliterate, which is certain to result in pressures on government to increase regulation. The health industries, given the rapidly escalating costs of health care, are likely to experience more regulation in the next few years. In these areas the willingness and ability of industry to police itself will probably affect the degree of government aggressiveness.

The root causes of increased regulation are in the very fundamental changes our advanced society is undergoing. George C. Lodge, of the Harvard Business School, sees American society going through a great ideological transformation no less significant than the transition that ended the medieval period. The traditional values surrounding property rights and individualism, he argues, are slowly being replaced by communitarianism and community needs.[3] These new ideas are powerful. They change the way society views both business and government. They change the demands people place on these institutions. What these demands will be or how they will emerge in terms of policy from government decision-making processes is difficult to predict. In the long run, they are likely to push governments to more regulatory activity.

The Forces Behind Deregulation

There is substantial pressure today to both improve the way government regulations are managed and to reduce the number of regulations in force. On balance though, this pressure probably will only slow the development of new regulations. Several groups active in promoting deregulation and better regulatory management have met with some success. The extent of that success can be measured partially in the intensity of interest in governmental, journalistic, and academic circles about the problems of regulation and in recent statements by public officials, including President Carter. There is a new journal called *Regulation*, published by the American Enterprise Institute, and major newspapers frequently report on regulatory matters. The *Washington Post* recently started a column called "The Regulatory Beat." University programs to study regulatory management and the economic impact of regulation are beginning to develop in both business and public affairs programs.

The results of these activities are seen in several areas. Some regulatory agencies have moved to cut back their regulatory programs and reduce the impact of regulations. The Environmental Protection Agency recently announced a major reduction in the particulate standards for urban areas. This change will save substantial sums of money by making it easier for communities and the industries located within them to comply with the reduced air-pollution-control standards. OSHA has also reduced the size and the scope of its regulatory program significantly.

The activities of the Carter White House in the field of regulatory management improvement are important developments. The Regulatory Advisory Review Group and the Regulatory Council taken together with the requirement that agencies file an impact statement when proposing new rules signifies, at the very least, awareness of the problems the nation has today in complying with federal regulations. Douglas M. Costle, the Chairman of the Regulatory Council, reflects this view in a recent speech:

> We are not regulatory entrepreneurs knocking out *Federal Register* notices for the sheer joy of it.
>
> We have no profit motive, no stockholders, no shares in the company, no year-end bonuses.
>
> If we cannot produce cost-effective regulations we are as bankrupt as the company that can't sell its product.
>
> I do think the Council will stimulate some significant new approaches in regulatory agencies: a greater emphasis on the big problems, on setting priorities, on pruning a way the undergrowth of regulation which has built up over the years, often obscuring the total landscape of purpose and objectives.[4]

George Eads, a member of the President's Council on Economic Advisors, and chairman of the Regulatory Advisory Review Group, seemed to agree with Costle when he indicated that one of the tasks of RARG is to encourage federal agencies to look at the impact of what they are doing. "It's hard to get agencies to see the links between what they're trying to do and its effects," said Eads. "We're trying to put administrators into the shoes of businessmen."[5]

Assessing the costs imposed on society by proposed regulations and streamlining the management of all regulations are now high priorities in government. The results of these activities are bound to be an improvement in the way regulations are managed, but it will take some time before the impact is felt. The regulatory programs of the government did not grow overnight. Furthermore, most are rooted strongly in a base of political support. There is no reason to believe that it will be any easier now to eliminate regulations or slow down the writing of new ones; it is always a difficult struggle. But there is unquestionably more focus on deregulation and better regulatory management now than there has been in the past.

Barbara Hackman Franklin, one of the original members of the Consumer Product Safety Commission, noted remarkable changes in government attitude toward regulation.

> What has changed is public sentiment toward regulation, which has colored the way the administration feels about things. . . . And how the administration feels about regulations is crucial, because the decisions are still made here in Washington, and the tone in the city, the climate about government regulation influences the kind of decision-making that goes on.[6]

The federal government is proposing some interesting innovations in regulatory management, such as a new program that would allow agencies to deregulate on an experimental basis for a short period of time. This authority would be used by agencies to test the results of deregulation. They would not, however, have to go through all of the changes in law and regulations that permanent deregulation would require. This novel approach is only one of a rather imaginative set of procedures designed to both study and implement major changes in regulatory management.

The proposal is part of the Regulatory Reform Act, which the administration submitted to Congress early in 1979. The act contains many important provisions to improve the regulatory process, including several new schemes to use economic incentives to achieve regulatory goals. Some of these proposals are controversial. In fact, the power to suspend regulations so that agencies may conduct deregulatory experiments could well prove to be unconstitutional. Laws passed by Congress or rules written by agencies under powers delegated by Congress probably cannot be suspended temporarily by agency action. The significance of the proposal, however, is that it is an innovative attempt to deal with certain difficulties in the regulatory process. It is an indication that the government itself is concerned about the criticism raised in many quarters about government regulation.[7]

Another possible force for deregulation is the courts, which might require several changes both in the extent of regulation and also in the way the government manages its regulatory programs. In early 1979, Sears, Roebuck & Co. filed a massive suit against ten federal agencies. The suit primarily involves equal employment opportunity regulations and the inconsistencies in the way these regulations are promulgated by government agencies. One interesting aspect of the case is that Sears claims that a number of contradictory government policies make it impossible to comply with the standards set by equal employment opportunity regulations. They ask "how to resolve existing conflicts between affirmative action requirements based on race and sex and those based on veterans' status, age and physical or mental handicaps."[8] Sears claims it has attempted to comply with government requirements but cannot because of the contradictions. The company also claims that the government's veterans' programs assured the country that the work force would be primarily male. Ninety-seven percent of World War II armed forces personnel were male, and 92 percent of them were white. According to the suit, this set into motion the process of male, white domination of the marketplace. Furthermore, the new federal retirement law barring mandatory retirement before age seventy has made it much more difficult for corporations to hire or upgrade women and minorities. The thrust of the suit is that the private sector is being called upon to correct labor force problems created over the years by government itself. This is a provocative argument. The U.S. District Court for the District of Columbia, however, dismissed the case on the grounds that the Sears allegations were not sufficiently concrete for the case to be argued on its merits. It is likely this case will be appealed and that other corporations will file similar suits.

There are other areas where court intervention could make significant changes in regulatory law. The courts have not generally involved themselves in the substance of regulatory policy as they are being required to do in the Sears case. A move in this direction by the courts would have important implications for both business and government in the regulatory field.

The most frequently discussed pressure for deregulation is the assertion that regulations are inflationary. By adding to the costs of management and production, regulations help fuel the fires of inflation. This controversial subject has been addressed elsewhere in this book. It is worth noting once again, however, because it is one of the major generators of opposition to various regulations. The whole issue of government spending is under closer scrutiny now than during most periods of American history. Proposals to balance the federal budget are heard from many quarters. One proposal would even call a constitutional convention to write an amendment requiring a balanced federal budget. Certainly the regulatory programs of the federal government will have to do their part in the fight to bring inflation under control, but the dollars saved here are not likely to be substantial.

The Years Ahead

The American public seems to want a better working relationship between government and business. In 1978 *Fortune* magazine reported that a number of polls indicated that "the American people want government and business to stop battling and start trying to work together on national problems."[9]

The major thrust of this book has been that even though government is large and complex, most issues can be followed by outsiders if they understand the nature of decision-making systems. The small, discrete decision-making systems process the majority of issues that reach the public agenda. As government policy becomes more important in the lives of business corporations, (contracts, grants, fiscal policy, regulations, and tarrifs just to name a few), businessmen must become more knowledgeable about the decision-making system. The corporations that have turned their attention to governmental actions and have begun to publicize their own activities are learning how government works and how best to work with it.[10]

Those who reject the decision-making system in the public sector as irrational, excessively deliberative, and unpredictable are missing the point. Public decision-making systems function the way they do precisely because that is the way our system processes issues of concern to all Americans. Government decision-making systems were not modeled after the private system, nor could they be.

Government decision-making systems have evolved over two hundred years and done so in a slow, incremental manner. Changing them to conform to an individual corporation or industry's concept of good management can be a long, time-consuming, and frustrating experience with few positive results. A much more productive and desirable approach is for business executives to learn how the system works and to seek to influence the key actors to produce favorable results.[11]

Business now has a vested interest in the public decision-making system at the city, county, state, and federal levels. These systems are under extreme pressure to work faster, process more and larger issues, become more open, satisfy more diverse clients, and respond to increased pressures from organized interests. Business organizations should be developing and implementing plans to insure the viability of the public decision-making systems by seeking to strengthen rather than weaken them.

The competition that business organizations experience in the marketplace is not markedly different from the competition among components of the public sector. Just as corporations compete for market shares, new products, outlets, and customers, so do public-sector bureaucracies, interest groups, and congressional committees vie for influence, jurisdiction, oversight, and budget allocations.

Competition among the different components of the public-sector decision-making systems often produces duplication, overlapping, and a lack of coordination. It is the duplication and contradiction which leads some to question whether or not the traditional decision-making systems can cope successfully in the future. Certainly the kinds of questions raised in the Sears case illustrate clearly how policy can be confused, costly, and ineffective when made by decision-making centers that have little contact with each other.

The effectiveness of traditional decision systems is also called into question when new and large problems present themselves to government. National energy and urban policies have not been developed well by government. The reasons for these failures are the size and complexities of the problems. No single decision-making system or small group of related systems can develop policy adequate to deal with the scope of these problems. If one ties international relations and inflation to energy, one can see that the decision-making centers described in this book are not equal to the task of adequate policy development for national issues. The current management improvement activities designed to overcome the deficiencies of the traditional government decision-making systems will yield some encouraging results, but whether or not these improvements will be adequate is uncertain.

More centralized planning, such as that which occurs in wartime, is an alternative to government decision-making as we now know it. It is unpopular in this country with most people, including presidents, who realize the great political costs involved in centralized decision-making. Yet, if the normal, competing decision-making centers cannot resolve the nation's big problems, we, as a nation, are likely to gravitate toward a more centralized system—centralized around the presidency. Economic planning has rarely been attempted in this country, except in cases of great emergency. The American public is opposed to it. Planning runs counter to the notions of limited government and decentralized, fragmented power which have been the basis of our system for two hundred years. While the views of the public are not likely to change soon, there is some evidence that government is moving towards a more centralized approach to decision-making, particularly in the area of funds allocation. The movement is far from extreme or alarming, however. The creation of the Office of Management and Budget and the budget committees in both houses of Congress are two attempts tc inject a little more planning and predictability into the resourse allocation process on the federal level.

Excluding times of national emergency, this is about as close as the U.S. government has come to economic planning. Centralized or command-type planning as exercised in some countries is not politically feasible in our pluralistic society. However, business executives, who spend a considerable amount of their time in planning corporate activities, know the value of indicative planning and rational goal-setting. These activities are more like informal goal-setting than centralized planning. Business organizations recognizing the importance of this type of planning will probably encourage government executives to move in this direction.[12]

American business corporations can be certain of a large role in decision-making processes of government when they use the framework discussed in this book. By doing so, they can keep decision-makers informed, and the decision-making systems themselves will better accomodate the business viewpoints expressed.

Ignoring the process or responding viscerally to government because it doesn't respond to private-sector needs has proved fruitless and frustrating. All the evidence we have gathered indicates an increasing role for government in the lives of all citizens and all organizations. The successful executives and corporations of the 1980s will be the ones who combine quality products, sound marketing practices, fair pricing, and consumer awareness with knowledgeable involvement in the activities of the public-sector agencies at the federal, state, and local levels.

Notes

1. Saul Alinsky, *Reveille for Radicals* (New York: Vantage Press, 1969), p. 224.
2. See "The Corporate Image," *Business Week*, 22 January 1979, p. 47, for an

interesting study of the attempts of several large corporations to improve their public image.

3. George C. Lodge, *The New American Ideology* (New York: Alfred A. Knopf, 1975).

4. Remarks by Douglas M. Costle, administrator, U.S. Environmental Protection Agency, before the Colorado Association of Corporate Counsels, 10 January 1979.

5. Quoted in Susan J. Tolchin, "Presidential Power and the Politics of RARG," *Regulation* 3, no. 4, (July-August 1979), pp. 44–49.

6. Larry Kramer, "End of a Chapter at Safety Agency," *Washington Post,* 8 February 1979.

7. Margot Hornblower, "White House to Propose 'Regulatory Experiment' Bill," *Washington Post,* 7 February 1979.

8. The issues of the case are outlined in an article by William Raspberry, "Sears v. Inconsistency," *Washington Post,* 2 February 1979. See *Sears, Roebuck and Co. v. Attorney General of the United States, et al,* U.S. District Court for the District of Columbia, 1979.

9. Hugh D. Menzies, "Union Carbide Raises Its Voice," *Fortune,* 25 September 1978, p. 87.

10. See "Public Relations and the Chief Executive," *Business Week,* 22 January 1979, pp. 50 and 54.

11. Menzies, "Union Carbide," p. 88.

12. For an interesting discussion of the problems of planning, see Murray Weidenbaum and Linda Rockwood, "Corporate Planning versus Government Planning," *The Public Interest* 46 (Winter 1977): 59–72

appendix a

Washington-Based Organizations of Interest to Business Executives

American Enterprise Institute for Public Policy Research

1150 17th Street, N.W.
Washington, D.C. 20036
202-296-5616

Association of Asian-American Chambers of Commerce

National Press Building
529 14th Street, N.W.
Washington, D.C. 20045
202-638-5568

Bankers Association for Foreign Trade

1101 16th Street, N.W.
Washington, D.C. 20036
202-833-3060

The Brookings Institution

1775 Massachusetts Avenue, N.W.
Washington, D.C. 20036
202-797-6000

Business-Industry Political Action Committee

1747 Pennsylvania Avenue, N.W.
Washington, D.C. 20006
202-833-1880

The Business Council

888 17th Street, N.W.
Washington, D.C. 20006
202-298-7650

The Business Roundtable

1801 K Street, N.W.
Washington, D.C. 20006
202-872-0092

Chamber of Commerce of the United States

1615 H Street, N.W.
Washington, D.C. 20062
202-659-6000

Committee for Economic Development (CED)

1700 K Street, N.W.
Washington, D.C. 20006
202-296-5860

The Conference Board

1755 Massachusetts Avenue, N.W.
Washington, D.C. 20036

Council of State Chambers of Commerce

499 S. Capitol Street, S.W.
Washington, D.C. 20003

Council of the Americas

1700 Pennsylvania Avenue, N.W.
Washington, D.C. 20006
202-298-9016

East-West Trade Council

1700 Pennsylvania Avenue, N.W.
Washington, D.C. 20006
202-393-6240

Emergency Committee for American Trade

1211 Connecticut Avenue, N.W.
Washington, D.C. 20036
202-659-5147

National Alliance of Business

1730 K Street, N.W.
Washington, D.C. 20006
202-457-0040

National Associated Businessmen, Inc.

1000 Connecticut Avenue, N.W.
Washington, D.C. 20036
202-296-5773

National Association of Manufacturers

1776 F Street, N.W.
Washington, D.C. 20006
202-331-3700

National Business League

4324 Georgia Avenue, N.W.
Washington, D.C. 20011
202-726-6200

National Contract Management Association

2001 Jefferson Davis Highway
Arlington, Va. 22202
703-521-2717

National Council for U.S.-China Trade

1050 17th Street, N.W.
Washington, D.C. 20036
202-331-0290

National Patent Council

2001 Jefferson Davis Highway
Arlington, Va. 22202
703-521-1669

National Planning Association

1606 New Hampshire Avenue, N.W.
Washington, D.C. 20009
202-265-7685

National Tax Equality Association

1000 Connecticut Avenue
Washington, D.C. 20036
202-296-5424

Tax Foundation, Inc.

1875 Connecticut Avenue, N.W.
Washington, D.C. 20009
202-328-4500

Trade Relations Council of the United States

1001 Connecticut Avenue, N.W.
Washington, D.C. 20036
202-785-4194

U.S. Council for an Open World Economy

1028 Connecticut Avenue, N.W.
Washington, D.C. 20036
202-659-2066

U.S.-Japan Trade Council

1000 Connecticut Avenue, N.W.
Washington, D.C. 20036
202-296-5633

Major Trade Associations

Aerospace Industries Association of America

1725 DeSales Street, N.W.
Washington, D.C. 20036
202-347-2315

Air Transport Association of America

1709 New York Avenue, N.W.
Washington, D.C. 20006
202-872-4000

American Advertising Federation

1225 Connecticut Avenue, N.W.
Washington, D.C. 20036
202-659-1800

American Apparel Manufacturers Association, Inc.

1611 N. Kent Street
Arlington, Va. 22209
703-524-1864

American Association of Advertising Agencies

1730 M Street, N.W.
Washington, D.C. 20036
202-331-7345

American Bankers Association

1120 Connecticut Avenue, N.W.
Washington, D.C. 20036
202-467-4097

American Bus Association

1025 Connecticut Avenue, N.W.
Washington, D.C. 20036
202-293-5890

American Coke and Coal Chemicals Institute

1010 16th Street, N.W.
Washington, D.C. 20036
202-296-5932

American Cotton Shippers Association

1707 L Street, N.W.
Washington, D.C. 20036
202-296-7116

American Farm Bureau Federation

425 13th Street, N.W.
Washington, D.C. 20004
202-637-0500

American Footwear Industries Association

1611 N. Kent Street
Arlington, Va. 22209
703-522-8070

American Gas Association

1515 Wilson Blvd.
Arlington, Va. 22209
703-524-2000

American Imported Automobile Dealers Association

1220 19th Street, N.W.
Washington, D.C. 20036
202-659-2561

American Institute of Food Distribution

1707 H Street, N.W.
Washington, D.C. 20006
202-298-6344

American Insurance Association

1025 Connecticut Avenue, N.W.
Washington, D.C. 20036
202-293-3010

American Iron and Steel Institute

1000 16th Street, N.W.
Washington, D.C. 20036
202-452-7100

American National Cattlemen's Association

425 13th Street, N.W.
Washington, D.C. 20004
202-347-0228

American Textile Manufacturers Institute, Inc.

1150 17th Street, N.W.
Washington, D.C. 20036
202-833-9420

Japanese Textile Importers Association

900 17th Street, N.W.
Washington, D.C. 20006
202-296-4484

Association of National Advertisers

1725 K Street, N.W.
Washington, D.C. 20006
202-785-1525

Computer and Business Equipment Manufacturers Association

1828 L Street, N.W.
Washington, D.C. 20036
202-466-2288

Computer and Communications Industry Association

1500 Wilson Blvd.
Arlington, Va. 22209
703-524-1360

Consumer Bankers Association

1725 K Street, N.W.
Washington, D.C. 20006
202-466-2590

Cotton Council International

1030 15th Street, N.W.
Washington, D.C. 20005
202-833-2943

Health Insurance Association of America

1750 K Street, N.W.
Washington, D.C. 20036
202-331-1336

Health Insurance Institute

1730 Pennsylvania Avenue, N.W.
Washington, D.C. 20006
202-393-3041

Independent Petroleum Association of America

16th Street, N.W.
Washington, D.C. 20036
202-466-8240

Information Industry Association

4720 Montgomery Lane
Bethesda, Md. 20014
301-654-4150

Interstate Natural Gas Association of America

1600 L Street, N.W.
Washington, D.C. 20036
202-293-5770

National Association of Chain Drug Stores, Inc.

1911 Jefferson Davis Highway
Arlington, Va. 22202
703-521-1144

National Association of Food Chains

1725 Eye Street, N.W.
Washington, D.C. 20006
202-331-7822

National Automobile Dealers Association

8400 Westpark Drive
McLean, Va. 22101
703-821-7000

National Business Aircraft Association

1634 Eye Street, N.W.
Washington, D.C. 20006
202-783-9000

National Cotton Council of America

1030 15th Street, N.W.
Washington, D.C. 20005
202-833-2943

National Council of Technical Service Industries

888 17th Street, N.W.
Washington, D.C. 20006
202-833-8540

National Farmers Organization

475 L'Enfant Plaza, S.W.
Washington, D.C. 20024
202-484-7075

National Grain and Feed Association

725 15th Street, N.W.
Washington, D.C. 20005
202-783-2024

National Grain Trade Council

725 15th Street, N.W.
Washington, D.C. 20005
202-783-8945

National Lumber and Building Materials Dealers Association

1990 M Street, N.W.
Washington, D.C. 20036
202-872-8860

National Retail Merchants Association

1000 Connecticut Avenue, N.W.
Washington, D.C. 20036
202-223-8250

National Security Industrial Association

740 15th Street, N.W.
Washington, D.C. 20005
202-393-3620

Pharmaceutical Manufacturers Association

1155 15th Street, N.W.
Washington, D.C. 20005
202-296-2440

Silver Users Association

1717 K Street, N.W.
Washington, D.C. 20006
202-785-3050

Tobacco Institute

1776 K Street, N.W.
Washington, D.C. 20006
202-457-4800

Public-Interest Groups

Academy for Contemporary Problems

1501 Neil Avenue
Columbus, O. 43201
614-421-7700

Washington Office:
444 North Capitol Street
Suite 349
Washington, D.C. 20001
202-638-1445

Airport Operators Council, International, Inc.

1700 K Street, N.W., Suite 602
Washington, D.C. 20006
202-296-3270

American Association of Port Authorities

1612 K Street, N.W., Suite 502
Washington, D.C. 20006
202-331-1263

American Association of School Administrators

1801 North Moore Street
Arlington, Va. 22209
703-528-0700

American Association of State Highway and Transportation Officials

444 North Capitol Street
Suite 225
Washington, D.C. 20001
202-624-5810

American Institute of Certified Planners

and the

American Planning Association

1313 East 60th Street
Chicago, Ill. 60637
312-947-2560

Washington Office:
1776 Massachusetts Ave., N.W.
Washington, D.C. 20036
202-872-0611

American Public Health Association

1015 18th Street, N.W., 7th Floor
Washington, D.C. 20036
202-467-5051

American Public Power Association

2600 Virginia Ave., N.W.
Room 212
Washington, D.C. 20037
202-333-9200

American Public Welfare Association

1155 16th St., N.W., Suite 201
Washington, D.C. 20036
202-833-9250

American Public Works Association

1313 East 60th Street
Chicago, Ill. 60637
312-947-2524

Washington Office:
1776 Massachusetts Ave., N.W.
Washington, D.C. 20036
202-833-1168

American Society for Public Administration

1225 Connecticut Ave., N.W.
Room 300
Washington, D.C. 20036
202-785-3255

American Public Transit Association

1100 17th Street, N.W., Suite 1200
Washington, D.C. 20036
202-331-1100

American Water Works Association, Inc.

6666 West Quincy Avenue
Denver, Col. 80235
303-794-7711

Washington Office:
704 National Press Building
Washington, D.C. 20045
202-628-8303

Building Officials and Code Administrators, International

17926 S. Homestead
Homewood, Ill. 60430
312-799-2300

Council for International Urban Liaison

818 18th Street, N.W., Suite 840
Washington, D.C. 20006
202-223-1434

Council for Urban Economic Development

1730 K Street, N.W.
Washington, D.C. 20006
202-223-4735

Council of State Community Affairs Agencies

444 North Capitol Street
Washington, D.C. 20001
202-624-5850

Council of State Governments

Iron Works Pike
P.O. Box 11910
Lexington, Ky. 40511
606-252-2291

Washington Office:
444 North Capitol Street
Washington, D.C. 20001
202-624-5450

Council of State Planning Agencies

444 North Capitol Street
Washington, D.C. 20001
202-624-5386

Institute of Transportation Engineers

1815 North Fort Meyer Drive
Arlington, Va. 22209
703-527-5277

International Association of Assessing Officers

1313 East 60th Street
Chicago, Ill. 60637
312-947-2065

International Association of Chiefs of Police

11 Firstfield Road
Gaithersburg, Md. 20760
301-948-0922

International Association of Fire Chiefs

1329 18th Street, N.W.
Washington, D.C. 20036
202-833-3420

International Bridge, Tunnel, and Turnpike Association

1225 Connecticut Ave., N.W.
Room 307
Washington, D.C. 20036
202-659-4620

International Institute of Municipal Clerks

160 N. Altadena Drive
Pasadena, Calif. 91107
213-795-6153

International City Management Association

1140 Connecticut Ave. 2nd floor
Washington, D.C. 20036
202-293-2200

International Municipal Signal Association

1511 K Street, N.W., Room 430
Washington, D.C. 20005
202-638-7283

International Personnel Management Association

1850 K Street, N.W., Room 870
Washington, D.C. 20006
202-833-5860

International Urban Technology Exchange Program, Ltd.

250 M Bedford Chambers, Covent Gardens
London, WC2, England
(01) 836-3281

Municipal Finance Officers Association

180 North Michigan Ave.
Chicago, Ill. 60601
312-977-9700

Washington Office:
1750 K Street, N.W.
Room 650
Washington, D.C. 20006
202-466-2014

National Academy of Public Administration

1225 Connecticut Ave., Room 300
Washington, D.C. 20036
202-659-9165

National Association of Attorneys General

444 North Capitol Street
Washington, D.C. 20001
202-624-5454

National Association of Counties

1735 New York Ave., N.W.
5th Floor
Washington, D.C. 20036
202-785-9577

National Association of Housing and Redevelopment Officials

2600 Virginia Ave., N.W.
Room 404
Washington, D.C. 20037
202-333-2020

National Association of Regional Councils

1700 K Street, N.W., Room 1306
Washington, D.C. 20036
202-457-0710

National Association of State Mental Health Program Directors

1001 3rd Street, S.W., Suite 114
Washington, D.C. 20024
202-554-7807

National Association of Schools of Public Affairs and Administration

1225 Connecticut Ave., N.W.
Room 300
Washington, D.C. 20036
202-785-3260

National Association of State Budget Officers

444 North Capitol Street
Suite 204
Washington, D.C. 20001
202-624-5382

National Association of Tax Administrators

444 North Capitol Street, N.W.
Washington, D.C. 20001
202-624-5890

National Association of Towns and Townships

1800 M Street, N.W.
Suite 1030-N
Washington, D.C. 20036
202-452-8100

National Conference of State Legislatures

1405 Curtis Street, 23rd Floor
Denver, Col. 80202
303-623-6600

Washington Office:
444 North Capitol Street, N.W.
2nd Floor
Washington, D.C. 20001
202-624-5402

National Governors' Association

444 North Capitol Street
2nd Floor
Washington, D.C. 20001
202-624-5300

National Institute of Governmental Purchasing

1001 Connecticut Ave., N.W.
Room 922
Washington, D.C. 20036
202-331-1357

National Institute of Municipal Law Officers

1000 Connecticut Ave., N.W.
Room 800
Washington, D.C. 20036
202-466-5424

National Institute of Public Affairs

1225 Connecticut Ave., N.W.
Room 300
Washington, D.C. 20036
202-659-9165

National League of Cities

1620 Eye Street, N.W., 4th Floor
Washington, D.C. 20006
202-293-6915

National Municipal League

47 East 68th Street
New York, N.Y. 10021
212-535-5700

National Recreation and Park Association

1601 North Kent Street
Arlington, Va. 22209
703-525-0606

National School Boards Association

1055 Thomas Jefferson Street
Washington, D.C. 20007
202-337-7666

National Training and Development Service

5028 Wisconsin Ave., N.W.
Room 321
Washington, D.C. 20016
202-966-3761

North American Urban Liaison Office

45, Wassenaarseweg
2596CG The Hague, Netherlands
(070)244032

Public Administration Service

1776 Massachusetts Ave., N.W.
Washington, D.C. 20036
202-833-2505

Public Technology, Inc.

1140 Connecticut Ave., N.W.
11th Floor
Washington, D.C. 20036
202-452-7700

Sister Cities International

1625 Eye Street, N.W., Suite 424
Washington, D.C. 20006
202-293-5504

United States Conference of Mayors

1620 Eye Street, 4th Floor
Washington, D.C. 20006
202-293-6796

Water Pollution Control Federation

2626 Pennsylvania Avenue
Washington, D.C. 20037
202-337-2500

appendix b

How a Bill Becomes Law

The following explanation of how a bill becomes law incorporates the changes made in the legislative process by the Legislative Reorganization Act of 1970. The act, which cleared Congress October 8, 1970, was designed to improve the operations of Congress in committee and on the floor, to provide Congress with better means of evaluating the federal budget, and with improved resources for research and information.

Introduction of Bills

A House member (including the resident commissioner of Puerto Rico and nonvoting delegates of the District of Columbia, Guam, and the Virgin Islands) may introduce any one of several types of bills and resolutions by handing it to the clerk of the House or placing it in a box called the hopper. A senator first gains recognition of the presiding officer to announce the introduction of a bill. If objection is offered by any senator, the introduction of the bill is postponed until the following day.

As the next step in either the House or Senate, the bill is numbered, referred to the appropriate committee, labeled with the sponsor's name, and sent to the Government Printing Office so that copies can be made for subsequent study and action. Senate bills may be jointly sponsored and carry several senators' names. In the House, until 1967, each bill carried the name of one sponsor only; however, the House on April 25, 1967, voted to allow cosponsorship of bills, setting a limit of twenty-five cosponsors on any one bill. A bill written in the Executive Branch and proposed as an administration measure usually is introduced by the chairman of the congressional committee which has jurisdiction.

Bills. Prefixed with "HR" in the House, "S" in the Senate, followed by a number. Used as the form for most legislation, whether general or special, public or private.

Joint resolutions. Designated HJ Res or SJ Res. Subject to the same procedure as bills, with the exception of a joint resolution proposing an amendment to the Constitution. The latter must be approved by two-thirds of both houses and is thereupon sent directly to the administrator of general services for submission to the states for ratification rather than being presented to the president for his approval.

Concurrent resolutions. Designated H Con Res or S Con Res. Used for matters affecting the operations of both houses. These resolutions do not become law.

Resolutions. Designated H Res or S Res. Used for a matter concerning the operation of either house alone and adopted only by the chamber in which it originates.

Committee Action

A bill is referred to the appropriate committee by a House parliamentarian on the Speaker's order, or by the Senate president. Sponsors may indicate their preferences for referral, although custom and chamber rule generally govern. An exception is the referral of private bills, which are sent to whatever group is designated by their sponsors. Bills are technically considered "read for the first time" when referred to House committees.

When a bill reaches a committee it is placed upon the group's calendar. At that time it comes under the sharpest congressional focus. Its chances for passage are quickly determined— and the great majority of bills fall by the legislative roadside. Failure of a committee to act on a bill is equivalent to killing it; the measure can be withdrawn from the group's purview only by a discharge petition signed by a majority of the House membership on House bills, or by adoption of a special resolution in the senate. Discharge attempts rarely succeed.

The first committee action taken on a bill usually is a request for comment on it by interested agencies of the government. The committee chairman may assign the bill to a subcommittee for study and hearings, or it may be considered by the full committee. Hearings may be public, closed (executive session), or both. A subcommittee, after considering a bill, reports to the full committee its recommendations for action and any proposed amendments.

The full committee then votes on its recommendation to the House or Senate. This procedure is called "ordering a bill reported." Occasionally a committee may order a bill reported unfavorably; most of the time a report, submitted by the chairman of the committee to the House or Senate, calls for favorable action on the measure, since the committee can effectively "kill" a bill by simply failing to take any action.

When a committee sends a bill to the chamber floor, it explains its reasons in a written statement, called a report, which accompanies the bill. Often committee members opposing a measure issue dissenting minority statements which are included in the report.

Usually, the committee proposes amendments to the bill. If they are substantial and the measure is complicated, the committee may order a "clean bill" introduced, which will embody the proposed amendments. The original bill then is put aside and the "clean bill," with a new number, is reported to the floor.

The chamber must approve, alter, or reject the committee amendments before the bill itself can be put to a vote.

Floor action

After a bill is reported back to the house where it originated, it is placed on the calendar.

There are five legislative calendars in the House, issued in one cumulative calendar titled Calendars of the United States House of Representatives and History of Legislation. The House calendars are:

The Union Calendar, to which are referred bills raising revenues, general appropriation bills, and any measures directly or indirectly appropriating money or property. It is the Calendar of the Committee of the Whole House on the State of the Union.

The House Calendar, to which are referred all bills of a public character not raising revenue or appropriating money or property.

The Consent Calendar, to which are referred bills of a noncontroversial nature that are passed without debate when the Consent Calendar is called on the first and third Mondays of each month.

The Private Calendar, to which are referred bills for relief in the nature of claims against the United States or private immigration bills that are passed without debate when the Private Calendar is called the first and third Tuesdays of each month.

The Discharge Calendar, to which are referred motions to discharge committees when the necessary signatures are signed to a discharge petition.

There is only one legislative calendar in the Senate and one "executive calendar" for treaties and nominations submitted to the Senate. When the Senate Calendar is called, each senator is limited to five minutes' debate on each bill.

Debate. A bill is brought to debate by varying procedures. If a routine measure, it may await the call of the calendar. If it is urgent or important, it can be taken up in the Senate either by unanimous consent or by a majority vote. The policy committee of the majority party in the Senate schedules the bills that it wants taken up for debate.

In the House, precedence is granted if a special rule is obtained from the Rules Committee. A request for a special rule is usually made by the chairman of the committee that favorably reported the bill, supported by the bill's sponsor and other committee members. The request, considered by the Rules Committee in the same fashion that other committees consider legislative measures, is in the form of a resolution providing for immediate consideration of the bill. The Rules committee reports the resolution to the House, where it is debated and voted upon in the same fashion as regular bills. If the Rules Committee should fail to report a rule requested by a committee, there are several ways to bring the bill to the House Floor —under suspension of the rules, on Calendar Wednesday, or by a discharge motion.

The resolutions providing special rules are important because they specify how long the bill may be debated and whether it may be amended from the floor. If floor amendments are banned, the bill is considered under a "closed rule," which permits only members of the committee that first reported the measure to the House to alter its language, subject to chamber acceptance.

When a bill is debated under an "open rule," amendments may be offered from the floor. Committee amendments are always taken up first, but may be changed, as may all amendments up to the second degree, i.e., an amendment to an amendment to an amendment is not in order.

Duration of debate in the House depends on whether the bill is under discussion by the House proper or before the House when it is sitting as the Committee of the Whole on the State of the Union. In the former, the amount of time for debate is determined either by special rule or is allocated with an hour for each member if the measure is under consideration without a rule. In the Committee of the Whole the amount of time agreed on for general debate is equally divided between proponents and opponents. At the end of general discussion, the bill is read section by section for amendment. Debate on an amendment is limited to five minutes for each side.

Senate debate is usually unlimited. It can be halted only by unanimous consent by "cloture," which requires a three-fifths majority of the entire Senate except for proposed changes in the Senate's rules. The latter require a two-thirds vote.

The House sits as the Committee of the Whole on the State of the Union when it considers any tax measure or bill dealing with public appropriations. It can also resolve itself into the Committee of the Whole if a member moves to do so and the motion is carried. The Speaker appoints a member to serve as the chairman. The rules of the House permit the Committee of the Whole to meet with any 100 members on the floor, and to amend and act on bills with a quorum of the 100, within the time limitations mentioned previously. When the Committee of the Whole has acted, it "rises," the Speaker returns as the presiding officer of the House, and the member appointed chairman of the Committee of the Whole reports the action of the committee and its recommendations (amendments adopted).

Votes. Voting on bills may occur repeatedly before they are finally approved or rejected. The House votes on the rule for the bill and on various amendments to the bill. Voting on amendments often is a more illuminating test of a bill's support than is the final tally. Sometimes members approve final passage of bills after vigorously supporting amendments which, if adopted, would have scuttled the legislation.

The Senate has three different methods of voting: an untabulated voice vote, a standing vote (called a division), and a recorded roll call to which members answer "yea" or "nay" when their names are called. The House also employs voice and standing votes, but since January 1973 yeas and nays have been recorded by an electronic voting device, eliminating the need for time-consuming roll calls.

Another method of voting, used in the House only, is the teller vote. Traditionally, members filed up the center aisle past counters; only vote totals were announced. Since 1971, one-fifth of a quorum can demand that the votes of individual members be recorded, thereby forcing them to take a public position on amendments to key bills. Electronic voting now is commonly used for this purpose.

After amendments to a bill have been voted upon, a vote may be taken on a motion to recommit the bill to committee. If carried, this vote removes the bill from the chamber's calendar. If the motion is unsuccessful, the bill then is "read for the third time." An actual reading usually is dispensed with. Until 1965, an opponent of a bill could delay this move by objecting and asking for a full reading of an engrossed (certified in final form) copy of the bill. After the "third reading," the vote on final passage is taken.

The final vote may be followed by a motion to reconsider, and this motion itself may be followed by a move to lay the motion on the table. Usually, those voting for the bill's passage vote for the tabling motion, thus safeguarding the final passage action. With that, the bill has been formally passed by the chamber. While a motion to reconsider a Senate vote is pending on a bill, the measure cannot be sent to the House.

Action in second House

After a bill is passed it is sent to the other chamber. This body may then take one of several steps. It may pass the bill as is—accepting the other chamber's language. It may send the bill to committee for scrutiny or alterations, or reject the entire bill, advising the other house of its actions. Or it may simply ignore the bill submitted while it continues work on its own version of the proposed legislation. Frequently, one chamber may approve a version of a bill that is greatly at variance with the version already passed by the other house, and then substitute its amendments for the language of the other, retaining only the latter's bill designation.

A provision of the Legislative Reorganization Act of 1970 permits a separate House vote on any nongermane amendment added by the Senate to a House-passed bill and requires a majority vote to retain the amendment. Previously the House was forced to act on the bill as a whole; the only way to defeat the nongermane amendment was to reject the entire bill.

Often the second chamber makes only minor changes. If these are readily agreed to by the other house, the bill then is routed to the White House for signing. However, if the opposite chamber basically alters the bill submitted to it, the measure usually is "sent to conference." The chamber that has possession of the "papers" (engrossed bill, engrossed amendments, messages of transmittal) requests a conference and the other chamber must agree to it.

Conference. A conference undertakes to harmonize conflicting House and Senate versions of a legislative bill. The conference is usually staffed by senior members (conferees), appointed by the presiding officers of the two houses, from the committees that managed the bills. Under this arrangement the conferees of one house have the duty of trying to maintain their chamber's position in the face of amending actions by the conferees (also referred to as "managers") of the other house.

The number of conferees from each chamber may vary, the range usually being from three to nine members in each group, depending upon the length or complexity of the bill involved. There may be five representatives and senators on the conference committee, or the reverse. But a majority vote controls the action of each group so that a larger representation does not give one chamber a voting advantage over the other chamber's conferees.

Theoretically, conferees are not allowed to write new legislation in reconciling the two versions before them, but this curb sometimes is bypassed. Many bills have been put into acceptable compromise form only after new language was provided by the conferees. The

1970 Reorganization Act attempted to tighten restrictions on conferees by forbidding them to introduce any language on a topic that neither chamber sent to conference or to modify any topic beyond the scope of the different House and Senate versions.

Frequently the ironing out of difficulties takes days or even weeks. Conferences on involved appropriation bills sometimes are particularly drawn out.

As a conference proceeds, conferees reconcile differences between the versions, but generally they grant concessions only insofar as they remain sure that the chamber they represent will accept the compromises. Occasionally, uncertainty over how either house will react, or the positive refusal of a chamber to back down on a disputed amendment, results in an impasse, and the bills die in conference even though each was approved by its sponsoring chamber.

Conferees sometimes go back to their respective chambers for further instructions, when they report certain portions in disagreement. Then the chamber concerned can either "recede and concur" in the amendment of the other house, or "insist on its amendment".

When the conferees have reached agreement, they prepare a conference report embodying their recommendations (compromises). The reports, in document form, must be submitted to each house.

The Legislative Reorganization Act of 1970 provides that Senate and House conferees must jointly prepare an explanatory statement for every conference report and that all conference reports and accompanying statements must be printed in both houses. Previously, conference reports were printed in the house with an explanatory statement prepared by the House conferees only.

The conference report must be approved by each house. Consequently, approval of the report is approval of the compromise bill. In the order of voting on conference reports, the chamber that asked for a conference yields to the other chamber the opportunity to vote first.

Final steps. After a bill has been passed by both the House and Senate in identical form, all of the original papers are sent to the enrolling clerk of the chamber in which the bill originated. He then prepares an enrolled bill which is printed on parchment paper. When this bill has been certified as correct by the Senate or the clerk of the House, depending on which chamber originated the bill, it is signed first (no matter whether it originated in the Senate or House) by the speaker of the House and then by the president of the Senate. It is next sent to the White House to await action.

How a bill becomes law

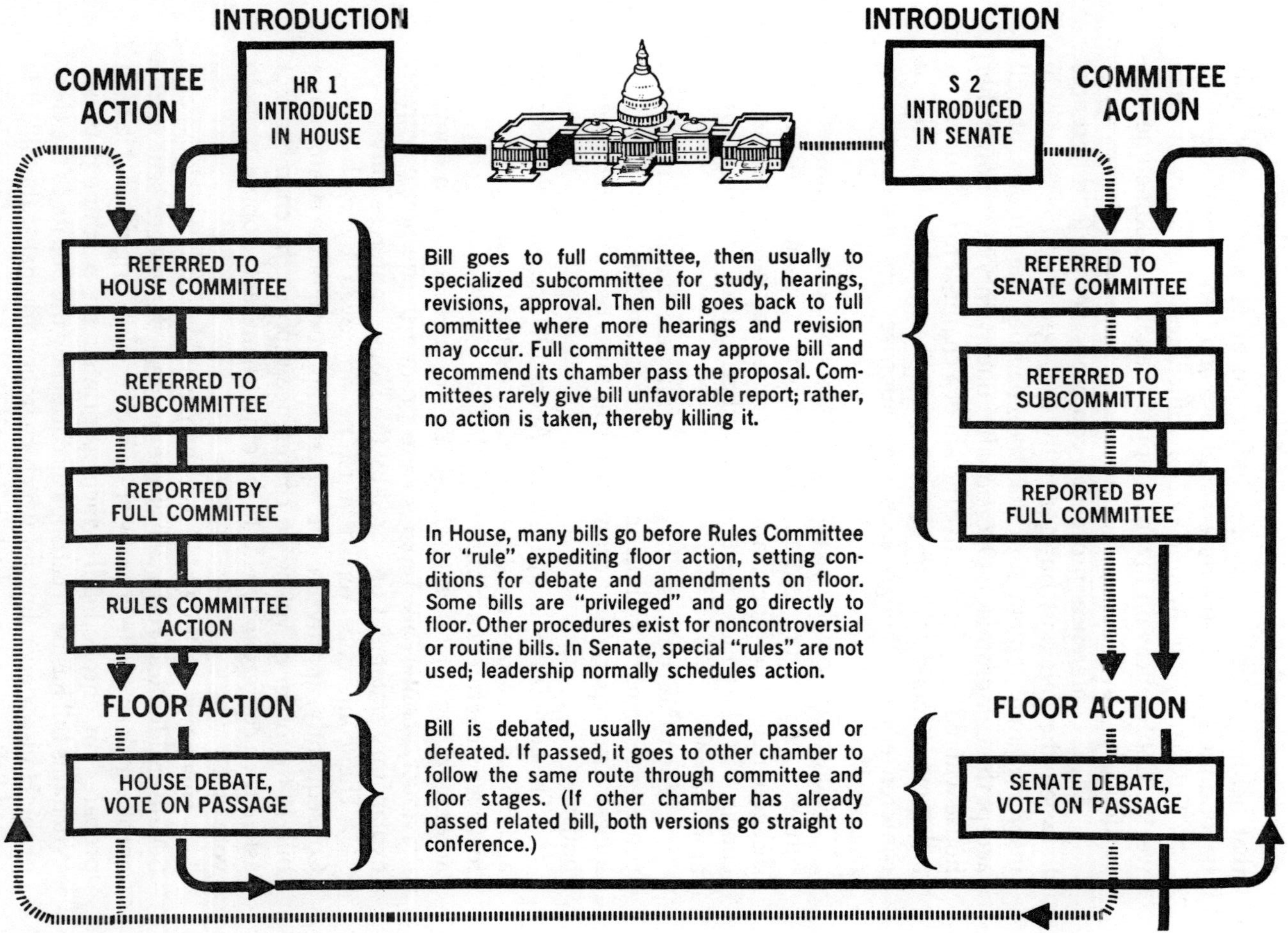

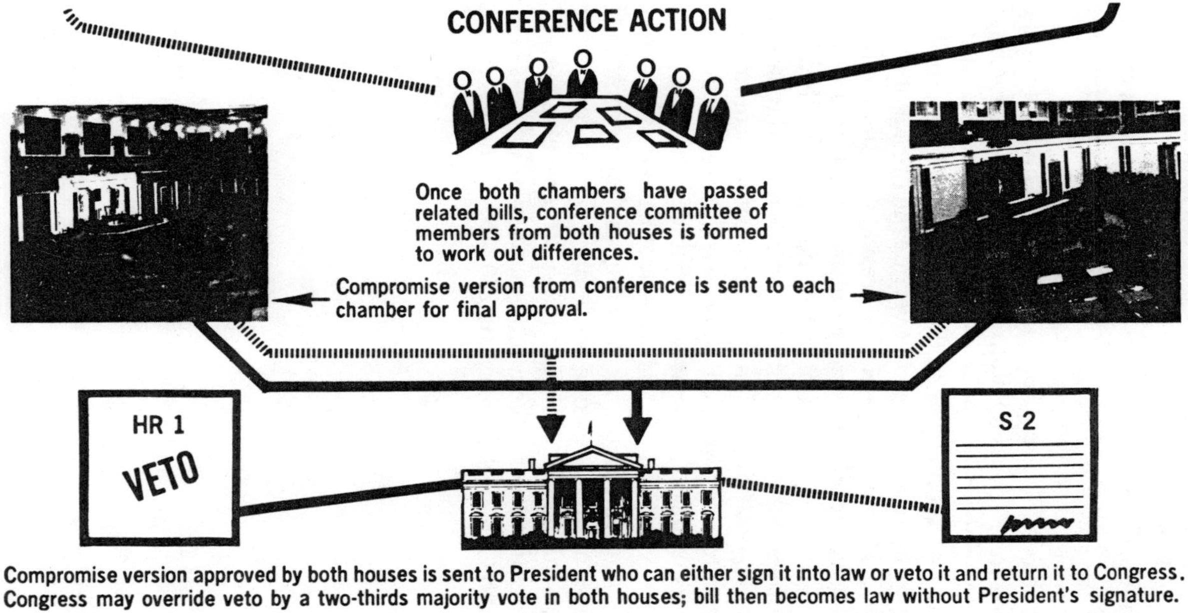

This graphic shows the most typical way in which proposed legislation is enacted into law. There are more complicated, as well as simpler, routes, and most bills fall by the wayside and never become law. The process is illustrated with two hypothetical bills, House bill No. 1 (HR 1) and Senate bill No. 2 (S 2). Each bill must be passed by both houses of Congress in identical form before it can become law. The path of HR 1 is traced by a solid line, that of S 2 by a broken line. However, in practice most legislation begins as similar proposals in both houses.

Source: *Congressional Quarterly Guide to American Government,* Washington, D.C., Spring 1979, pp. 139–144. Reprinted with permission.

If the president approves the bill he signs it, dates it and usually writes the word "approved" on the document. If he does not sign it within ten days (Sundays excepted) and Congress is in session, the bill becomes law without his signature.

However, should Congress adjourn before the ten days expire, and the president has failed to sign the measure, it does not become law. This procedure is called the pocket veto.

A president vetoes a bill by refusing to sign it and before the ten-day period expires, returning it to Congress with a message stating his reasons. The message is sent to the chamber which originated the bill. If no action is taken there on the message, the bill dies. Congress, however, can attempt to override the president's veto and enact the bill, "the objections of the president to the contrary notwithstanding." Overriding of a veto requires a two-thirds vote of those present, who must number a quorum and vote by roll call.

Debate can precede this vote, with motions permitted to lay the message on the table, postpone action on it, or refer it to committee. If the president's veto is overridden by a two-thirds vote in both houses, the bill becomes law. Otherwise it is dead.

When bills are passed finally and signed, or passed over a veto, they are given law numbers in numerical order as they become law. There are two series of numbers, one for public and one for private laws, starting at the number "1" for each two-year term of Congress. They are then identified by law number and by Congress—i.e., Private Law 21, 90th Congress; Public Law 250, 90th Congress (or PL 90–250).

appendix c

How to Use the Federal Register

What is the *Federal Register?*

The *Federal Register* is a legal newspaper in which the Executive Department of the United States Government publishes regulations, orders, and other documents. A citizen is thereby informed of his rights, his obligations, and, often, the benefits of his government. The *Register* is issued weekdays by the Office of the Federal Register. It is published in softcover and issues usually run between 150 and 300 pages.

Who reads the *Register?*

If you are in business and subject to regulation by a federal agency, if you are an attorney who might represent a client before a regulatory agency, or if you have a need to know the day-to-day operations of the federal government, the *Federal Register* will be useful, even vital, reading for you. There are many other citizens—such as those involved with consumer, conservation, and other special-interest groups—who will profit from reading the *Register.*

How is the *Register* organized?

Each issue has four sections: "Presidential Documents," including executive orders and proclamations; "Rules and Regulations," including on occasion policy statements; "Proposed Rules;" and "Notices," including scheduled hearings and meetings open to the public. Each issue has a "Highlights" section starting on the front page in which a brief statement describes the principal subject of selected documents. Anything appearing in the *Register* may be freely copied.

Is *Register* information available in advance?

Highlights of key documents scheduled to be published the following day can be obtained by telephoning the Office of the Federal Register at 202–523–5022. Documents are also available for inspection and may be copied the day before publication in Room 8401, 1100 L Street, N.W., Washington, D.C. *Register* business hours are 8:45 A.M. to 5:15 P.M., Monday through Friday. The office is closed on official holidays.

Why is the *Register* important?

Because advance notice of rule-making must be given by departments and agencies in the *Register,* citizens can influence the decision-making process of the government. The procedure is simple. An interested individual or organization concerned with a pending regulation may comment on it directly, either in writing or orally at a hearing, to the office drafting the rule. The comment period varies, but is usually thirty, sixty, or ninety days. In each instance, the *Register* gives detailed instructions on how, when, and where a viewpoint can be expressed. As an aid to this "town-crier" function, the *Federal Register* each Wednesday publishes a reminder list of comment deadlines for the following week.

Where is the *Register* available?

Most public libraries and all Federal Depository Libraries in major cities have copies of the *Federal Register* on file. A sample copy may be obtained by writing the Office of the Federal Register, 1100 L Street, N.W., Washington, D.C. 20408, or at GPO bookstores around the nation. Each copy is $.75; checks or money orders should be made out to the Superintendent of Documents. Subscriptions to the *Federal Register* are $5 for a month or $50 per year. Write the U.S. Government Printing Office, Washington, D.C. 20402.

The *Federal Register* is published by the Office of the Federal Register, National Archives and Records Service, a component of the U.S. General Services Administration.

Source: *Federal Register*
Superintendent of Documents
U.S. Government Printing Office
Washington, D.C. 20402

appendix d

How to Use the Code of Federal Regulations

What is the *Code of Federal Regulations?*

The *Code of Federal Regulations (CFR)* is a codification of the current general and permanent rules of the various federal agencies. Name a subject from "air" to "zoological parks" and chances are the *CFR* will contain a regulation about it. All such official regulations are grouped together in the approximately 140 volumes that comprise the *CFR*. The United States is a complex industrial nation, and this body of regulations reflects both its size and complexity.

What is its purpose?

The purpose of the *CFR* is to present the *complete text* of agency regulations in one organized publication and to provide a comprehensive and convenient reference for all those who may need to know the text of general and permanent federal regulations.

How is the *Code* organized?

The *CFR* is organized into fifty titles representing broad areas subject to regulatory action, for example, Title 20—Employee Benefits. Each title is divided into chapters, which are assigned to agencies or subagencies issuing regulations pertaining to that broad subject area, for example, Title 20 contains Chapter III—Social Security Administration, Department of Health, Education, and Welfare. Each chapter is divided into parts covering specific functions or programs of the agency. Each part is divided into sections, the basic unit of the *CFR*. Note that some agencies may issue regulations that appear in more than one title, for example, "Trucking" may be subject to rules found both under Title 23—Highways and Title 49—Transportation.

How does the *Code* work?

The *CFR* is keyed to and kept up to date by the daily *Federal Register.* These two publications must be used together to determine the latest version of any given rule. When a federal agency publishes a regulation in the *Federal Register,* that regulation usually is an amendment to the basic *CFR* in the form of a change, an addition, or a deletion. To research all of the regulations in effect on a particular day concerning a particular subject, it would be necessary to refer both to the appropriate title(s) of the *CFR* and those *Federal Registers* that contain amendments to the title(s). This is not as complicated as it sounds. The Office of the Federal Register prepares various finding aids and guides that assist users in determining which issues of the *Federal Register* are needed to update specific regulations.

When is the *Code* published?

The approximately 140 *CFR* volumes are revised at least once a year on a quarterly basis as follows: Titles 1–16 as of January 1; Titles 17–27 as of April 1; Titles 28–41 as of July 1; Titles 42–50 as of October 1.

Where is the *Code* available?

Most law libraries, some public libraries, and all Federal Depository Libraries in major cities have copies of the *CFR.* Individual copies or subscriptions to the entire *CFR* are available from the Superintendent of Documents, U.S. Government Printing Office, Washington, D.C. 20402. Subscription price is $400 a year ($100 additional for foreign mailing). Individual copies are separately priced, and price inquiries may be made to the Superintendent of Documents or the Office of the Federal Register.

The *CFR* is published by the Office of the Federal Register, National Archives and Records Service, a component of the U.S. General Services Administration.

Source: *Code of Federal Regulations*
Superintendent of Documents
U.S. Government Printing Office
Washington, D.C. 20402

appendix e

Rules and Regulations for Registering as a Lobbyist

Registering to become a lobbyist requires filing three copies of the Preliminary Report form, one with the Secretary of the Senate and two with the Clerk of the House of Representatives.

To obtain forms, contact the Office of the Secretary, United States Senate, Washington, D.C., 20510, (202-224-0758). This office will mail sufficient copies of the form, with mailing labels and a section of the pertinent law.

Who must register

A. Person(s) who directly or indirectly solicits, collects, or receives money (or any other thing of value) to be used to aid in the passage or defeat of legislation by the United States Congress.

B. Person(s) whose principle function is to aid in the passage or defeat of legislation by the United States Congress.

Requirement for preliminary report

A. Employers and employees must file separate reports.

B. One copy of the report is to be filed with the secretary of the Senate, and two copies are to be filed with the clerk of the House of Representatives.

C. Identifying data:

1. The name, address, and nature of business of employer.
2. Approximate duration of lobbying activities.

3. Statement of general and specific legislative interests.
    a. Short titles of statutes and bills, House and Senate number of bills, citations of statutes, and stand (for or against) on such statutes and bills.
4. Description of publications to be received or distributed in connection with legislative interests.
    a. Quantity distributed, date of distribution, name of printer or publisher, and name of donor if publications were a gift.
5. Statement of anticipated expenses:
    a. Nature and amount of expenses and salary of agent or employee.

Quarterly report requirements

A. A report must be filed at the end of each calendar quarter (between the first and tenth day) in which money has been received or spent in connection with legislative interests.

B. One copy of the report is to be filed with the secretary of the Senate and two copies are to be filed with the clerk of the House of Representatives.

C. Receipts (other than loans):

1. Gifts of money and printed or duplicated material, and receipts from sales of printed or duplicated material.

D. Loans received:

1. Total amount presently owed, borrowed, and repaid this quarter.

E. Contributions (including loans):

1. Name and address of each person who has made a contribution of $500 or more, and the amount contributed.

F. Expenditures (other than loans):

1. Public-relations and advertising services, wages, salaries, fees and commissions, gifts or contributions, printed or duplicated material, office overhead, telephone

and telegraph, and travel, food, lodging, and entertainment.

G. Loans made to others:

1. Total amount presently owed to person filing, lent this quarter, and payments received.

H. Recipients of expenditures:

1. Name and address of recipients of $10 or more, and purpose and date of expenditure.

Penalties

A. A person convicted of violating the provisions of Title III of the Legislative Reorganization Act of 1946 will be considered guilty of a misdemeanor and will be punished by either a maximum fine of $5,000 or a maximum prison sentence of 12 months, or both.

B. Any person convicted of such a misdemeanor is prohibited from lobbying for three years from the date of conviction; violation of this is considered a felony and is punishable by either a maximum fine of $10,000 or a maximum prison sentence of 5 years, or both.

Source: *Federal Regulation of Lobbying Act (PL.601)*
U.S. Government Printing Office
Washington, D.C., 1976

appendix f

Rules and Regulations Governing the Creation of Political Action Committees (PACs)

Registering to create a PAC requires filing with the Federal Election Commission (FEC). To obtain the necessary forms, contact the Federal Election Commission, 1325 K Street, N.W., Washington, D.C. 20463, (202-523-4068, or toll free, 800-424-9530). The commission will supply the copies of the pertinent law and a registration guide.

The Chamber of Commerce of the United States has developed guidelines for Corporate Action Committees. For copies, write their Public Affairs Department, 1615 H Street, N.W., Washington, D.C. 20062, (202-659-6152). These guidelines explain the complexities involved in organizing a political action committee.

Who must register

A. A political committee established by a national bank, corporation, labor organization, trade association, cooperative, or membership organization to raise or spend more than $1,000 to influence federal elections.

Requirements of registration (statement of organization)

A. Identifying data:

1. name and address of the parent organization
2. name and address of treasurer
3. mailing address of committee
4. officers of committee
5. name and address of committee's bank
6. name and address of candidates supported by committee

B. Committees must file ten days after committee is organized or ten days after committee raises or spends $1,000 or anticipates doing so.

C. Amendments of statement of organization

1. must be reported within ten days

2. must amend statement when:

   a. support new candidate

   b. change bank

   c. change name and/or address of committee

   d. elect new officers

Monthly or quarterly report requirements

A. A report must be filed with the Federal Election Commission (either monthly or quarterly) listing receipts and expenditures used to influence Federal elections.

1. Monthly reports are due no later than the twentieth day of the month.

2. Quarterly reports are due April 10, July 10, and October 10 and must list total contributions received or total expenditures made which exceed $1,000 during the quarter.

B. Pre-election and post-election reports

1. Committees must file a pre- and post-election report if they support federal candidates in either general or primary elections.

2. A report must be filed with the secretary of the State in which the committee supports a candidate for federal office.

Prohibited contributions

A. Contributions from government contractors

B. Contributions from foreign nationals who are not permanent residents of the United States

C. Contributions of more than $100 per person per campaign period

D. Contributions made in the name of another person

Contribution limits

A. Initial limits on political action committees

1. $1,000 per election to a candidate
2. $20,000 to a national party committee per calendar year
3. $5,000 to any other political committee per calendar year

B. An individual can contribute $5,000 to a political action committee. When a political action committee attains status as a multicandidate committee (committee with more than fifty contributors) and has been registered for at least six months, and with the exception of state party committees, has made contributions to five or more federal candidates, then contributions are limited to:

1. $15,000 to a national party committee per calendar year
2. $5,000 to any other political committee per calendar year. (Contributions between affiliated committees and committees of the same party are unlimited).

Penalties

A. A committee found to be in violation of the Federal Election Campaign Act Amendments of 1976 may be required to pay a fine not to exceed the greater of $5,000 or an amount equal to the amount of the contribution or expenditure involved in the violation.

B. If the FEC has established proof that a committee was involved in a knowing and willful violation of the Act it may be required to pay a fine not to exceed the greater of $10,000 or 200 percent of the amount of the contribution or expenditure involved in the violation.

appendix g

Publications of Interest to Business Executives

The Almanac of American Politics

Published annually. It includes senators, representatives, governors and information on their voting records, states, and districts.
Available from E.P. Dutton, 201 Park Avenue South, New York, N.Y. 10003

Antitrust and Trade Regulation Report

Federal Trade Commission activities and the Justice Department's antitrust division activities. Issued weekly.
Available from Bureau of National Affairs, 1231 25th Street, N.W., Washington, D.C. 20037.

Business and Economics

Abstracts of research reports concerned with economics and business. Issued weekly.
Available from National Technical Information Service, Commerce Department, Springfield, Va. 22151.

Business Condition Digest

Review by Bureau of Economic Analysis, Commerce Department, of national income and production, wages, prices, and balance of payments. Issued monthly.
Available from Government Printing Office, Washington, D.C. 20402.

Business Statistics

Statistical information regarding the gross national product, industrial production and trade, and the balance of international payments. Issued biannually.
Available from Government Printing Office, Washington, D.C. 20402.

Catalog of Federal Domestic Assistance

Federal services and programs for which individuals and communities can apply. Issued annually by Office of Management and Budget.
Available from Government Printing Office, Washington, D.C. 20402.

Census of Business

Information concerning business organizations. Issued every five years by Bureau of the Census, Commerce Department.
Available from Government Printing Office, Washington, D.C. 20402.

Census of Manufacturers

Data on manufacturing industries, their products and material consumption. Issued every five years by Bureau of the Census, Commerce Department.
Available from Government Printing Office, Washington, D.C. 20402.

Commerce Business Daily

Government contract awards and opportunities, sales and procurements standards. Issued by Bureau of Field Operations, Industry and Trade Administration, Commerce Department.
Available from Government Printing Office, Washington, D.C. 20402.

Congressional Directory

Biographies of Congressional and Supreme Court members. List of committees and press covering Congress. Issued each new Congress.
Available from Government Printing Office, Washington, D.C. 20402.

Congressional Information Service Index to Publications of the United States Congress, Washington, D.C.

Analyzes major policy issues before Congress each year. Indexes hearings and reports by subject so researchers can follow specific issues and identify pertinent committee members and witnesses.
Available from the Congressional Information Service, Washington, D.C.

Congressional Quarterly Almanac

Review of congressional action, voting studies, reports on lobbying, the executive branch, and the Supreme Court. Issued after each session.
Available from Congressional Quarterly, 1414 22nd Street, N.W., Washington, D.C. 20037.

Congressional Quarterly Weekly Report

Presidential programs and activities, political developments, and congressional actions.
Available from Congressional Quarterly, 1414 22nd Street, N.W., Washington, D.C. 20037.

Congressional Record

Official record of congressional debates and proceedings. Issued daily when Congress is in session.
Available from Government Printing Office, Washington, D.C. 20402.

Congressional Staff Directory

Comprehensive guide to personal and committee staff members, elected members of Congress, and key personnel in the executive departments.
Available from Post Box 62, Mount Vernon, Va. 22121.

County and City Data Book

Statistical data on U.S. counties and metropolitan areas. Issued by Census Bureau, Commerce Department, 1972.
Available from Government Printing Office, Washington, D.C. 20402.

Daily Report for Executives

Factors affecting business, such as investments and government controls.
Available from Bureau of National Affairs, 1231 25th Street, N.W., Washington, D.C. 20037.

Daily Tax Reports

Federal court rulings, congressional and executive laws and regulations affecting taxes and fiscal affairs.
Available from Bureau of National Affairs, 1231 25th Street, N.W., Washington, D.C. 20037.

Digest of Public General Bills

Summaries of public bills and resolutions. Includes subject, author, and specific title. Issued by Congressional Research Service, Library of Congress, five times, with biweekly supplements during every session.
Available from Government Printing Office, Washington, D.C. 20402.

Directory of Washington Representatives of American Associations and Industry

Lists representatives of major national associations, labor unions, lobbyists, law firms, and special-interest groups. Issued annually.
Available from Columbia Books, Inc., 734 15th St., N.W., Washington, D.C. 20005.

Doing Business with the Federal Government

Procurement of government goods and services. Includes pertinent offices and specifications. Issued by Business Service Center, General Services Administration, 1975.
Available from Government Printing Office, Washington, D.C. 20402.

Economic Indicators

Information concerning wages, prices, credit, money, business activity, and government finance. Issued by Council of Economic Advisers for the Joint Economic Committee, U.S. Congress, monthly.
Available from Government Printing Office, Washington, D.C. 20402.

Environment Regulation Handbook

Guide to environmental law and regulations. Monthly updates issued.
Available from Environment Information Center, Inc., 124 E. 39th Street, New York, N.Y. 10016.

Federal Contracts Report

Federal procurement procedures and standards, and deadlines for industry's response to regulatory proposals. Issued weekly.
Available from Bureau of National Affairs, 1231 25th Street, N.W., Washington, D.C. 20037.

Federal Environment Law

Includes federal laws, regulations, and programs concerned with the environment.
Available from West Publishing Company, 50 W. Kellog Boulevard, St. Paul, Minn. 55102.

Federal Funds for Research, Development, and Other Scientific Activities

Research and development programs funded by federal agencies. Includes type of research, field of science, and other pertinent data. Issued annually.
Available from Government Printing Office, Washington, D.C. 20402.

Federal Register

Published daily. It contains new and revised rules and regulations proposed by federal agencies.

Available from the Office of the Federal Register, National Archives, GSA, Washington, D.C. 20408.

Federal Regulatory Directory

A guide to the powers, responsibilities, organizations, and officials of federal agencies engaged in regulatory practices.

Available from Congressional Quarterly, Inc., 1414 22nd Street, N.W., Washington, D.C. 20037.

Government Publications and Their Use

Describes the basic guides to government publications. Discusses the uses, limitations, and availability of catalogues and bibliographies.

Available from the Brookings Institution, 1775 Massachusetts Avenue, N.W., Washington, D.C. 20036.

Guide to Record Retention Requirements

U.S. statutes and agency regulations governing record-keeping for individuals and business organizations. Compiled by the Office of the Federal Register, General Services Administration, 1977.

Available from Government Printing Office, Washington, D.C. 20402.

Guidelines for Corporate Political Action Committees

Includes the organization of a political action committee, reporting requirements, laws, tax considerations, and other pertinent data. Issued 1977, with updates when changes in law or regulations occur.

Available from Chamber of Commerce of the U.S., Public Affairs Department, 1615 H Street, N.W., Washington, D.C. 20062.

International Monetary Fund Publications

Describes the Fund's publications on economic and financial topics. Issued annually.

Available from the Secretary, International Monetary Fund, 700 19th Street, N.W., Washington, D.C. 20431.

The Metropolitan Association Handbook

Lists local and national associations and non-profit organizations with offices in metropolitan Washington. Issued 1977.

Available from the Metropolitan Washington Board of Trade, 1129 20th Street, N.W., Washington, D.C. 20036.

The Monthly Catalog of U.S. Government Publications

Divided into author, title, and subject indexes. Periodicals issued by the government are listed in an appendix once a year.
Available from Shoe String Press, Hamden, Connecticut.

National Journal

Weekly publication covering politics and public policy at the federal level. Analyzes the actors, groups, and organizations that influence and shape government policy.
Available from National Journal, 1730 M Street, N.W., Washington, D.C. 20036.

National Trade and Professional Associations of the United States and Canada and Labor Unions

Lists trade and professional associations. Includes addresses, phone numbers, history, and publications. Issued annually.
Available from Columbia Books, Inc., 734 15th St., N.W., Washington, D.C. 20005.

One Hundred Companies Receiving the Largest Dollar Volume of Prime Contracts Awards

Lists business organizations by net value of military contract awards. Issued annually by Directorate for Information Operations, Office of Assistant Secretary of Defense.
Available from Office of Information, Defense Department, the Pentagon, Washington, D.C. 20301.

Policy and Supporting Positions (Washington, D.C.: Committee on Post Office and Civil Service, House of Representatives, published yearly)

A listing of all top-level executive branch positions by agency, including names and salaries.
Available from U.S. Government Printing Office, Washington, D.C. 20402.

Regulation

AEI Journal on Government and Society. Monthly publication containing articles of interest in the area of government regulation.
Available from the American Enterprise Institute, 1150 17th Street, N.W., Washington, D.C.

Regulatory Eye

A newsletter for policy makers in business and government discussing major changes in government regulation and the structure of the regulatory process.

Available from *Regulatory Eye*, 1625 Eye Street, N.W., Suite 125, Washington, D.C. 20006.

A Researcher's Guide to Washington

Includes a federal telephone directory of experts in the government and a list of all members of Congress and all committees with addresses and phone numbers. Issued annually.

Available from Washington Researchers, 910 17th St., N.W., Washington, D.C. 20006.

Selling to the United States Government

Federal government buying practices and procedures. Issued by Small Business Administration, 1975.

Available from Small Business Administration, U.S. Department of Commerce, Washington, D.C. 20416.

Special Analyses: Budget of the United States Government

Contains numerous special analyses designed to highlight specified program areas or other significant aspects of budget data.

Available from U.S. Government Printing Office, Washington, D.C. 20402.

Survey of Current Business

Statistical data on national income, business, and industry trends and projections, and other pertinent information. Issued by Office of Business Economics, Commerce Department, monthly.

Available from Government Printing Office, Washington, D.C. 20402.

Trade Regulation Reports

National and state laws concerned with fair trade, price discrimination, and antitrust laws. Issued weekly.

Available from Commerce Clearing House, 4025 W. Peterson Avenue, Chicago, Ill. 60646

The United States Budget in Brief

Provides a concise, less technical review of the current annual budget than the budget. Summary and historical tables of the budget are provided along with charts and graphs.

Available from U.S. Government Printing Office, Washington, D.C. 20402.

United States Government Manual

Describes the purposes and programs of most government agencies and lists the top officials in each.
Available from U.S. Government Printing Office, Washington, D.C. 20402.

U.S. Industrial Outlook

Data on industrial production, marketing, planning, and investments, and factors affecting the industry. Issued annually by Bureau of Domestic Commerce, Commerce Department.
Available from Government Printing Office, Washington, D.C. 20402.

Washington Financial Reports

Analysis of federal regulations affecting financial organizations. Issued weekly.
Available from Bureau of National Affairs, 1231 25th Street, N.W., Washington, D.C. 20037.

Washington Information Directory

Information on executive branch agencies, Congress, and private or nongovernmental organizations. Issued annually.
Available from Congressional Quarterly, Inc., 1414 22nd St., N.W., Washington, D.C. 20037.

Washington Representatives, 1979

A guide to individuals, public relations firms, organizations and foreign governments engaged in influencing government decision-making and legislation.
Available from Columbia Books, Inc., Suite 601, 734 Fifteenth Street, N.W., Washington, D.C. 20005.

The Weekly Regulatory Monitor

A summary of proposed and adopted regulations by federal agency.
Available from The Washington Monitor, Inc., 499 National Press Building, Washington, D.C. 20045.

Who's Who in American Politics: A Biographical Directory of United States Political Leaders

Biographies of members of Congress, state and local officials, presidential appointees, and former national leaders. Issued biannually.
Available from R. R. Bowker, P. O. Box 1807, Ann Arbor, Michigan 48106.

Who's Who in Government

Lists federal government officials. Issued biannually.
Available from Marquis Who's Who, Inc., 200 E. Ohio Street, Chicago, Ill. 60611.

Suggestions for Further Reading

ALTSHULER, ALAN A., and NORMAN C. THOMAS
Politics of the Federal Bureaucracy, 2nd ed. New York: Harper and Row, 1977.

BAUER, RAYMOND A., ITHIEL DE SOLA POOL and LEWIS ANTHONY DEXTER
American Business and Public Policy: The Politics of Foreign Trade. New York: Atherton Press, 1968.

BLOUGH, ROGER MILES
The Washington Embrace of Business. New York, New York: Columbia University Press, 1975.

CARY, WILLIAM L.
Politics and the Regulatory Agencies. New York: McGraw-Hill, 1967.

COCHRAN, THOMAS C.
Business in American Life: A History. New York: McGraw-Hill, 1972.

CORSON, JOHN J.
Business in the Humane Society. New York: McGraw-Hill, 1971.

CAYER, N. JOSEPH
Public Personnel Administration in the United States. New York: St. Martin's Press, 1975.

DAVIDSON, ROGER H. and WALTER J. OLESZEK
Congress Against Itself. Bloomington, Indiana: Indiana University Press, 1977.

DIMOCK, MARSHALL E.
Business and Government: Issues of Public Policy, 4th ed. New York: Holt, Rinehart and Winston, Inc., 1961.

DOWNS, ANTHONY
Inside Bureaucracy. Boston: Little, Brown and Co. 1967.

DRUCKER, PETER F.
The Future of Industrial Man: A Conservative Approach. New York: New American Library, 1970.

ELAZAR, DANIEL L.
American Federalism: A View from the States, 2nd ed. New York: Harper and Row, 1977.

EPSTEIN, EDWIN M.
The Corporation in American Politics. Englewood Cliffs, N.J.: Prentice-Hall, 1969.

EPSTEIN, EDWIN M.
Corporations, Contributions, and Political Campaigns; Federal Regulation in Perspective. Berkeley: University of California, 1968.

FENNO, RICHARD F., JR.
Congressmen in Committees. Boston: Little, Brown and Co., 1973.

FIORINA, MORRIS P.
Congress—Keystone of the Washington Establishment. New Haven: Yale University Press, 1977.

FISHER, LOUIS
The Constitution Between Friends: Congress, the President and the Law. New York: St. Martin's Press, 1978.

——— *President and Congress.* New York: Free Press, 1972.

FOX, HARRISON W., JR., and SUSAN W. HAMMOND
Congressional Staffs: The Invisible Force in American Lawmaking. New York: Free Press, 1977.

FREEMAN, J. LEIPER
The Political Process: Executive Bureau–Legislative Committee Relations. New York: Random House, 1965.

FRITSCHLER, A. LEE
Smoking and Politics: Policy Making and the Federal Bureaucracy, 2nd ed. Englewood Cliffs, N.J.: Prentice-Hall, 1975.

GALBRAITH, JOHN KENNETH
The New Industrial State, 3rd ed. Boston: Houghton Mifflin, 1978.

GLENDENING, PARRIS M., and MAVIS MANN REEVES
Pragmatic Federalism: An Intergovernmental View of American Government. Pacific Palisades, Calif.: Palisades Publishers, 1977.

GREEN, MARK J., ED.
The Monopoly Makers: Ralph Nader's Study Group Report on Regulation and Competition. New York: Grossman, 1973.

GREENWALD, CAROL S.
Group Power: Lobbying and Public Policy. New York: Praeger Publishers, 1977.

GUTTMAN, DANIEL, and BARRY WILLNER
The Shadow Government: The Governments' Multi-Billion Dollar Giveaway of its Decisionmaking Powers to Private Management Consultants, Experts, and Think Tanks. New York: Pantheon, 1976.

HAIDER, DONALD H.
When Governments Come to Washington: Governors, Mayors and Intergovernmental Lobbying. New York: The Free Press, 1974.

HAVEMANN, JOEL
Congress and the Budget. Bloomington, Indiana: Indiana University Press, 1978.

HECLO, HUGH
Government of Strangers: Executive Politics in Washington. Washington, D.C.: The Brookings Institution, 1977.

HESS, STEPHEN
Organizing the Presidency. Washington, D.C.: The Brookings Institution, 1976.

HUGHES, JONATHAN R. T.
The Governmental Habit: Economic Controls from Colonial Times to the Present. New York: Basic Books, 1977.

JACOBY, NEIL H.
The Business-Government Relationship: A Reassessment. Santa Monica, Calif.: Goodyear, 1975.

JOHNSON, EDGAR
The Foundations of American Economic Freedom: Government and Enterprise in the Age of Washington. Minneapolis: University of Minnesota Press, 1973.

JOHNSON, ARTHUR M.
Government-Business Relations: A Pragmatic Approach to the American Experience. Columbus: Merrill, 1965.

KALVELAGE, CARL, and MORLEY SEGAL
Research Guide in Political Science, 2nd ed. Morristown, N.J.: General Learning Process, 1976.

KAUFMAN, HERBERT
Are Government Organizations Immortal? Washington, D.C.: The Brookings Institution, 1976.

——— *Red Tape: Its Origins, Uses and Abuses.* Washington, D.C.: The Brookings Institution, 1977.

KOENIG, LOUIS W.
The Chief Executive, 3rd ed. New York: Harcourt Brace Jovanovich, Inc., 1975.

KOHLMEIER, LOUIS M., JR.
The Regulators: Watchdog Agencies and the Public Interest. New York: Harper and Row, 1969.

KRANZ, HARRY
The Participatory Bureaucracy. Lexington, Mass.: Lexington Books, 1976.

LINDBLOM, CHARLES E.
Politics and Markets: The World's Political-Economic Systems. New York: Basic Books, Inc., 1977.

LODGE, GEORGE C.
The New American Ideology: How the Ideological Basis of Legitimate Authority in America is Being Radically Transformed. New York: Knopf, 1975.

LOWI, THEODORE J.
The End of Liberalism: Ideology, Policy and the Crisis of Public Authority, 2nd ed. New York: W. W. Norton, Inc., 1979.

MCCONNELL, GRANT
The Modern Presidency, 2nd ed. New York: St. Martin's Press, 1976.

——— *Private Power and American Democracy.* New York: Vintage Books, 1966.

MCGRATH, PHYLLIS S.
Action Plans for Public Affairs. New York: The Conference Board, Inc., 1977.

MILLER, ARTHUR S.
The Modern Corporate State: Private Governments and the American Constitution. Westport, Conn.: Greenwood Press, 1976.

MUND, VERNON A.
Government and Business, 4th ed. New York: Harper and Row, 1965.

NADER, RALPH, ET AL.
Taming the Giant Corporation. New York: Norton, 1976.

NEUSTADT, RICHARD E.
Presidential Power: The Politics on Leadership with Reflections on Johnson and Nixon, 2nd ed. New York: Wiley, 1976.

NOLL, ROGER G.
Reforming Regulation. Washington, D.C.: The Brookings Institution, 1971.

NORTH, DOUGLAS C., and ROGER L. MILLER
The Economics of Public Issues, 2nd ed. New York: Harper and Row, 1973.

OLESZEK, WALTER
Congressional Procedure and Policy Process. Washington, D.C.: Congressional Quarterly, 1978.

ORNSTEIN, NORMAN J., and SHIRLEY ELDER
Interest Groups, Lobbying and Policymaking. Washington, D.C.: Congressional Quarterly, 1978.

PEGRUM, DUDLEY F.
Public Regulation of Business, rev. ed. Homewood, Ill: Irwin, 1965.

PHILLIPS, ALMARIN, ED.
Promoting Competition in Regulated Markets. Washington, D.C.: The Brookings Institution, 1975.

PIOUS, RICHARD M.
The American Presidency. New York: Basic Books, 1979.

REAGAN, MICHAEL D.
The Managed Economy. New York: Oxford University Press, 1963.

REDFORD, EMMETTE S.
Democracy in the Administrative State. New York: Oxford University Press, 1969.

——— *American Government and the Economy.* New York: Macmillan, 1965.

——— *The Regulatory Process.* Austin: University of Texas Press, 1969.

RIPLEY, RANDALL
Congress: Process and Policy. New York: W. W. Norton, 1976.

RIPLEY, RANDALL B. and GRACE A. FRANKLIN
Congress, the Bureaucracy and Public Policy. Homewood, Ill: Dorsey Press, 1976.

RIVLIN, ALICE M.
Systematic Thinking for Social Action. Washington, D.C.: The Brookings Institution, 1971.

ROURKE, FRANCIS E.
Bureaucracy, Politics, and Public Policy, 2nd ed. Boston: Little Brown and Co., 1976.

SANFORD, TERRY
Storm Over the States. New York: McGraw-Hill, 1967.

SCHNITZER, MARTIN C.
Contemporary Government and Business Relations. Chicago: Rand McNally, 1978.

SCHRIFTGIESSER, KARL
Business and the American Government. Washington, D.C.: R. B. Luce, 1964.

SCHULTZE, CHARLES
Public Use of Private Interest. Washington, D.C.: The Brookings Institution, 1977.

SCHULTZ, GEORGE P., and KENNETH W. DAM
Economic Policy Beyond the Headlines. New York: W. W. Norton, 1977.

SEIDMAN, HAROLD
Politics, Position and Power: The Dynamics of Federal Organization, 2nd ed. New York: Oxford University Press, 1975.

SILK, LEONARD, and DAVID VOGEL
Ethics and Profits: The Crisis of Confidence in American Business. New York: Simon and Schuster, 1976.

SOBEL, ROBERT
The Age of Giant Corporations: A Micro-Economic History of American Business, 1914–1970. Westport, Conn.: Greenwood Press, 1972.

STEINER, GEORGE A.
Business and Society, 2nd ed. New York: Random House, 1975.

SUNDQUIST, JAMES L., and DAVID W. DAVIS
Making Federalism Work: A Study of Program Coordination at the Community Level. Washington, D.C.: The Brookings Institution, 1969.

TIMBERG, THOMAS A.
Federal Executive: The President and the Bureaucracy. New York: Irvington Publishers, 1978.

TOLCHIN, MARTIN, and SUSAN TOLCHIN
To the Victor . . . Political Patronage from the Club House to the White House. New York: Random House, 1971.

TORRENCE, SUSAN WALKER
Grass Roots Government: The County in American Politics. Washington, D.C.–New York: Robert B. Luce, Inc., 1974.

TUGWELL, REXFORD G.
The Economic Basis of Public Interest. New York: Kelley, 1968.

VOGEL, DAVID
Lobbying the Corporation: Citizen Challenges to Business Authority. New York: Basic Books, Inc., 1979.

WEIDENBAUM, MURRAY L.
Business, Government, and the Public. Englewood Cliffs, N.J.: Prentice-Hall, 1977.

WILCOX, CLAIR
Public Policies Toward Business, 4th ed. Homewood, Ill.: Irwin, 1971.

WOLL, PETER
American Bureaucracy, 2nd ed. New York: W. W. Norton, 1977.

WRIGHT, DEIL
Understanding Intergovernmental Relations. N. Scituate, Mass.: Duxbury Press, 1978.

index

A

B

C

P

Q

R

S